W9-AVE-719

A LIFETIME IN JERUSALEM

AUTHOR'S PUBLICATIONS

A Primer on Palestine; Junior Hadassah, New York, December, 1932 (reprinted April and December, 1931, 123 pp. and map).

*A Handbook of the Jewish Communal Villages;*Zionist Organization Youth Department, Jerusalem, 1938: 92 pp., with appendices and map (and in German); second edition, 1945 (and in French).

The Theory of Administration; Rubin Mass, Jerusalem, for the Middle East College of Public Administration, 1947: 131 pp. (and in Hebrew, translated by Gila Uriel).

Problems of Government in the State of Israel; Rubin Mass, Jerusalem, 1956: 107 pp. (and in Spanish as *Israel por Dentro*, Editorial Candelabro, Buenos Aires, 1957).

British Traditions in the Administration of Israel; Vallentine, Mitchell, London, for the Anglo-Israel Association, 1957, 52 pp.

Britain's Legacy to Israel; Leeds University Press (the Fourth Selig Brodetsky Memorial Lecture), 1962, 19 pp.

The Social Structure of Israel; Random House, New York, 1969.

COLLECTED SHORT STORIES

A Cottage in Galilee (illustrated by Gabriella Rosenthal); Vallentine, Mitchell, London, 1957, 227 pp.

A Coat of Many Colours; Abelard Schuman, New York, 1960, 246 pp.

My Friend Musa; Abelard Schuman, New York, 1963, 248 pp.

The Cucumber King; Abelard Schuman, New York, 1965, 253 pp.

His Celestial Highness; Abelard Schuman, New York, 1968, 222 pp.

Captain Noah and His Ark (children's story illustrated by Lola Fielding); Abelard Schuman, New York, 1965, 46 pp.

A LIFETIME
IN JERUSALEM

THE MEMOIRS
OF THE SECOND VISCOUNT SAMUEL

VALLENTINE, MITCHELL — LONDON

First published in Great Britain in 1970 by
VALLENTINE, MITCHELL & CO., LTD.,
18 Cursitor Street, London, E.C.4

Copyright © Edwin Samuel, 1970

SBN: 85303016 2

ALL RIGHTS RESERVED
No part of this publication may be reproduced, stored
in a retrieval system, or transmitted in any form or by
any means, electronic, mechanical, photocopying,
recording or otherwise, without the prior permission in
writing of Vallentine, Mitchell & Co. Ltd.

This book has been composed, printed and bound
at the Keter Publishing House Ltd., Jerusalem, Israel, 1970

To my father's memory

LIBRARY
FLORIDA STATE UNIVERSITY
TALLAHASSEE, FLORIDA

CONTENTS

LIST OF ILLUSTRATIONS

FOREWORD

I arrived in Palestine for the first time in December, 1917, and, later, visited Jerusalem. Half a century later, my home is still in Jerusalem. From 1920 till 1948, I was a British colonial civil servant in the Palestine administration. During those 28 years I worked in five different departments. Two of these — the District Administration and the High Commissioner's Secretariat — were considered to be part of the Political Service. In 1934, I left the Political Service to become Deputy Commissioner of Migration (though that was political enough). During World War II, I was in the Imperial Censorship in Palestine and eventually became Chief Censor. After World War II, I ran the Palestine Broadcasting Service for the last three years of the British administration. Most British colonial civil servants serve in the same department in a succession of colonial territories: I served during the whole of my career in different departments in the same territory. I may nevertheless have gained in depth what I lost in breadth.

I have now reached the age of seventy which is a good time in life to write one's memoirs. My friend Gershon Agron, founder and editor of the daily *Palestine* (now *Jerusalem*) *Post* was once asked by a woman to mention her husband's 50th birthday. He said that was nonsense. "When he's sixty, I'll give him a line: when he's seventy, I'll give him a paragraph: when he's eighty — who cares?" I hope to get this out before then.

These are memoirs, not an autobiography carefully compiled from diaries, letters and other documents. Apart from during World War I, I have never kept a diary. Even then, my diary was merely a series of letters sent home to my parents for family circulation: it is now extremely dull reading. No, what I have written is what I remember; and the older I get, the less I shall remember; which is another reason for writing these memoirs now. If, today, I don't remember something in the past, no-one else is likely to be interested in it.

Memory is not very objective: it retains pleasant things and tries to forget the unpleasant ones. I have tried to check as far as possible the dates, names and places I have quoted. But this is not meant to be a political history of Palestine. 'John Marlowe' (in real life Jack Collard), Christopher Sykes and many others have adequately traversed those arid wastes. Mine is a more personal approach. I start with a chapter on my father, by far the most important member of our family. He rose to be a Cabinet Minister, a leader of a political party, High Commissioner in Palestine and a peer. Then I describe the curious chain of circumstances that led to my ever getting involved in Palestine, Zionism and Israel. This is followed by a series of chapters dealing successively with the work in which I was involved at different periods and what life was like at the time. I have put at the end a short chapter on my childhood: it is only of interest to explain the origin of some of the developments I have discussed in previous chapters.

I am grateful to Elie Mizrahi of the Israel State Archives, for checking some of the factual material with my personal papers now in those archives; to Norman Bentwich, Max Nurock and several members of my family who read the manuscript and made many helpful suggestions. I am also grateful to my friends David Kessler, Managing Director of Vallentine Mitchell in London, the joint publishers of this book. He has made several improvements in it, as have Lew Schwartz, one of the owners of Abelard Schuman in New York, Mrs. Nina Watkins, at that time of Vallentine Mitchell, and Derek Orlans, chief editor of Israel Universities Press.

Jerusalem
April, 1969   EDWIN SAMUEL

CHAPTER I

MY FATHER

My father, who died in 1963 at the age of ninety-two, wrote his own biography in 1945*. In the early 1950's, he asked me to go through his private papers, after his death, and to write a biography of him. I declined the invitation, first, because writing anyone's biography is an undertaking which requires skill and experience, neither of which I possessed. Secondly, to write a good biography of one's own father is exceedingly difficult. Either one is critical and unfilial, or one uses too much whitewash. I suggested instead that a professional biographer be invited to go through my father's papers in his own lifetime. The biographer would have the advantage of my father's oral explanation of his documents, and my father would himself derive much pleasure from the collaboration. Roger Fulford (who was appointed one of my father's literary executors, together with myself) was unable to accept my father's invitation to undertake this biography at that time. John Bowle, like my father once a student at Balliol College at Oxford, and subsequently professor at the *College de l'Europe* in Bruges, was, however, interested. The first draft of his

* *Memoirs of the Rt Hon Viscount Samuel, P.C., G.C.B., G.B.E.,* Cresset Press, London, 1945.

book was gone through by my father with a fine comb; and, inasmuch as any man is an authority on his own life, John Bowle's book* is factually correct. But the definitive work can only be written when all the Cabinet papers and other official documents of this period are open for public inspection. Under the new ruling, public records will now be open after thirty years, instead of fifty, as previously. This will shortly enable historians to examine the Cabinet papers of Herbert Samuel's last period of office — 1931-32.

Meanwhile, Roger Fulford and I, after my father's death, decided that his private papers should be divided. Those concerned with Palestine, Zionism and Jewish affairs generally should go to the Israel State Archives in Jerusalem. His private papers concerned with his political life in Britain, as well as his philosophical and other literary papers, should go to the House of Lords archives. This has been done and scholars in both countries are already studying them.

★ ★ ★

My father was born in Liverpool in 1870, the youngest son of Edwin Samuel (after whom I am named) and his wife Clara (née Yates).** Edwin Samuel moved to London in the early 1870's and, with his brother Montagu Samuel (who

* *Viscount Samuel: A Biography*, John Bowle, Gollancz, London, 1957.

** Three genealogical works include Herbert Samuel's ancestry. They are:

a. *The History and Genealogy of the Jewish Families of Yates and Samuel, from materials collected by Stuart M. Samuel, M.P.*, edited with an introduction, addition and notes by Lucien Wolf (past president of the changed his name to Samuel Montagu), founded the banking firm of Samuel Montagu and Co. Unfortunately, Edwin Samuel died in 1876, when my father was six, and he was brought up by his very discerning mother. Jews (and Catholics) were only admitted to Oxford in 1870; but his mother arranged for him to go there and, of all colleges, to Balliol, then still under that redoubtable Master, Benjamin Jowett. At Oxford he did well and took a first in history. Being sufficiently well off, thanks to a legacy from his father, not to have to earn a living, he entered politics as a Liberal.

On 17th November, 1897, he married his cousin, Beatrice Miriam Franklin, whose father was partner in another family bank—Keyser and Co. Her dowry increased my father's private means and established him even more firmly in the upper middle class. They had five children, of whom one died in infancy.

★ ★ ★

I find it difficult to describe my father, except at the end of his life. I do not remember much about his looks when I

Jewish Historical Society of England, etc.); London, 1901; for private circulation (printed by the Wardour Press, 140 Wardour Street, London, W1);

b. *Records of the Franklin Family*, collated and compiled by Arthur Ellis Franklin; George Routledge and Sons, London (second edition), 1935; and

c. *The Samuel Family of Liverpool and London from 1755 Onwards.* A Biographical and Genealogical Dictionary of the Descendants of Emanuel Samuel. Foreword by Viscount Samuel. Edited by Ronald J. d'Arcy Hart; Routledge and Kegan Paul, London, 1958: with Supplement, 1966.

was young, save his moustache and stubbly cheeks, He was never as tall as I am now. Even my mother gave the impression that she herself was taller than he was, perhaps because she was slender. In his later years he was portly and moved slowly, with the aid of a stick. Then, he looked very Jewish; and his eyes seemed small in relation to his face. His complexion was ruddy and never paled from lack of sun. · To the end of his life he had masses of hair, pure white, of course; and he was proud of it. If a good crop of hair is hereditary, then I am lucky in my ancestry: so far, at seventy, there is no sign of baldness.

Herbert Samuel's temperament was more equable than that of anyone else I have ever known. He was essentially rational in his thinking and well-balanced. I can only remember seeing him really angry once, when I was a boy, and a dealer complained that I had stolen some postage stamps. For that, my father walloped me — with a shoe, I think. Otherwise he never struck anyone, or even raised his voice against a fellow-creature. On one occasion, when I asked him, casually, whether something had not upset him, he replied firmly: 'Such a word does not exist in my vocabulary.' One of his maxims, on which we were all brought up, was: 'Don't waste good agony'; the implication being that everyone has a limited stock at his or her disposal, and that it should be reserved for big occasions. As far as his own life was concerned, there were few occasions big enough for agony. Only the death of his wife in 1959, when she was 88 and he 89, shook him severely. For the remaining four years of his life he could hardly ever speak of her without a catch in his voice and tears in his eyes. They were a singularly devoted couple; although her fussiness and hypochondria were a sore trial. He had the patience of an angel.

4

Perhaps because she constantly took pills for every kind of ailment, real or fancy, he developed a stern hostility to medication of all sorts. He would never himself take an aspirin to subdue a headache: he realised, rightly, that headaches came largely from strain. So he was careful to lead a rational life, without strain, and, consequently, enjoyed good health, apart from increasing deafness in his old age. Even at ninety-one he enjoyed going with me to Covent Garden to see and hear Stravinsky's *Sacre du Printemps*. It had been first performed in Paris exactly half a century earlier. He had heard the music much later, apparently on the radio, and had not approved. Now, at last, he made his peace with it.

His own dislike of medicines extended to a disapproval of anyone else who relied on them. At the end of his life, his doctor prescribed vitamin tablets for him and he took them regularly: but he insisted that they were food and not medicine. He was also proud of being able to sleep well, even in extreme old age. But he must have known that the tablets given to him at bedtime were mild sedatives.

To everyone, of whatever age or station in life, he was courteous — a gentleman of the old school. He was a meliorist and believed firmly in human perfectibility. This was the basis of his social and political philosophy and comes out strongly in his books. By nature he was optimistic, in large things as well as in small. When the weather was uncertain and we children debated whether to go out for a projected country walk, his maxim was always: 'When in doubt, go out'. That he was optimistic even about English weather says a lot.

His own optimism may perhaps have been strengthened by his wife's more pessimistic attitude towards life. He had to cheer her up and hence developed the necessary anti-bodies to enable him to do so. My own definition of an optimist is someone who is married to a pessimist.

He relished good stories and jokes (if not improper) and was a lifelong subscriber to *Punch*. His chuckle was infectious, his laughter hearty. He belonged to an older generation to whom even puns were permissible: I am afraid I have inherited that habit. Whenever he was due for a holiday and released himself from his old-fashioned roll-top desk, puns flowed fast and furious. We then knew that he had begun to relax. Essentially his temperament was buoyant, or sanguine as it would have been called in an earlier age.

He always led an active life, with plenty of exercise. He lived in Bayswater for some eighty years and was proud of being an honorary citizen of the Borough of Paddington. During all the years when he was in Parliament, he enjoyed walking there across the four royal parks — Kensington Gardens, Hyde Park, Green Park and St. James's Park — a good two miles each way. On Sundays, when I was a boy, he used to take me bicycling out of London, pedalling endlessly along the Harrow Road (I hated it). He played a good game of tennis; and one of my few complaints against him was that, just when I was able to beat him, he was advised by his doctor to give it up. In his younger years he enjoyed suimming and was once carried out to sea and nearly drowned while I, as a small child, was, it seems, dancing up and down on the beach, almost beside myself with terror. He belonged to a group of friends who called themselves the Sunday Tramps, with whom he used to go out by train, walk across country for hours, with a picnic lunch, and return in the evening by another suburban railway line, tired and happy. An even more exhausting sport was glorified 'hare and hounds' played for a whole week in the Lake District with another group of friends.

As a townsman, he kept few pet animals. There may have been cats in my childhood, but I do not remember any dogs. He liked birds, however, and always had some bird-food in the small garden outside his Bayswater study. Once, immediately after World War II, when everything was scarce, I managed to find a coconut in Soho to hang up outside his library window for the tits: his gratitude was profound. He became quite knowledgeable about London's birds, which is why a group of his fellow-peers chose a book on ornithology in five volumes to be specially bound and presented to him on his birthday on the 6th of November, 1952, to commemorate the fiftieth anniversary of his first election to Parliament on the 6th of November, 1902, on his 32nd birthday.

Being a rational man, my father was abstemious. He hardly ever drank cocktails or between meals. He liked a glass or two of light wine with his food but would dilute it with water, to the horror of the connoisseur. During World War I, he followed the King's example and gave up all alcohol 'for the duration.' But this self-denial did not extend to an occasional liqueur chocolate, which he enjoyed all the more. Apparently, as a young man, he had smoked, and oversmoked: so he gave it up completely and never indulged again during the rest of his long life. His strength of will made him somewhat contemptuous of those lesser mortals unable to throw off the vice. He once wrote a letter to *The Times*, when this subject was being discussed, and said: 'The only way to stop smoking is to stop.'

He never swore or used strong language of any kind. Nor did he gamble or even play any game for money. The most innocent sweepstake was taboo, being a method of getting something for nothing. I find it impossible, even today, to throw off these ingrained inhibitions. His ideas of morality in general were puritanical in the extreme, and his speech against homosexuality in the House of Lords in November, 1953, in the debate on the moral state of the nation, was stern and unbending. He received many letters from like-minded people from all over Britain, to his great satisfaction. He would have been dismayed to know that, as his successor, I voted for the Bill on homosexuality which has now become law.

He was well-read, especially in the standard works, and he had good literary taste. He liked the theatre and would listen, in old age, to much good music on his radio (he never installed TV). But he was not, I think, really musical; and his wife was completely unmusical. In the arts he was old-fashioned in his likes and dislikes. I remember taking him to see the Picasso exhibition at the Tate Gallery in 1960. He was horrified, and said (in the loud, carrying voice of which some deaf people are unaware): 'Ridiculous! Preposterous!' as he stamped along with his walking-stick. Many elderly ladies present, who had privately come to the same conclusion but were too awed, or shy, to say so, actually applauded.

Many of these qualities — which made him in some respects the Last of the Romans — can be summed up in one word — integrity. But they were also responsible for his never quite arriving at the top of the tree. He lacked the ambition, the ruthlessness, that might have given him even higher office. He never advertised himself; nor did he complain if his qualities were overlooked. In one who had reached so high an eminence in British public life — a viscountcy and the Order of Merit — it is perhaps unfair to expect more. But his moderation sometimes expressed itself in caution when boldness and 'damn-the-consequences' were what the country needed. I remember an occasion when the position of Viceroy of India was vacant. This was then possibly the most responsible public office in the Commonwealth, after that of the Prime Minister himself. The Marquess of Reading, another Jew, had once been viceroy and there was no bar on Herbert Samuel's holding this high office. He once told me he very much wanted the nomination, and I was present when he received a summons to the Prime Minister's office. But it was about some minor matter and he came back very disappointed; yet he never showed it. Even his private letters to his wife rarely betray any hidden turmoil (I don't think she ever destroyed any of them). So his equanimity may be the reason for his being only a leader, never *the* leader.

★   ★   ★

My father's political formation began early in his life, before I was born. By birth, he belonged to the upper middle class which, in the nineteenth century, increasingly dominated the Government of Britain. By historical accident, largely derived from early struggles between Protestant and Catholic and between Crown and Parliament, two large political parties developed — Tory and Whig. These, in the nineteenth century, became Conservative and Liberal. No trade unionist or socialist MP's were elected until the beginning of the twentieth century. The choice for Herbert Samuel as a young man was thus between Liberal and Conservative, and he chose Liberalism as the more progressive. He describes in his own autobiography the awakening of his social conscience at Balliol and outside. He was something of a political prodigy, first standing for Parliament at the age of 25 for the hopelessly Conservative rural constituency of North Oxfordshire: failure to be elected was inevitable. But in 1902, at the age of 32 he did manage to secure election for the Yorkshire mining constituency of Cleveland and his progress thereafter was rapid. In 1902, he also wrote his first book, a sound analysis of contemporary Liberalism,★ and became thereby one of the younger theoreticians of the Party. In 1905, when the Liberals at last got back to power, after ten years in the political wilderness, Herbert Samuel was appointed a junior Minister in the Government as Under-Secretary of State for the Home Office and, in 1908, a Privy Councillor (usually reserved only for full Cabinet Ministers). Winston Churchill received *his* first appointment at the same time, as Under-Secretary of State for the Colonies. At the end of his life, my father was proud of the fact that, after Churchill, he himself was the most senior Privy Councillor in the list.

His political advancement included appointment as Chancellor of the Duchy of Lancaster, 1909-10 and 1915-16, Postmaster-General, 1910 and 1915-16; President of the Local Government Board, 1914-15; and Secretary of State for Home Affairs, 1916. But his political career received a mortal blow when the more dynamic Liberal leader Lloyd George brought down Asquith as Liberal Prime Minister

★ *Liberalism: An Attempt to State the Principles and Proposals of Contemporary Liberalism in England* (with an introduction by the Rt Hon H. H. Asquith, K.C., M.P.) Grant Richards, London, 1902.

in 1916. My father remained loyal to Asquith and refused reappointment by Lloyd George. He spent the rest of the war out of office, except for chairmanship of the committee on war expenditure.

The Liberal Party never recovered from this internecine rivalry and eventually split into three fragments — Lloyd George Liberals, Samuel Liberals and Simon Liberals. What was more significant was the rise of the Labour Party as the progressives on the Left. From only two MP's out of 670 in 1902, the Labour Party reached 288 out of 615 in 1929. Many educated and progressive young men entering politics joined the Labour Party: few joined the Liberals. Some established Liberals also went over to the Labour Party; others to the Conservatives. Liberalism as a political force disintegrated after World War I and Herbert Samuel's political future with it. My father always predicted a revival of Liberalism; but there is no room in the British system of constituency elections for more than two parties.

Representative government in Britain, with an alternative Cabinet always ready in the wings, requires two big political parties, as in the United States. Having only one party leads to dictatorship: a coalition of several small parties produces only weak Governments. But Herbert Samuel did not accept this analysis. He regarded Liberalism as a permanent force, long after the Labour Party began to represent progressive opinion. When he realised that the Liberal Party was unlikely ever to secure a majority of seats in a general election, he fell back on the hope that it would hold the balance of power. He did not agree that it would be undemocratic for the smallest of three political parties to dominate in this way.

Perhaps, as leader of a dwindling party, he should have led

the remnant out of the political wilderness into either the Labour Party or the Conservative Party. But he was opposed on principle to such a solution. To him, Liberalism had a distinct policy of its own, although, with the passage of time, in actual fact this became less and less true. In any country, there are basically two natural political groupings — those who want to advance more rapidly and those who want to advance more slowly. A third rate of advance, between the other two, is a luxury.

Herbert Samuel considered that the Labour Party represented the working class and the Conservatives the upper classes, whereas the Liberal Party alone was above all class distinctions. This may or may not be true, but it helps to explain his refusal to join either. Actually, he was closer to Labour than to Conservative: but he was never a socialist. In fact, a determining factor in his political career was his refusal as a young man formally to join the Fabian Society to which many of his political friends belonged. He would not accept the idea that the State should control key industries in *principle*. When, later, in 1926, he was chairman of the Coal Commission, he refused to recommend nationalisation of the mines, although the earlier Sankey committee in 1919 had done so. These, then, are some of the reasons why his political career faltered after 1916. If he had had less integrity, greater ambition and more ruthlessness, he would have deserted the Liberals and joined up with either Labour or Conservatives and have risen higher in their ranks, as did several of his former Liberal colleagues.

As it was, with the exception of one year, he was out of office from 1916 till 1963, when he died. From 1920 to 1925, as High Commissioner for Palestine and Trans-Jordan, he was out of British politics altogether. On his return to

Britain, he stood as a Liberal in the Lancashire constituency of Darwen and got back in 1929 to the House of Commons, where he was the leader of a handful of Liberals till 1935.

In 1931, when Ramsay Macdonald's Labour Government ran on the rocks and Britain went off the gold standard, Herbert Samuel proposed the formation of a coalition Government, including Baldwin and the Conservatives, together with himself and the Liberals, under Macdonald as Prime Minister. The King accepted this advice and my father again became Home Secretary. But, a year later, when Imperial Preference was introduced under the Ottawa Agreement, the Liberal Party withdrew from the coalition on the issue of free trade. Herbert Samuel never again held Cabinet office.

In the general election of 1935, he even lost his seat at Darwen. Only seventeen Liberals were returned to Parliament, and the chance of his winning any future election as a Liberal in Darwen — or in any other constituency — was remote. He had twice been offered a peerage and had twice refused, both because he disliked the idea of hereditary titles and also because it meant the end of an active political career in the Commons. But, by 1935, he was already sixty-five years of age; so, in 1937, he accepted a viscountcy (the rank customarily accorded to former senior Cabinet Ministers) and led the diminished Liberal Party from the House of Lords from 1944 till 1955.

He was much beloved in the Upper House. His speeches were cogent and polished. He always spoke from hand-notes that he had carefully prepared, no matter how minor the occasion. He possessed an uncanny intuition of what would move the House and, even more, of what would hit the headlines the next day.

His wit was proverbial. In a House where political leaders were in their seventies, he decided, when he himself reached eighty-five, that it was time for him to hand over the leadership of the Liberal Party in the House of Lords to Philip Rea, then aged sixty. In introducing him, my father said: 'Your Lordships will be glad to know that Lord Rea is a representative of the *younger* generation: his grandchildren are still at school.'

Whenever I was in England, I used to go down to the House and, from the steps of the Throne, listen to his speech. He had a beautiful speaking voice and, when he was in his eighties, he seemed to throw off at least twenty years when he got up to address the House. Even in extreme old age, it was rash for anyone to challenge him. Sitting one afternoon on the Liberal front bench, as former Leader, he had his eyes closed. This annoyed another peer who was speaking. He interrupted his speech and said: 'The noble Viscount opposite is asleep!' My father opened one eye and said: 'Unfortunately not.'

Being so deeply involved in British politics, my father had little time, or inclination, to participate in Anglo-Jewish communal affairs. He did, however, assume leadership of the Central British Fund for German Jewry in 1936, and went to the United States with Sir Simon Marks and Lord Bearsted to raise funds for this purpose.

★　★　★

My father was proud of being Jewish. But, as a rational man, and interested in the relationship between religion, ethics, philosophy and science and politics, he could not be expected to adhere completely to Jewish orthodoxy. Nevertheless, having been born into an observant family and his wife even more so, he maintained the basic rules of *kashrut* both at home and outside. He did not accompany my mother every Sabbath to the New West End Synagogue, but only on the High Holydays. However, he never worked or travelled on the Sabbath but sat at home and read, or went for a walk. Since his father died when he was six, he became a seat-holder of the Synagogue in his own right at an early age and, at the end of his long life, was by far the oldest congregant. He appreciated, not without a little vanity, the respect paid to him by the congregation who, whenever he was called on to open the Ark of the Law, stood up as he passed. Under the influence, I think, of my mother, he strongly objected to intermarriage. When three out of four of his daughter's children 'married out', he refused to have anything more to do with them. Even after his wife's death, I had great difficulty in persuading him to agree to allow one of them to come and visit him with her first baby.

His chief connection with Jewish life came from his five years as High Commissioner for Palestine. He had had no great interest in Zionism until the outbreak of World War I. Then, as a member of the Cabinet, he realised that, if Turkey were defeated by British arms, the future of Palestine might lie in British hands. In 1915, thinking well ahead, he wrote a confidential memorandum to the Prime Minister on the various possibilities. It was printed and circulated to his colleagues as a Cabinet paper. In it he recommended a British protectorate over Palestine (the League of Nations and the Mandatory system had not then been thought of) with provision for Jewish immigration, investment and settlement. As this was a secret Cabinet paper, the terms of this document were not known publicly during the years when the author was High Commissioner and the object of, at times, violent Zionist criticism. The document was first published, with Crown permission, in John Bowle's biography of 1957. Since then, my father's reputation as an early Zionist has undergone considerable rehabilitation. Among his private papers on his death, I found his own copy of the Cabinet paper: it is now in the Israel State Archives.

The fact that he favoured what eventually became the policy of a Jewish National Home in Palestine led (after 1916, when he was already out of office) to his association with Chaim Weizmann in the negotiations with the British Government that led to the Balfour Declaration in November, 1917. (It is curious that the issue of such a Declaration was bitterly fought by the only Jew in the Cabinet at the time, my father's first cousin, Edwin Montagu, the Secretary of State for India.)

Lloyd George, then Prime Minister, had true Celtic imagination and chose the other Jew — Herbert Samuel — to go out to Palestine in the spring of 1920 to report on the measures to be taken to transform its military administration into a civil government of the Crown Colony type, but under League of Nations supervision. Samuel having so reported, Lloyd George then asked him to go out again to Palestine and put his own recommendations into effect as the first of what eventually turned out to be seven High Commissioners over a period of 28 years. My father was originally appointed for the standard four years of a colonial governor, but was later invited to stay on for a fifth year.

Zionism was ill-prepared for both of its great moments

— the Balfour Declaration of 1917 and the Independence of the State of Israel in 1948. In 1917, out of all the millions of Jews in the world, only 100,000 were members of the Zionist Organization. Apart from a few realists, such as Dr Arthur Ruppin, who had been head of the Zionist Organization's Jaffa office before World War I, Zionism was not only weak as a whole and further riven by factions, but also quite unrealistic. Zionists had messianic hopes but wholly inadequate means to put them into effect. The same month — November, 1917 — when it was declared that the gates of Palestine would be opened to Jewish immigration, the gates of Russia, from which the most fervent Zionists came, were closed by the Russian October Revolution. The wealthy Jews of America and of Britain (including *all* my father's brothers and brothers-in-law) would have nothing to do with Zionism. Weizmann managed to raise only one per cent of the capital that he had confidently anticipated. From the very outset, immigrants were few, but still outstripped the capital needed for their settlement on the land. The Jewish Home got off to a bad start.

After four hundred years of Turkish misrule, this small and obscure province of the Ottoman Empire, now called Palestine, was derelict. Its first State budgets were only just over £1,000,000 a year. The British Government was not prepared to subsidise it to any great extent, so there was little Palestine Government money available for development. Even in the early years, Arab nationalism was strong enough to block Sir Herbert Samuel's well-meant efforts, as a Liberal statesman, to introduce joint Arab-Jewish parliamentary institutions. There were outbreaks of Arab rioting and temporary stoppages of Jewish immigration. He made several bad political mistakes—the grant of large tracts of valuable, well-watered land near Beisan to Arab squatters who promptly *sold* them to Jews; and the recognition as Mufti of Jerusalem of Haj Amin el Husseini, who subsequently turned out to be an implacable enemy not only of Zionism but also of Britain.

Herbert Samuel's five years of office were, however, a period of advance, as his final report showed.★ Although he had had no previous experience in colonial government, it was not difficult for him, as a former Cabinet Minister, to manage a complex administrative system. By personal correspondence with the Secretary of State for the Colonies, and even with the Prime Minister himself when necessary, he was able to circumvent Colonial Office red tape and get his policies, legislation and budgets approved.

As High Commissioner also for Trans-Jordan, he established a friendly working arrangement with the Amir Abdallah, whose British advisers in Amman came under the control of the High Commissioner in Jerusalem.

After the termination of his five years of office, he dreamed of establishing himself on Mount Carmel as a private citizen, and to concentrate there on his philosophical writings. But the presence of a former High Commissioner in a territory now under the management of his successor did not commend itself to Field Marshal Lord Plumer, the new High Commissioner, and the Colonial Secretary prevailed upon Sir Herbert to abandon his plan.★★ Mount Carmel was,

★ *Report of the High Commissioner on the Administration of Palestine, 1920–5*, H.M. Stationery Office, London; Colonial No. 15, 1925.

★★ I have recently discovered amongst his papers a confidential letter to his wife written while he was in Palestine in the spring of 1920 to make his report on setting up a civil administration. He then suggested to her that, even if he was not appointed head of the new administration, however, to form part of his title when he became a peer. He maintained his contact with Palestine and visited it on occasion, especially after 1936 when he became chairman of the Palestine Electric Corporation. I myself remained in Palestine after he left and my reports to him in a series of letters—and his comments—are now in the Israel State Archives.

He was firmly opposed to the partition of Palestine and wrote to the Colonial Secretary to that effect, after it had been recommended by the Peel Commission in 1937. But, once Palestine had fallen apart in 1948, he immediately established personal relations with the representatives of the new State of Israel, both in Jerusalem and London. He was one of the few persons whom Dr Chaim Weizmann, the first President of Israel, in his book *Trial and Error*★ consistently and warmly appreciated. My father was a governor of the Hebrew University and President of the Friends of the Hebrew University in Britain, for whom he did much valuable work.

★   ★   ★

In addition to his career as a British political leader and as High Commissioner for Palestine, Herbert Samuel had a third career as a broadcaster and writer, particularly in the realm of philosophy. It is strange to note that the more his own party disintegrated, the higher his own personal

they should come out to Jerusalem as private citizens. He himself might become a British liaison with the Palestine Zionist Executive. Thus, neither of his attempts to settle in Palestine succeeded.
★ Harper, New York 1949.

reputation stood in Britain. As a member of the BBC's Brains Trust, his ideas became known to a large circle of listeners. At the end of his days he was affectionately regarded as an elder statesman by millions of his fellow-citizens. He had a remarkable memory: even when he was over ninety, he could clearly recollect the minutest details of events in his youth. At family games, such as 'Famous Men beginning with (say) the letter M' he was unbeatable. Every Sunday, he and my youngest brother Godfrey used regularly to do the quiz in the *Sunday Times*, and it was a rare occasion when my father did not obtain the higher score. When I was in London, I frequently took him for a short stroll along the streets and squares surrounding Porchester Terrace where he had spent so much of his life. He knew the occupants, present and past, of many houses, and to listen to his stories of them was a fascinating insight into the social history of England.

As a writer, he was methodical. He would begin with spilling out on sheets of paper all that he wanted to say on the subject in hand, without any order. Then, later, he would rearrange these ideas in the exact sequence in which he would use them, adding new ones in their right places and eliminating those that did not fit. He loved quoting from other people's writings and, in fact, had compiled a valuable anthology, based on sixty years of reading and selection, all copied out by my mother in her lovely script and subsequently published.* It contained a number of his own aphorisms, some of which (such as 'Don't waste good agony') have passed into common use. Personally, I always thought

* *Viscount Samuel's Book of Quotations;* James Barrie, London (second edition, 1954).

that his own style could stand up well by itself and did not need embellishment with other men's jewels: but he belonged to an older school of writing. When he had finished the final draft of his manuscript, it was typed by one of a series of women private secretaries who served him faithfully at different periods of his career. His handwriting was somewhat crabbed, in spite of his gallant attempts, late in life, to adopt italic script. (He even became the president of the society formed to promote it.)

Apart from his book on Liberalism, his autobiography and his book of quotations, most of his other writings dealt, in one way or another, with the relationships between religion, ethics, philosophy, politics and science. Even his utopian *An Unknown Land** (a singularly drab title) was merely a vehicle for putting some of his ideas into popular form. His other works were: *The War and Liberty* (1917); *Philosophy and the Ordinary Man* (1932); *The Tree of Good and Evil* (1933); *Practical Ethics* (1935); *Belief and Action, An Everyday Philosophy* (1937); *Creative Man and Other Addresses* (1949); *Essay on Physics* (1951); and *In Search of Reality* (1957).

Herbert Samuel, in his later years, found great solace in his writing, even though he suffered the fate of all philosopher-statesmen: the statesmen thought him a good philosopher, and the philosophers an excellent statesman. But he had early decided to allow his name to be connected with more than one field of learning. From 1918 to 1920, he was president of the Royal Statistical Society, though no statistician; in 1953 of the Classical Association, though no classicist. He did not consider it strange that, from 1931

---

* George Allen and Unwin, London, 1942.

to 1959, he was president of the British (now Royal) Institute of Philosophy, though not a professional philosopher. To all these societies he brought the prestige of his name and his long experience in the management of affairs.

His thinking was illumined by a sturdy common sense. He believed nothing that his reason could not apprehend. Those academic philosophers who proved mathematically things which seemed alien to experience he wholly rejected. This attitude, of course, secured for him great acclaim from the man in the street who is normally put off by the esoteric approach of many academics.

Although Herbert Samuel was not equipped mathematically or statistically, he did equip himself, by wide reading, to understand the various schools of philosophy. Anything that was a mystery he brooded on until he could find a solution: for example, his revival of the ether theory in order to provide an adequate explanation of the mechanics of motion through empty space. On this he had a long correspondence with the redoubtable Albert Einstein, whom he had known since they had first met at Government House in Jerusalem in 1924, when the Einsteins were his guests. Einstein's letter was published as an appendix to my father's book *In Search of Reality*.★

As a result of his challenge to professional scientists to disprove his ether theory, Herbert Samuel engaged in a dialogue with the physicist Professor Herbert Dingle. Their discussion was published as a book, *A Threefold Cord*★★ (another ambiguous title).

My father had the courage of his convictions in

★ Basil Blackwell, Oxford, 1957, pp. 169–171.
★★ George Allen and Unwin, London, 1961.

philosophy, ethics, science and religion, just as he had always had in politics. The professionals in all those fields sometimes looked on at his efforts with an air of tolerant amusement. But he regarded the award to him of the Order of Merit in 1958 as a vindication of his philosophical beliefs; although it was probably more of a tribute to his general public activities over half a century.

He often discussed his books with me; and I read most of them in typescript. I did not agree with his views on free will, being more influenced myself by Spinoza's determinist approach. My father maintained that an acceptance of the theory of free will was an essential basis for any code of ethics. My inevitable answer was 'Is it true? Is it likely? How can you get round the law of cause and effect?' We never found common ground in this discussion.

★   ★   ★

Our relations were always friendly and affectionate and as close as the differences in age and experience would allow. The truth is that I went in great awe of my father. It is not easy to be the eldest son of a famous man. I showed him, in the 1950's I think, some autobiographical essays I had written (but have never published) of which the first was entitled *How I Learned to be the Son of a Famous Man*. He had never realised till then that, for me, there had been any such problem.

I owe, of course, an immense amount to him. It was he who decided that I should go to school at Westminster in 1911 and who eventually agreed to let me switch from the classics, which I loathed, to science which I adored. But

I saw little of him when I was a boy: he was not up by the time I went to school; and he came back from late sittings in the House of Commons long after I had gone to bed. But, during the holidays, the family was usually together, especially in the summer, which we invariably spent in Cleveland, his constituency, with its wonderful beaches and glorious moors.

From the age of nineteen I was but rarely in London. In the spring of 1917, at eighteen and a half, I joined the Royal Field Artillery and went out to Allenby's Egyptian Expeditionary Force in Palestine. It was my father who later insisted that I should go to the University. So, when I returned to England in 1919, I went straight to Balliol, but, as soon as I graduated, I went out to the Palestine Civil Service, married, and set up my own household in Jerusalem. For five years he also lived in Jerusalem, on the Mount of Olives; but he was the High Commissioner and I was almost the lowest form of animal life — a district officer. Although some of the more feudal-minded Palestinians and the more self-seeking British officials tended to treat me as Crown Prince, I do not think that I ever benefited from my father's favouritism. If anything, he leaned over backwards to prevent any such imputations.

While kind, he was spartan, especially in money matters. He never indulged himself and brought us all up to be economical in our turn. On my marriage, he generously gave me a small private income (£300 a year, then quite an appreciable sum) and increased it to £500 a year on the birth of my first son. But it was not easy, even with this, for me to live for 28 years on my salary as a colonial civil servant. I found it difficult to go on leave to England every two years with a wife, two children and a nurse, before the days of Government passage grants. For most of my life I was just out of debt again by the time I was due to go on leave once more. He would assist me with a loan to cover my debts, but he was strict in expecting repayment by the dates agreed on.

He was, I think, proud of my doings, as he was of those of his other three children. But he was never emotional; he always seemed embarrassed when, on our meeting again after a long absence, I kissed him lightly on his stubbly cheek.

As the eldest son of a very distinguished man, I sometimes felt rather like a sapling growing up in the shadow of a massive oak. One of the subconscious reasons for my deciding not to return to England after I left the Colonial Service but to stay on in the new Israel and teach at the Hebrew University may have been my desire to keep out of the shadow of that tree. I have recently realised that this was the real reason why I shortened my name many years ago, for all practical purposes, from 'Edwin Herbert Samuel' to 'Edwin Samuel'.

CHAPTER 2

PALESTINE, 1917–19

I first got to Palestine in December, 1917, a month after the Balfour Declaration was published. Most people who arrive in Palestine — or, today, in Israel — come because of Zionist convictions, or because they have fled from oppression and have nowhere else to go. I came for an odd and unique reason. As a mounted artilleryman in the British army, I did not wish to be separated from my horses.

I had been at Westminster School when the war broke out, and was madly keen on science. I tried to enlist in 1916 in a chemical warfare battalion but was rejected as too young. In the spring of 1917, I volunteered for the Royal Field Artillery, then horse-drawn. Here my mathematics helped (in calculating ranges) and the combination of men, horses and machines enchanted me. Having been in the school officers' training corps, I went straight to an artillery officers' cadet school and, after six months, was commissioned as a second lieutenant. Like my fellow cadets, I was due to go to France and bought all my equipment for a winter in the trenches—gum-boots, a wool-lined trench-coat with a fur collar, fur-lined leather gloves, a woollen scarf and so on. The fact that the average life of an artillery subaltern in France in 1917 was about six weeks did not seem to have worried me. I was merely sorry that

I was to be involved in the stalemate of trench warfare and would be separated from my beloved horses.

Not that I was a famous rider: as a Londoner I had had little opportunity for riding. But my imaginative grandmother used regularly to give me, as birthday presents, twelve tickets enabling me to tittup of a Sunday morning round Hyde Park for an hour on a docile and disinterested mare, hired from a local livery stable. On arriving at the cadet school, any cadet who could ride was ordered to step one pace forward. I, supremely confident, did so, to find — too late — that, apart from a regular mounted sergeant-major of many years standing, I was the only cadet who could ride. The N.C.O. riding master mounted me on a fierce and gigantic stallion and instructed me to jump over a five-barred gate in the riding school, without saddle or bridle. I had never jumped before in my life. I went over the jump all right, but without the horse. So I was put in the infants' class, the butt of all the riding instructors as the aspirant for an artillery commission who had said he could ride. Since then, I have never made the mistake of stepping one pace forward in any circumstance whatsoever.

But I did learn to ride in the cadet school and delighted in being one of the three mounted gunners, each with a pair of horses, all harnessed to an eighteen-pounder gun. We practised daily galloping into action across Regent's Park with all the shiny steel shackles jangling. Woe betide anyone who fell off under the bounding wheel of the gun or its attached ammunition limber!

So it was with interest that I heard by accident one day in the mess at Woolwich, when I was already awaiting an overseas posting to France, that General Fox was going out from Canterbury with artillery reinforcements for Allenby's

Egyptian Expeditionary Force. There was to be a big 'push' in Palestine.

I hardly knew where Palestine was: I had never heard of Zionism. But the idea of galloping into action across the desert and winning the Victoria Cross seemed to me far preferable to life in the water-logged trenches of Flanders. So I asked a fellow-officer called Sexton, who claimed to have friends at the War Office, to get me transferred to the E.E.F. I did not really believe that he could pull such strings: in those days I was very innocent. But, in a couple of weeks, orders came through posting 2nd Lt. E. H. Samuel, R.F.A. to the E.E.F. So back I went to my military outfitters and exchanged my gum-boots, my trench-coat, my gloves and my scarf for the latest in tropical pith helmets, mosquito nets and special khaki shirts with a buttoned-on spine protector against the non-existent menace of spinal sunstroke. (I have by now spent fifty years in Palestine and Israel and never wear an ordinary hat even at noon-time on the hottest summer day. I have long ago discovered that a pair of cheap dark glasses is all that one needs.)

So, in November, 1917, I started off from Southampton, after two false alarms. Each time our sailing was cancelled, I was welcomed home again by a tearful mother. On my third departure from home, she did not even trouble to kiss me good-bye and we were both relieved.

I found that I was now the proud officer in charge of a detachment of artillery reservists, all of whom were at least twice my age. We crossed the Channel and landed at Le Havre, to see, for the first time, a detachment of American soldiers drawn up on the quay-side. They were tall, slender young men, in strange olive-green uniforms and slouch hats, with sausage-shaped packs on their backs and curious water-bottles. Even I realised what an immense asset America's entry into the war must be. Here were virile young men arriving by the tens of thousands across the Atlantic, while we were already scraping the bottom of our man-power barrel.

Owing to a German breakthrough on the sector held by Gough's Fifth Army, we made a detour by rail round Paris and went via Orleans to Marseilles. It was at Orleans that we celebrated the *entente cordiale* with a trainful of French troops coming home on leave from the front. We exchanged water-bottles, but I found, too late, that my French comrade's was filled with something neat and fiery. Being unused to alcohol, all I remember is getting back to my own compartment, announcing to my fellow officers that I would shortly be very drunk indeed and waking up many hours later with my first and only hangover.

It was an unforgettable journey, along the Côte d'Azur, in sunny weather, in and out of tunnels, overlooking the little bays and the gorgeous blue Mediterranean. No subsequent journey anywhere has ever seemed so magical.

At Marseilles I lost a man in the brothels. I expected — and imagined all the way to Egypt — that I would be court-martialled for this on arrival. This fear rather took the gilt off the ginger-bread derived from my doubly exalted position on board our troopship. The artillery-men, and their officers (myself included) were roped in to help man the anti-submarine guns. So I messed with the ship's staff and had to try to decipher our course on the charts supplied by our Japanese destroyer escorts. The other cause for my special position was the fact that mine was the only unit on board which had its own lending library. This stemmed from the fact that, as a schoolboy of sixteen, I had been walking down our London street one day with my father. I noticed an old lady struggling to wrap up in brown paper, and address, a book that she wanted to post to the War Libraries for troops at the front. My father was then Postmaster-General and I suggested to him that it would be much simpler if books could be posted unwrapped and unaddressed, and that all books found in the pillar-boxes be sent automatically to the War Libraries. My father passed on the idea and it was adopted. I was subsequently told that the number of books received each month had vastly increased in consequence. So, when I was due myself to take a unit overseas, being then a very serious young man I wrote to the War Libraries office and asked whether I, as originator of the idea, could have a box of books for my men. A box was duly delivered on board at Marseilles. We became the only unit to have anything to read, so our status rose considerably.

My first taste of the East was Alexandria, not a place I would recommend to the romantically inclined. We were all sent to some base camp to await our regimental postings. Gradually, everyone went up to the front, then around Gaza, except me. Eventually I received a telegram instructing 2nd Lieut. E.H. Samuel, R.F.A., to proceed at once to G.S.I., G.H.Q., First Echelon. I was then so ignorant of military terminology that I had no idea that G.S.I. meant General Staff Intelligence, or that First Echelon meant Allenby's advanced headquarters in the field (as contrasted with Second Echelon, his base at Cairo). I was much too shy to ask anyone what G.S.I., G.H.Q., First Echelon, meant. So I just thrust the slip of paper through the little window of the railway transport officer's hut on the platform of the Alexandria railway station. The strange thing was that he did not know either where to send me, as the troops were advancing into Palestine and Allenby was continually moving up his own headquarters just behind the forward units. Eventually I caught up with his headquarters near the Arab village of Dair el Balah, south-west of Gaza.

It was only after the war that I discovered why I had been posted to the Intelligence Corps in Palestine. My father was still then an M.P., though out of office. One day, in the Commons he met another member, Sir Mark Sykes, an expert on the Middle East (the Sykes-Picot Agreement enshrines his name for ever), and one of the under-secretaries of the War Cabinet. He asked my father why he looked so sad, and my father said that his eldest son had just gone overseas. Sir Mark politely asked to which front and was told the Middle East. Sykes, apparently thinking that I was a university graduate in my late twenties, exclaimed: 'Just the man we want!' He at once had me posted to Allenby's political intelligence section at G.H.Q. under Lt-Col. Wyndham Deedes, as — of all things — an expert on Jewish affairs.

I caught up with Allenby's headquarters on December 10th, the day after the capture of Jerusalem. The Turks had launched a counter-attack to recapture Nebi Samwil (called after the Prophet Samuel whose tomb is still shown in the local mosque). This village, to the north-west of Jerusalem, is even higher than the city and commands the whole countryside. The counter-attack was repelled, and some members of the junior intelligence officers' mess were reading the evening bulletin when I appeared. I had just announced myself as 'Second Lieutenant Samuel reporting for duty' when the mess wag, a captain said: 'Here is Nebi

Samuel himself!'; and the nickname has stuck to me in Palestine and Israel ever since.

The tented G.H.Q. camp at Dair Balah was on a sandy plain. I had a small grey Arab pony allotted to me on which I used to ride every morning at dawn. My career was nearly cut short at its beginning when I was out riding with another officer, disregarding Allenby's strict regulation that no soldier was ever to ride in shorts. Riding breeches or, at a pinch, slacks, must be worn to prevent the rider's knees being chafed and the soldier rendered unfit for subsequent duty, hence a court-martial offence. By ill chance we ran into the Commander-in-Chief himself, who—known as the Bull — was promptly enraged. My companion manfully lied and said he had ordered me at short notice to accompany him. Allenby could not have believed this; but I was not court-martialled.

Wyndham Deeds, that most remarkable of men* was a regular British army officer who had been seconded in peace time to the Ottoman gendarmerie in North Africa and knew excellent Turkish. (At G.H.Q. he kept his most secret notes in Turkish, on the ground that enemy spies would be German, not knowing Turkish.) He became almost a second father to me and I was devoted to him. From 1920 till 1922, he was Chief Secretary in Palestine and I again served under him; he influenced me a great deal. As a devout Christian he could not stand the bickering over the Holy Places and went to live in the East End of London, becoming assistant secretary to the National Council for Social Service. Every time I went on leave, I used to call on him at his office in Bedford Square. He would take me out to lunch but never

* See *Deeds Bey*—John Presland; Macmillan, 1942.

ate anything himself. He never married, ending his days in Hythe, where he devotedly visited bed-ridden old men hardly younger than himself: he was a saintly figure. He immediately realised that I was no expert on Jewish affairs; or on anything else, either. I was put to writing up the Intelligence Corps war diary, then much in arrears. But, never having seen even a file before, I had not the slightest idea how to go about extracting the relevant data. So I was soon taken off this, too, and set to dealing with translated reports from British agents behind the enemy line. Everything was new to me — the geography of the Middle East, the sub-divisions of the Ottoman Empire, Turkish military and civil titles and terminology and the organization of modern armies. I cannot think that my contribution to the war effort was of any value whatsoever: but I certainly learnt a great deal that helped to fit me for a Colonial Service career in Palestine for a subsequent twenty-eight years.

Among the reports that I handled were those of the Aaronsohn organization. This had been built up by the well-known agricultural scientist Aaron Aaronsohn, based at his experimental station at Athlit, on the coast south of Haifa (then still behind the enemy lines). Aaron had escaped to the Allies, leaving his sister Sarah behind to collect the material from spies in the field. Every month, when there was no moon, an Admiralty sloop from Port Said would take Aaron's brother, (Captain) Alex Aaronsohn, up the coast, drop him off near Athlit to pick up the reports from his sister and take him back again. (On one of these expeditions he lost the pistol I had lent him.) But this was too slow for Captain George Lloyd (later Lord Lloyd) of G.S.I. He arranged for messages to be brought out by land. Naaman Belkind, one of the messengers, disguised as a Beduin, was captured by a pro-Turkish tribe. He was tortured and gave away the names of the whole organization, many of whom were then arrested and hanged. Sarah shot herself to avoid torture and is now a national heroine among ultra-nationalists in Israel.

After some weeks, Allenby's headquarters moved forward once more to a valley bottom west of Jerusalem. The site — then called Junction Station—had been chosen by an experienced senior staff officer, Lieutenant-Colonel Guy Dawnay, But, as soon as the rains restarted, many of the tents were washed away, leaving all the surrounding lanes deep in mud and impassable. Allenby had the colonel on the mat to explain why he had chosen a valley bottom for G.H.Q. Dawnay explained that one of his ancestors had been a Crusader and had camped on that very site. Allenby is reported to have roared: 'But did he have motor transport?!'

Just about this time, my eyes began to give trouble. There was no military oculist yet in Palestine and I had to go down to Egypt for examination. As luck would have it, the rains flooding the Wadi Ghuzzeh had washed away the recently-built military railway line from Egypt. So I had to motor from Junction Station to Jerusalem, from Jerusalem to Hebron and from Hebron south of the Wadi Ghuzzeh to catch a train for Egypt. My travelling companion was a Lieutenant-Colonel Meinertzhagen, and our drive from G.H.Q. to the effective railhead took three days. During this time I regaled the colonel with items of recently acquired information (mostly inaccurate, I am sure) on the geography, archaeology, history, ethnology, flora and fauna of the countryside through which we were passing. It was only when I got to Cairo that I discovered that Richard Meinertzhagen was the greatest living authority on the birds of the Middle East, about which he had written the standard work.

Shortly after I came back from Cairo, we moved camp again to Bir Salem, near the main Jaffa-Jerusalem road. This was in the centre of the famous Jaffa orange belt. The red soil, when watered, is immensely fertile: one day I counted no less than thirty different kinds of small spring flowers in the few square yards around my bell-tent. Being city-bred, this seemed to me miraculous. Many mornings, at sunrise, I would see Allenby himself in the fields, picking flowers and putting them in a large envelope (which he held in his arthritic hand, his arm in a sling) for despatch to Lady Allenby in Cairo.

From Bir Salem I was within easy riding distance of some of the older, larger and most prosperous Jewish settlements in Judaea. I had already visited Ruchama, then the most southerly of all the Jewish settlements. After three years of war, it was miserably poor and neglected, but it was my first direct contact with Jewish colonisation. Now I was able to see Rishon LeZiyyon ('The first in Zion'), the centre of the Jewish wine industry. Believing that, in the East, one should do things in Eastern style, I remember making my first entry into Rishon on camel-back. It was not only most uncomfortable but gave the impression that I must be a lunatic. For, outside the desert, the camel is used solely as a beast of burden—to carry sacks.

Still, I got to know several well-to-do Jewish farmers in Rishon, and their families. An Anglo-Jewish army officer was then a novelty and I had everywhere a most friendly reception. I knew no Hebrew, Arabic, Yiddish or Russian; they knew no English, but we managed to get on in a mixture of French and German.

I was having tea one day at Rishon when a series of British motor-cycle despatch-riders came roaring through the village, looking for me. In the office that morning I had been sent the top secret file on the Sykes-Picot Agreement which embodied the Anglo-French plan for the division of the Ottoman Arab provinces at the end of the war between the two Powers. By the time I had finished with it, the N.C.O. in charge of the secret registry had gone off to lunch; so I, very intelligently as I thought, had locked up the file in my kit-bag. Again, as ill-luck would have it, the C-in-C wanted the file after lunch: it was marked out and to 2nd Lieutenant Samuel, and 2nd Lieutenant Samuel had disappeared. But the C-in-C was so relieved to find that I had neither lost nor stolen the file that I again heard nothing more after this escapade.

My direct contact with Jewish settlers in Rishon LeZiyyon and Rehovot had naturally whetted my desire to learn a little Hebrew, for purely utilitarian reasons. I was still no Zionist, and had no intention of remaining in the country after the war. There was a little Jewish settlement adjacent to Allenby's headquarters at Bir Salem ('The well of Salem' in Arabic.) It was called Be'er Ya'aqov ('The well of Jacob' in Hebrew.) There, I found an elderly Jewish schoolteacher, wearing a high-buttoned and embroidered shirt, who agreed to give me lessons. Every afternoon I walked across the *wadi*★ into the village, along the unpaved street between the rickety, unpainted wooden palings, to my teacher's house. I had just got as far as being able to say '*Bait lavan im gag adom*' ('A white house with a red roof') when, by another

★ A river bed, dry in the summer (Arabic).

sudden turn of fate, I found myself one of the four military officers attached to Dr Chaim Weizmann. He had come out to Tel Aviv with the first Zionist Commission in order to put the Balfour Declaration into effective operation.

By this time, I had begun really to know something of Jewish affairs and had been handling the telegrams at G.H.Q. announcing the arrival of Dr Weizmann and his colleagues. Most of them I had never heard of; but, providentially, Lt-Col Norman Bentwich, who had married my mother's niece, was stationed some miles from G.H.Q. He had been an early Zionist who had gone out as a British legal adviser to the Egyptian government before the war. He hoped thereby to be able to walk into the Promised Land as soon as the gates were opened, as he firmly believed they would be. By 1918, he most improbably commanded an Egyptian camel transport company in Palestine. He was sixteen years my senior, but I had met him casually at the first *Seder* (Passover service) for Jewish troops held in Jerusalem in the spring of 1918. So, whenever I was asked at G.H.Q. some question about Jewish affairs to which I did not have the answer (of course we had no encyclopaedia or reference books, beyond the Holy Bible) I used to ride over to Norman to get the information and be back before anyone knew that I had been out of the camp. So it was he who supplied me with all the particulars of Weizmann and his colleagues. I was to spend the next three months with them in Tel Aviv, then a suburb of Jaffa with a population of about 6,000. Except for a few schools, it was composed entirely of little one and two-storey cottages, many set in neglected gardens, surrounded by unpainted fences. The streets were all sandy and most were unpaved.

My going to Tel Aviv had been Weizmann's own idea.

He knew my father in London: they had collaborated in the negotiations with the British Government that led to the Balfour Declaration. Weizmann always had an eye cocked towards the future. Here was a young English Jew, son of an ex-Cabinet Minister, so he decided to try and make a Zionist out of me. At that time, the senior British political advisers to Weizmann were Major William Ormsby-Gore (later Colonial Secretary and Lord Harlech) and Major James de Rothschild (only son of Baron Edmond de Rothschild, of Paris, father of the *Yishuv* — the Jewish community of Palestine.) They had come out from England with him; but two more British officers were to be attached locally. One was Captain Eric Waley, who, before the war, had been in business in Egypt. Weizmann asked Deedes to second me to Ormsby-Gore as the other. I was much the youngest of the four officers and soon became virtually A.D.C. to Weizmann. (I kept a daily record of his interviews and visits and have recently given it, with all my other papers, to the Israel State Archives in Jerusalem.) He had a bewitching personality and it was not difficult for him to convert me to Zionism. I had already become somewhat starry-eyed about the early Jewish villages, especially the children.★ I had never seen sturdy blond Jewish peasant children before. As I accompanied Weizmann on his semi-royal tours of the Jewish settlements of Judaea (central and northern Palestine still being in Turkish hands), the jubilant reception he received everywhere added to the excitement. It was spring: I was all of nineteen and I converted easily, it seems.

★ See photograph between pages 148 and 149.

38

Somehow I got hold of a book — Dr Arthur Ruppin's *The Jews of Today*.★ Ruppin was a German-Jewish sociologist and an early Zionist. He had come out to Jaffa in 1907 to found the Palestine office of the World Zionist Movement. As such, he had undertaken the establishment of the first Jewish villages from publicly-controlled Jewish funds (as contrasted with the private Rothschild and Hirsch foundations.) His book convinced me that the Jewish people, caught between persecution in the east and assimilation in the west, could be saved only by Jewish nationalism and the establishment of a Jewish national home in Palestine.

It must be remembered that, by the spring of 1918, the Balfour Declaration favouring the establishment of such a national home in Palestine was only four months old. Everything then seemed possible and, like everyone else around me, I was swept along by messianic hopes.

One of the great events at that time was the laying of the foundation stones of the Hebrew University on Mount Scopus in Jerusalem. This was an early Zionist dream — a Jewish university in the Promised Land, teaching once again in the Holy Tongue. In the spring of 1918, the war was still in progress on all fronts. While General Allenby and Weizmann laid their stones in the midst of a vast crowd that had streamed on foot up the mountain, we could hear the British and Turkish guns faintly booming some fifteen miles to the north. That ceremony was an act of faith indeed.★★

There was another and more personal reason why I became so attached to Palestine. It was in Tel Aviv, in the

★ G. Bell & Sons, London, 1913.
★★ See photograph between pages 148 and 149.

spring of 1918, that I first met my future wife: we were married two and a half years later, after I had taken my degree at Oxford and had returned to Palestine as a British colonial civil servant.

We could not really escape meeting, as the vacant upper floor of her parents' house in Tel Aviv had been requisitioned by the British Army for use as quarters for the four officers attached to the Zionist Commission (who were themselves housed not far away.) Hearing the piano being played one day, I thought: 'where there is music there is youth!' I boldly walked downstairs and knocked at the door: it was opened by a slim, dark, shy girl. We had no common language except French: one cannot get very far in Hebrew with 'A white house with a red roof'.

At that time, my future wife's father had been exiled by the Turks to Damascus, more or less as a hostage for the good behaviour of the Jewish community in Palestine, then suspected (and rightly) of being strongly pro-British. He himself had come to Palestine from Lithuania in the 1880's and had earned his living, first as an agricultural labourer, later as a schoolteacher. A most erudite man, he was, in fact, a graduate of the famous Jewish religious seminary at Volojin in Lithuania, although he later became strongly anti-clerical. One of his pupils in the school at Ekron, in the south, where he taught, had come to Palestine as a child with her parents from Rumania. They married later and had five children, of whom my wife was the second. Later still, my future father-in-law entered the service of the Anglo-Palestine Bank and had been for some years branch manager in Beirut (where my future wife had learned French). Eventually, he became deputy manager at the main office of the bank in Jaffa.

Unlike most European Jewish immigrants in Palestine, who preferred to retain their foreign nationality and foreign consular protection, Yehuda Grasovsky had become an Ottoman citizen. (He had to prove that he had been born in the Ottoman Empire: such certificates were not difficult to obtain, for a consideration.) As an Ottoman citizen he could hold land; and vast areas of Jewish public and private land were registered in his name. But, being a man of sterling integrity, he was a faithful steward of this property, all of which was registered later, during the British Mandatory Administration, in the names of the rightful owners. But his real loves were pedagogy and philology. He had already written some of the first Hebrew school-books: they were published in Warsaw and had given him quite an appreciable income in royalties before World War I. Later in life, he was engaged in compiling — with David Yellin of Jerusalem, and then alone — a whole series of Hebrew dictionaries. He and his sons Hebraised their surname to Goor ('a lion cub': c.f., Ben-Gurion) and his dictionaries, published by Dvir of Tel Aviv, are commonly known under this name.

He was a most modest and yet far-sighted man. He realised, long before World War I that the future of Jewish settlement in Palestine would largely depend on the availability of trained Palestinian Jewish agriculturists. There were then no post-secondary agricultural facilities in Palestine. He sent his eldest son all the way to study horticulture at Berkeley University in California, where the climate and soil somewhat resembled those of Palestine.

When I first came to Tel Aviv, there were there only Mrs. Grasovsky, her second son Amihud (who later also went to Berkeley and Yale to study forestry), her elder daughter Hadassah (my future wife), and two younger children — a girl, Nechama, and a boy, Shai (who later took a degree in veterinary medicine at Edinburgh). Mrs. Grasovsky viewed with some perturbation her elder daughter's association with a British officer. When I asked Hadassah if she would give me Hebrew lessons, her mother flatly forbade it, thinking that this would merely be an excuse for two young people to stare into each other's eyes. But the end result, two and a half years later, was the same, even without the Hebrew lessons.

My Hebrew has never been perfect; and in those early years it was treacherous. For some reason I was deputed, in the spring of 1918, to represent the C-in-C at the first conference in Tel Aviv of Jewish schoolteachers from southern Palestine since its 'liberation'. I carefully prepared a short Hebrew speech; but, being unable then to read my own Hebrew script fast enough, I transliterated it into English lettering. I began well enough: '*Ani* (I) *sameach* (am glad) *lehipagesh* (to meet) *hayom* (today) *im* (with) *histadrut* (the organization of) — and then, instead of *hamorim* ('the teachers') I used the more guttural *chamorim*, which unfortunately means 'donkeys'. There was a wave of hilarious laughter; and, for years after, whenever I visited a Jewish school in Palestine, some teacher would be sure to come up and introduce himself as 'one of your donkeys'.

In the spring of 1920, on his first visit to Palestine, my father called on Rachel Grasovsky in Tel Aviv. Both families by now warmly approved of the match. My mother-in-law was a woman whose integrity fully matched her husband's. She was a wonderful manager and brought up her family successfully. I was devoted to her.

★ ★ ★

By the time Dr Weizmann returned to London in the summer of 1918, I had developed into an ardent Zionist. In addition to the other attractions of Palestine there was now Hadassah. She and her mother were staunch nationalists and strong supporters of the proposal to recruit in Palestine a third Jewish battalion — the 40th Royal Fusiliers. It was to take its place beside the 38th Battalion, recruited largely in Britain, and the 39th, recruited largely in America. The British Army affectionately nicknamed the 38th 'The King's Own Schneiders'. The 39th was given the regimental motto 'No advance without security', while the 40th was called, not the Gordon Highlanders, but the Jordan Highlanders. The raising of these battalions had been the work of a number of Jewish leaders, including the young David Ben-Gurion, then an exile in America from Palestine; Vladimir Jabotinsky, later to be the Revisionist leader; and Pinhas Rutenberg, the future promoter of the Palestine Electric Corporation.

As soon as Weizmann had left Palestine, I thought it was about time that I did some real fighting. I am not a naturally brave person; but I still hankered after that Victoria Cross. If I could not get it by galloping into action with my battery, I would try the infantry. So, under the inspiration of Hadassah and her mother, I asked Colonel Deedes if he would allow me to be seconded to the 40th Royal Fusiliers as a training officer. I had had an infantry training myself, in the Westminster School O.T.C., and I knew a little Hebrew. Deedes, who was a most understanding man, gave his consent. I took down from the lapels of my tunic the green tabs of the Intelligence Corps, put up the red *Magen David* sleeve patches and went down to Egypt to the camp of the 40th (Jewish) Battalion of the Royal Fusiliers, first at Helmieh,

43

near Cairo, and then at Tel el Kebir, some 25 miles west of the Suez Canal. The 38th and 39th Battalions were already in action in the Jordan Valley.

I was such an ardent Hebraist in those early days that I seem to have insisted on giving Hebrew names to all the 'streets' in our camp and having painted signs put up at each corner. I have also recently found among my World War I papers (now with the Israel State Archives) a small printed pamphlet entitled 'Parts of the Rifle, in English and Hebrew'. The authors are, unbelievably, Lieutenant Vladimir Jabotinsky and 2nd Lieutenant Edwin Samuel.

The 40th Royal Fusiliers was a most unusual battalion. Many Palestinian Jewish labour leaders (including David Ben-Gurion and the late Levi Eshkol, future Prime Ministers of Israel, and the late Itzhak Ben-Zvi, its second President) were in the ranks as privates or N.C.O.'s. A great deal of nationalist ferment went on in the men's tents late at night. In spite of the normal rules against too much fraternisation between officers and men, I used to go in and listen. They explained to me at length the ideals and organization of the then nascent labour movement and of the *kibbutz*. This may help to explain my membership of the Parliamentary Labour Party in the House of Lords today.

We were a very mixed crowd. Apart from the hard core of Labour Zionists, physically tough, there were a number of frail talmudical students, with long side-locks, from Jerusalem. They were equally fired with messianic enthusiasm; but it was not so easy to turn them into fighting men. Major James de Rothschild had been sent on a recruiting campaign in the Jewish quarters of Cairo and Alexandria, as well as in Palestine, and we soon received large numbers of Arabised Jews, in fezzes and long *galabiyas* (resembling

44

nightgowns), not knowing any language but Arabic. All training had to be done through translators. But the worst thorn in my flesh was a group of Turks. All Turkish prisoners-of-war in Egypt had been offered release; if Arab, to join Col. T. E. Lawrence's irregulars, or, if Jewish, the 40th Royal Fusiliers. A group of Moslem peasants from Anatolia who, I am sure, had never in their whole lives even seen a Jew, decided to become honorary Jews for the duration and were sent to me for retraining. They hardly knew their left foot from their right. Commands given were translated by one interpreter from English into French, by a second from French into Arabic and by a third from Arabic into Turkish. Orders to 'about turn' had to be given when the squad reached the centre of our small parade-ground to ensure — after allowing for successive translations — that it did not pile up at the boundary-wall before it received the command in Turkish.

It was all very hard work; but morale was high and I felt that, at last, I was earning my keep. We all looked forward to going up to Palestine to join our sister battalions in the final push that Allenby had launched in September. I would then win my Victoria Cross at last. But, unfortunately, the Turks crumpled without our assistance and, at the end of October, sued for an armistice.

There was clearly no further need for my services with the Battalion; so I returned to G.H.Q. at Bir Salem, this time to the staff of Brigadier-General Gilbert Clayton, chief political advisor to Allenby. It was here that I first met Colonel Lawrence and other members of the brilliant team that Clayton had collected around him, including Father Philip Waggett, of the Cowley Fathers (an Anglican order) and our expert on the Holy Places. I was now anxious myself to enter O.E.T.A. (the Occupied Enemy Territory Administration), staffed by British officers, until the future of the country had been decided at the Peace Conference.

But here my father put his foot down. He had no objection to my working in Palestine; but I must first come back to England and get a university degree. So, at the beginning of 1919, I was repatriated in one of the earliest demobilisation classes, that of teachers and students. We waited for weeks on the Canal at Kantara, then a tented city of over 100,000 inactive men. The available shipping first took back the ANZACs (men of the Australian and New Zealand Army Corps) who were the most rebellious. Eventually my turn came. We were landed at Taranto in southern Italy, whence we started on a week's nightmare railway trip to Le Havre in tropical uniforms in mid-winter in unheated carriages, the window panes missing. Every two days we were taken out and bathed. Before going through the Alps, we were given whale oil with which we smeared our bodies as a protection against frostbite. But it was my first sight of the snow-covered Alpine peaks. There was a full moon in a clear sky and I sat up all night at the open window, revelling even in the biting cold.

My father having been to Balliol, I went there, too. (My youngest brother followed me and, later, my own two sons.) I caused a sensation in 1966 by asking the Master to consider in due course one of my grand-*daughters*, then five. There is now a mixed men and women's graduate school in which Balliol and the women's college of St Anne's are participating: I may not be so far out as I seemed. I had wanted to become an electrical engineer: the only difficulty was that, in Palestine, there was then no electricity, nor any immediate prospect of any. So I decided to switch to the future Palestine civil service and, as a preparation, read modern history, political science and comparative government for my B.A.

This was my second switch, having started at Westminster as an unhappy classicist, followed by four years' blissful concentration on science to the exclusion of almost everything else. At Oxford, I had to start all over again. I did not even know in which *century* major events had occurred. But I was lucky enough to meet the historian Lewis Namier, then briefly tutor at Balliol, who taught me to look at Europe from Vienna and not from London. I was also fortunate having Francis Urquhart and Kenneth Bell as my regular tutors. They were very patient; for, in addition to my abysmal ignorance at the beginning, I suffered — like most of the young demobilised officers who had exercised too much authority abroad too early — from an immense difficulty in sitting down, hour after hour, and reading a book.

Post-war Oxford was bleak: there was little coal and little food. Most of the time we were cold and hungry. The famous social life of an Oxford college had not been fully restored, even by the time I graduated in 1920. It was all a terrific grind, even though I was given credit for a year and a half war service. It meant working through all the vacations (one Easter with David Fyfe, later Lord Chancellor, in a farmhouse in Kent). How I got through my examinations I really do not know. Luckily, the successful candidates were not divided into classes; so I shall never know how well — or badly — I did. But I do know that this shortened course left me very inadequately educated. I knew no economics or statistics; and it was not until 1932, when I was 33, that I got an American Commonwealth Fund fellowship, went to Columbia University and studied these two subjects. Only then I really began to feel prepared for an administrative career.

It was at Oxford that I had my next meeting with T.E. Lawrence, whose acquaintance I had first made at Allenby's G.H.Q. in Palestine in 1918. Although Lawrence refused resolutely to talk in public about the Middle East, for some reason he accepted my invitation to come up to Oxford and speak at the Labour Club. We both addressed the club the same evening, he on Arab nationalism, I on Jewish. He then walked me up and down the High until all hours, describing at length his manoeuvres to oust Lord Curzon, the Foreign Secretary, under whom Lawrence was then serving. I, still very naive, was shocked.

The only other time I met Lawrence was one day in the 1930's when I was on leave from Palestine. I went for a walk with my father: when we passed the house of George Bernard Shaw, an old friend of his, he suggested that we pay a call. Lawrence was there in R.A.F. uniform. While my father chatted with G.B.S., I stood with T.E.L. by the fireplace. I asked him why people were saying that he was an anti-Zionist. He replied that that was nonsense, as *he* had invented the slogan 'Arabia for the Arabs, Judaea for the Jews, Armenia for the Armenians'. He gave no support for any Arab claim to Palestine. When I asked if I might quote him, he said 'of course'. This was just before he left the Air Force: he was killed shortly thereafter in a motorcycle accident.

When I was still at Oxford, I decided to fulfil a promise I had made to myself while at Kantara in 1919, waiting to be repatriated to England. I had very little direct information about how Jews lived in England, outside my own narrow family circle. So I decided to spend a fortnight in Whitechapel to see what real Jewish life there was like. With the connivance of Basil Henriques, I joined his St George's boys' club incognito as a 'boy'. I was boarded out in the house of a Jewish butcher where I slept four in a bed with his three young sons. I claimed to be a demobilised soldier — an officer's batman (to explain my accent) — looking for work at a railway station nearby. In the evenings I hung around the billiard saloons in the drizzling rain. It was all rather squalid and confirmed me in my resolve to make my life in sunny Palestine. After ten days I could stand it no longer and came back to my parents' house. My disguise was so lifelike that our cook turned me away from the backdoor.

In the spring of 1920, my father was invited by Lloyd George, then Prime Minister, to go out to Palestine and report on the measures to be taken for transforming the war-time military administration into the British Mandatory civilian Palestine Government. On the way, he visited Hadassah, then studying at Geneva, and formed a most favourable impression. My mother invited her, although we were not then formally engaged, to stay with us while while I was still at Oxford. She rapidly learned English.

Later, my father was invited to put his own recommendations into practice and to go out to Jerusalem in July, 1920, as the first High Commissioner for Palestine and for Trans-Jordan. I came out myself in October, 1920, bringing my mother and sister; my two younger brothers remained at school in England. I immediately joined the staff of the District Commissioner of Jerusalem and am one of the few who served in the Palestine Administration from almost the beginning to the end.

CHAPTER 3

JERUSALEM, 1920–25

During the five years that my father served as High Commissioner, he lived in state on the Mount of Olives. His official residence was the *Augusta Viktoria Stiftung*—a vast German hospice which also served as government offices. Colonel Deedes, later Sir Wyndham Deedes, with his special knowledge, had been persuaded to return as Civil Secretary, while Norman Bentwich was the Legal Secretary. Some of the senior British civil servants were taken over from the military administration; others were career Colonial Service men transferred on promotion from British dependencies elsewhere. Although Palestine was legally a Mandated Territory, it was administered more or less as a Crown Colony. Because of the Jewish National Home policy, there were, in the early years, quite a number of British Jews in the administration, in addition to my father, Bentwich and myself. Few Palestinian Jews at that time knew any English.* Later, when a new generation grew up knowing English, some with English university degrees, British Jews were no

---

* Few Moslems knew English either. The majority of the Palestinians in the administration were Christian Arabs, although they formed only a tenth of the population. They had learned English in the mission schools.

longer necessary. But, in those early years, they formed a bridge between the Government and the Palestinian Jewish community.

For the first five years of my service, I was on the headquarters staff of Sir Ronald Storrs, the Governor (later District Commissioner) of the Jerusalem District. Palestine adopted the usual Crown Colony system of district administration with British district commissioners in the principal towns and British district officers in the smaller towns. This fitted in well with the former Ottoman administrative system, with its *Mutessarifs* and *Kaimakams*.

Storrs first came up from Egypt (where he had served as Oriental Secretary to the High Commissioner) to become Military Governor of Jerusalem and stayed on in a civilian capacity. The City owed much to him in those early days, in particular for the Pro-Jerusalem Society: it raised funds abroad (largely from non-Jews) for the preservation and restoration of the City and the re-establishment of some of its traditional crafts. He was a man of the widest culture, as his memoirs *Orientations*★ amply show. Music was a favourite relaxation and he could whistle many operas, accompanying himself on the piano. It was he who founded the Jerusalem Music Academy, under Sidney Seal, an Englishman who eventually settled in Jerusalem. Storrs also started a club in Jerusalem for playing chess, which he adored. He used to play at Amman against the Amir Abdallah, who cheated: but when Storrs quietly removed the captured queen that Abdallah had surreptiously replaced on the board, the Amir would roar with laughter at being found out.

★ Ivor Nicholson and Watson, London, 1947.

Storrs looked down on his cousin, Archer Cust, who was another of the district officers on his staff. It is true that, owing to World War I, Archer did not get a university education. But his family was of ancient origin and his father had been a courtier and confidant of King Edward VII. So Archer looked down on Storrs as an upstart.

Although he was quite a good linguist, Storrs pretended that he knew far more than he actually did — dropping a few words of Hebrew to visiting Italian ecclesiastics, and a few words of modern Greek to bemused Palestinian Jews. He would take up anyone who he thought would promote his interests, dropping him coldly as soon as he had outlived his usefulness. Storrs was thoroughly unscrupulous and often behaved like an Italian Renaissance prince: nothing he said could be wholly trusted. For example, he was determined to remove an unsightly partition in the Church of the Nativity at Bethlehem. He played on the well-known rivalry between the Patriarchs and persuaded the Latin Patriarch to sign an agreement by saying that the Orthodox Patriarch was opposed to the removal. He then induced the Orthodox Patriarch to sign another agreement by saying that the Latin Patriarch disliked the idea. It was this trickery that won for Storrs the nickname 'Oriental Storrs', an allusion to a shop in Cairo — Morum's Oriental Stores — where customers would be cheated.

But he had a quick eye; and, when I presented a draft letter to him, would give it one rapid glance and point out some error of phrasing half way down. To his own letters he appended an outsize signature in green ink boldly written with a broad-nibbed Onoto pen. Now, in the Colonial Service, the use of green ink is reserved for the auditor, and Storrs was asked to desist. He paid no attention to several hints: the Colonial Office lost patience and sent a formal despatch to my father *ordering* Storrs not to use green ink any more. They instructed the High Commissioner to transmit a copy of the despatch to Storrs and to get his signed acknowledgement of receipt, which he signed — in green ink. He knew very well that he could not be dismissed or otherwise penalised for such a peccadillo. So he did not care a damn about anything. In fact, he was thoroughly bored with administration: what he really enjoyed was political intrigue. He found chairmanship of the Jerusalem town-planning commission particularly exhausting (I was its secretary). After one such meeting, when most of the other members had left, he turned to Henderson, the British district medical officer of health, and said 'Hendy, can't you prescribe something for such occasions? What about a bullock's heart mashed up in iron wine?' That was rather a tragic remark as, although he had a florid complexion, he was found later to have pernicious anaemia and lived on a diet of raw liver.

He had great wit and audacity. Once he started a speech in Jerusalem: 'As was ably said by my predecessor, Pontius Pilate . . .' He entertained munificently, especially after he had married, rather late in life, the widow of Lieutenant-Colonel H. A. Clowes. His house in Jerusalem, with vaulted rooms, lent itself to his personal collection of antiquities. He took them with him to Cyprus when he became High Commissioner there. Unfortunately, they were destroyed when Government House was burnt down by rioters. No British colonial Government House had been burnt down since the American Revolution, and Storrs, with Archer Cust as his A.D.C., was sent into virtual exile as Governor of Northern Rhodesia (now Zambia).

His deputy, Sir Henry Luke, a dapper man, was the only one in the Jerusalem District who had worked in the Colonial Service before the war. He had started his career in Sierra Leone in 1908 and, in 1918, had been a (district) commissioner in Cyprus. He was also a man of wide culture, knowing Turkish and Greak and the niceties of maintaining the *status quo* in the Holy Places, one of our constant preoccupations.

There were half-a-dozen district officers at Jerusalem district headquarters, two being British Christians — Noel Law and Archer Cust; three Jews — one from Egypt (Ralph Harari), one from Palestine (Peretz Cornfeld), and myself, and one Moslem — Ruhi bey Abdul Hadi, a member of a leading family of Jenin, in Samaria, who had been in the Ottoman consular service in Salonika before the war. Our offices were in the St Paul's Hospice outside the Damascus Gate, later to become Government offices. We had a British chief clerk: the rest of the clerical and accountancy staff was Palestinian. There were British district officers, with Palestinian assistants and staff at Hebron* and Ramallah, and Palestinian district officers in the smaller sub-districts of Bethlehem and Jericho.

In December, 1920, I got married in great state at Government House on the Mount of Olives (my two sons were born there). It was the first big official reception my father had given, as, shortly after he had come to Palestine in July, his mother had died in London. But, by December, he was no longer in mourning. So some 800 guests assembled in the great hall—senior civil and military officials, religious dignita-

---

* The district officer at Hebron was Reginald Champion, who eventually became Governor of Aden and Sir Reginald, later taking holy orders.

ries and representatives of all the various communities of Palestine, both urban and rural. The Jewish marriage ceremony was performed by the two Chief Rabbis of Israel. Max Nurock (see later), then my father's assistant private secretary, was best man.

After the ceremony, to my surprise, I was hustled into a corner by a group of Beduin sheikhs and invested with the ceremonial robes and sword of an honorary sheikh of the tribes of Beersheba. Our only group wedding photograph shows me in this regalia.*

Noel Law arranged for the Government House bells to be rung for the first time since the British occupation as we set off in a Government House car for our honeymoon in Galilee (which I had never visited). Our first stop was ten miles away at Ramallah in the house of James Pollock, the District Officer,** as it was too late for us to venture in the dark through the then brigand-infested mountains of Samaria.

On our return to Jerusalem we set up on our own in a little stone-built cottage to the south of the city, in a suburb originally built by the German Templars near the railway station and known as the German Colony. On the British occupation, all its occupants had been deported as enemy aliens to Egypt. Most of the British civil servants in Jerusalem were allotted houses there.

We had two Yemenite Jewish servants — a woman cook and a house boy. When, before our departure from London,

---

* See photograph between pages 148 and 149.
** Towards the end of his life he became a Senator in Northern Ireland.

my fiancée told my grandmother in London what domestic staff we proposed to keep, she said: 'But how can you manage with only two servants?' There was just room for the Bechstein grand piano that she had given us for a wedding present (my wife played a little). All our mahogany furniture had been bought in London, at Heal's, at inflated post-war prices and shipped out to Jerusalem at vast expense. But there was no central heating: we had to burn olive wood in locally-made sheet-iron stoves. There was no bath-room: we bathed in a galvanised hip bath in a stone out-house. There we heated up water in a cauldron and mixed it with cold water from the pump: it was quite an operation. As there was no electricity — or gas — everyone used kerosene lamps which invariably smoked at the worst possible moments (as at Ramallah, on our wedding night). Cooking was done on a patent 'Primus' stove, using vaporised kerosene under pressure from an air-pump.

But we were happy in this cottage. It had a small garden, with shady trees, which was a great asset when our first child, David, was born in 1922. I worked about two miles away at the north-east end of the town and was provided with official means of transportation in the shape of a motor-cycle. I found this enchanting, except when the rains turned the dusty roads into greasy quagmires (tarring and asphalt had not then reached Palestine). When one went down to the coast at Jaffa, at infrequent intervals, the journey by road took four or five hours (today it takes just over the hour), so it was more convenient to go by train, winding slowly down the valleys. The journey by car to Haifa, through Nablus and Nazareth, took a whole day (today $2\frac{1}{2}$ hours.) There was then no motor-road at all between Jaffa and Haifa, owing to the opposition of the railway administration who feared losses if their own line to Haifa had a competitor. The City of Jerusalem then had a population of only 66,000, compared with 280,000 today. Jews were in a majority; but, as so many of them were foreign citizens and had no vote, the mayor was always an Arab and, by tradition, a Moslem. In the 1920's, he was Ragheb bey Nashashibi.★ His wife, Madame Nashashibi, as she was called, was Christian and came from Constantinople. She spoke French and was one of Jerusalem's hostesses in my father's day. Ragheb bey was a connoisseur of Persian rugs and had a fine private collection: but in all western furnishings their taste was lamentable.

The Nashashibi family and their allies controlled most of the municipalities of Palestine and some of its villages. They were the great rivals of the anti-government Husseinis, who controlled the Moslem religious establishment and the majority of the villages. As secretary of the Jerusalem town-planning commission for several years, I had much to do with Ragheb bey. He was an engineer by profession and had built Beersheba as an Ottoman frontier outpost (population today: 70,000). In the shortlived Turkish Parliament at Constantinople, he had been one of Palestine's two representatives. The municipality of Jerusalem was still run on traditional Ottoman lines, according to which every kind of favour was obtainable, at a price. This was difficult for a British colonial administration to accept. My work as district officer included the supervision of municipal affairs: I handled all the correspondence dealing with its by-laws, budgets and accounts. This required me to know

★ See photograph between pages 180 and 181.

all parts of the City, and I made extensive use of the opportunity. I got to know the Old City well, both the raucous, colourful life of its stone-vaulted markets, and the quiet beauty of its churches and mosques. My favourite was the little Crusader Church of St Anne; while the Armenian Cathedral of St James, with its rare wall tiles, had all the opulence of the East. I attended major religious ceremonies in the Holy Places whenever I could, especially the Washing of the Feet in St James, when the Armenian Patriarch, divested of his robe, knelt, washed, anointed and blessed one foot of each of his twelve bishops and priests.

Even though I was Jewish, as a district officer and son of the High Commissioner, I was allowed freely to enter the Haram esh Sherif, the Mosque of el Aksa and the Dome of the Rock — one of the most beautiful of all Moslem sanctuaries. Sitting in the wide stone-paved courtyard that Herod had built around the Temple, in the shade of the cypresses, one could hear the thunder of history.

Sir Harry Luke himself co-ordinated all the police and other arrangements that had to be made throughout the year for Moslem, Jewish, Orthodox, Latin and Armenian ceremonies in and around Jerusalem. These included the midnight mass in the Church of the Nativity in Bethlehem when the huge hanging lamps were set swinging in the nave. Then there was the wild Moslem peasant mob that came in to celebrate the festival of Nebi Musa (the Prophet Moses) along the Jericho road. Throughout the Day of Atonement there were continuous Jewish prayers at the Wailing Wall. Such occasions were always tense: the army stood by, the police were on non-stop duty, especially in Easter week, moving from one Holy Place to another. We district officers took it in turns to man a control point, day and night, in the district commissioner's offices. Once the ceremonies were over, Luke assembled for a *post mortem* every government official who had taken part in handling the ceremonies. Everything that had gone wrong was recorded, with a note what should be done the following year to prevent it. This was filed away until the next occasion. In consequence, as the years passed, the management of the religious ceremonies in and around Jerusalem grew more and more expert. Thanks to Luke, I have used this method of *post mortem* for the proper organization and management of every kind of recurrent event, both in Palestine and Israel.

Another magnificent building in the Old City is the Citadel that covers entrance through the Jaffa Gate. Built on a foundation of giant Herodian stone blocks, it contains several vaulted halls in perfect condition. Storrs, and his Pro-Jerusalem civic adviser—Charles Ashbee—had the Citadel cleared of the debris left by the Turkish garrison and turned into a public garden. In 1921, the first exhibition of indigenous Palestinian arts and crafts, largely peasant ware, was held in the Citadel, and I was made the organizer. What I learned in the process I used ten years later when I founded 'The Peasant House' at Nazareth (see page 141.)

Annie Landaus was then the jolly headmistress of the Evelina de Rothschild girls' school in Jerusalem. Her annual fancy dress ball was famous. With my penchant for authentic local costume and the help of my Christian Arab clerk, Mathieu Marroum, I won the first prize in four successive years — as successively a lemonade seller, water carrier, shepherd and beggar. The last was so convincing that, on arrival, I was turned away from the door.

My mother was a very devout Jewess. It pained her that

Jerusalem's only movie house should be called the Zion Cinema: so she used her influence to persuade the owner to rename it the Zion Hall. Similarly with the hotel originally started by one of the German Templars named Albrecht Fast. She had its name changed from the Fast Hotel to the Hotel Fast.

It was in the Fast Hotel that my future wife and her family had taken refuge from the British gunfire on the outskirts of the City in December, 1917. Sitting up all night, she watched the Turks pull out along the road below her window. Long straggling lines of infantry and artillery, and heavily-loaded pack-animals and baggage-wagons, passed hour after hour. From midnight there was nothing in the street: only distant dogs barked. Then, with the dawn, the first British patrols crept in, bayonets fixed, officers with their pistols drawn, examining side streets for snipers. A page of history had turned.

It was not easy for my mother to be wife of the High Commissioner: the official entertaining was onerous. She was never very strong and my father made many trips around Palestine alone, with his staff. As High Commissioner also for Trans-Jordan, he was on friendly terms with the then Amir Abdallah and paid several visits to Amman. On one occasion, Hadassah and I accompanied my father to a great banquet in the Amir's palace in honour of *his* father, King Hussein of Mecca, shortly to become a refugee when Ibn Saud took over his kingdom. (I called on the former King one summer when I had to visit Cyprus on duty and he was in exile there. He lived in a small villa, the doors and windows wide open, with tame gazelles and autumn leaves filtering in and out — a pathetic sight.) As usual, far too many guests from Trans-Jordan and Palestine had been invited. The wide tables, covered with broad belts of tiny dishes, were set so close to the walls that there was no room for the Beduin servants to pass. So they walked *on* the table in their stockinged feet. When you wanted some of the main dish—whole roasted sheep stuffed with rice—you handed your plate to a Beduin who walked along the table and cut off a choice morsel from the animal lying on one of the big copper trays in the centre.

The Amir was a jovial man with an odd sense of humour. He had purchased some fun-fair distorting mirrors and had them put up in the hall of his palace. As his guests filed in, he stood and roared at their discomfiture.

On another occasion, my wife and I were invited to accompany my father to stay in the Amir's temporary camp on the floor on the Petra valley. We detrained at Maan and rode horseback through the Sik, the narrow entrance defile. The Nabatean tombs cut out of the rose-red sandstone, in the form of temples, are one of the archaeological wonders of the world. To see them was a privilege: to be there as the Amir's guests was doubly so. We had fresh fish brought up daily on camel back from the Red Sea. (At this date, no fresh fish was obtainable even in Jerusalem.) We slept on brass-railed bedsteads under embroidered marquees (hired, I suspect, from Thomas Cook's in Cairo). At dawn, the Amir's personal muezzin on a rock peak summoned the faithful to prayer.

My father took me with him as his A.D.C. when he visited Egypt as the guest of his 'opposite number', the High Commissioner, then Field Marshal Allenby. My mother and Hadassah came too. We went up the Nile by train to visit Luxor and were then taken to see the recently discovered tomb of Tutankhamen, with the treasures (now in the Cairo

Museum) still in place, but all piled up higgledy-piggledy, as in an attic. Covering the Pharaoh's mummy-case was a purple linen awning, studded with tiny rosettes of solid gold. As the air filtered in from outside, the awning slowly collapsed into dust, before our eyes.

But, of all events in which my father participated, none could compare with the official opening of the Hebrew University in Jerusalem. The amphitheatre, cut out of the eastern slope of Mount Scopus, has, as its backdrop, the tawny lunar landscape of the Wilderness of Judaea — a unique site. Many years later, I discovered that the President of the university from 1962, Eliahu Elath, had also been present at the opening. He was then a penniless agricultural labourer at Rehovot, some forty miles away on the coastal plain. With a group of fellow workmen, he *walked* to Jerusalem through the night. Arriving on Mount Scopus, he found all seats occupied by thousands of invited guests. He climbed a pine tree at the edge of the amphitheatre and, pushing aside the branches, saw the inauguration of the institution where he would eventually study and of which, forty years later, become President.

Much as I loved Jerusalem, I hankered for an administrative command, however small, of my own. I spent two years learning Arabic with a dear old Arab inspector of Government schools — Habib Khoury. At the end of the two years, I passed my elementary Arabic examination, a prerequisite to appointment as district officer in a rural Arab area. (For the first half of my Colonial Service career, Arabic was more useful to me than Hebrew. I only began seriously to study Hebrew when I became deputy commissioner of migration at the age of 36. This was much too late: as a consequence I have been studying Hebrew ever since.)

I used to be able not only to speak and read Arabic but also to write it: I have since lapsed into illiteracy for lack of practice. I also studied administrative law — the Ottoman laws and British military and civil ordinances then in force, the rules of evidence, court procedure and so on — and came out top in the examinations, a prerequisite to holding a British magistrate's warrant. All British district officers then had powers, similar to those of the regular Palestinian magistrates, of sentence up to six months imprisonment and a fine of P£ 50 (£ 50 sterling).

In 1922, it was suggested that I replace Sidney Moody at Safad, the most northerly sub-district in Palestine and one of the wildest and most beautiful. (It also had the advantage of being the furthest removed from Jerusalem and its supervisory authorities.) But, at the last moment, the Huleh Valley and the headwaters of the Jordan River were ceded to Palestine by the French Mandatory authorities in Syria and the Lebanon. A more experienced officer than I was needed to incorporate the new territory. So Moody stayed on and I had to wait another three years until I was posted to be district officer at Ramallah, in the mountains north of Jerusalem.

CHAPTER 4

RAMALLAH, 1925–26

For a junior colonial administrator there is nothing to compare with one's first independent territorial command.* I was lucky to get Ramallah, one of the four sub-districts into which the Jerusalem district was then divided (the others being Hebron, Bethlehem, Jericho and the many villages around Jerusalem, which we called the Home Farm). In those days, the district officers in charge of the larger sub-districts were British: later they were all gradually replaced by Palestinians. I succeeded Pollock and already knew something about his area from handling his correspondence and monthly reports at district headquarters. Storrs was still my district commissioner and all the rest of his headquarters staff former colleagues.

My new charge consisted of some 30,000 hill-folk, all Arab, living in villages and hamlets. Of these villages, five were Christian, including the small town of Ramallah, my headquarters, with a population then of 3,000. (In 1967, before military occupation by Israel, it had a population of 30,000. Its Arabic name means The High Place of God.)

---

* For example, see *Growing*, the second volume (1904–11) of Leonard Woolf's autobiography, Hogarth Press, London, 1961.

The rest were all Moslems. Each village was composed of two or more clans, called in Arabic *hamulehs*, which were usually on bad terms with each other. One or two men in each village were selected by the Government as *mukhtars*, or head men (the name in Arabic means 'he who is chosen'). Their simple duties were to keep the village registers of births and deaths, to report infectious diseases to the Government doctor at Ramallah, and breaches of the peace to the police station, also at Ramallah, a day's journey by horse or mule from the most distant villages. They collected the tithe on cereal crops and were allowed to keep a fraction for their pains.

I arrived at Ramallah only eight years after the end of four centuries of Ottoman misrule, ending with World War I which had further ravaged the countryside. As the import of European coal had been stopped by the war, the Turks had cut down much of the few remaining forests as fuel for the railway that ran as far as Nablus and Tulkarm, with spurs to supply their eastern front that had crossed the Ramallah sub-district. To keep themselves from starving, the peasants had also felled many flourishing olive trees, which normally supplied olives and olive oil, and sold them as firewood. Olives were then still an essential part of peasant diet, and one of the basic raw materials for the production of rough kitchen-soap in the Moslem town of Nablus to the north.

Unlike the more fertile coastal plain, where individual Arab landlords each held large areas of land, farmed by hired labour, most of the hill country was cultivated by peasant owners. Many had stony hillside holdings of shallow soil which they scratched with wooden ploughs drawn by oxen for a meagre yield of wheat or barley. The seed

65

then used by the peasants was degenerate, as was the live-stock (cattle, goats and poultry). We in the district administration spent much time helping the agricultural field officers to establish demonstration plots and persuading the less conservative peasants to come and see them.

I was materially helped in dealing with these Arab villages by my friendship with Ragheb bey Nashashibi, the Mayor of Jerusalem. He and his family, and their allies, had considerable political influence in many of the villages in my sub-district. The word went out from Jerusalem to some of the leading peasants in many villages that they were to co-operate with me as far as possible; and they certainly did. When I asked Ragheb bey, before I took up office, what I should do if a *mukhtar* refused to come and see me when summoned, he laughed and said: 'The Turks would have flogged him. You won't; but he isn't sure enough of that to run the risk that, if he doesn't come, you'll send the police to arrest him. So he'll come as soon as you call.'

The hill country in Palestine was then in a terrible state. The terraces built in Roman times to retain soil for vineyards and olive groves had largely collapsed during the centuries and had not been repaired through lack of energy and gradual depopulation through emigration. The heavy winter rains had washed away much of the soil, exposing bare rock on which little would grow. Elsewhere the natural forest had been cut back by the ubiquitous goat and we had to help the forest rangers to police those areas in which villagers were, in the interest of forest regeneration, not allowed to graze their flocks and herds.

As the mountains grew more and more barren, the younger and more virile peasants emigrated, largely to the United States. As the population declined, the cultivated area decreased still further: it was a vicious circle. There were few roads for vehicles: surplus produce had to be carried to market by donkey, mule or camel. Apart from one or two water-pumps, flour-mills and oil-presses, there was no power-driven equipment in the whole area. I tried to revive some of the village crafts; but the craftsmen were undercut by cheaper, stronger, imported, mass-produced articles. For example, big pottery water-jars in which the women brought up water from the village well were soon replaced by the lighter and unbreakable four-gallon petrol tin (there were no petrol-pumps then).

It was difficult to know where to begin with agricultural development. No one had any money and almost every peasant was in debt to money-lenders, chiefly in Nablus, at interest rates up to five per cent *a month* (60 per cent a year!). This was absolutely illegal; but the debts were disguised as unpaid bills for the fictitious supply of soap and we were powerless to get the usurious agreements declared invalid in the courts. There was little bank capital for investment: credit co-operatives had not yet taken root. No-one in any case would lend money on mortgage, as some of the Ottoman property registers had been lost. Even where the registers were available, no maps were attached: the boundary descriptions were so vague as to be valueless. In order to reduce the land tax assessment, peasants had grossly under-declared the area of their property, with the aid of judicious *bakshish* to the Ottoman registrars. The registered area in consequence was far too small to support any application for a mortgage loan for agricultural betterment.

As I have said, my offices were in the little Christian Arab town of Ramallah with its three thousand inhabitants. Next door was the Moslem Arab village of Bireh (from the Hebrew *Beeroth* ('wells') of the Bible and hence many thousands of years old) with a further thousand inhabitants. Many of the inhabitants of Ramallah and Bireh were farmers owning vineyards in the neighbourhood. I myself lived in a roomy two-storey house built by a Ramallah man who had gone to the United States and had returned with some money. This was exceptional. I calculated that only about a third of the emigrants came back with money (and promptly bought a horse, a wife and a house). One third came back penniless: the remaining third were too broke even to come back. Nevertheless, about a third of the income of my area was in the form of remittances from the U.S.A.

From the upper floor of my house one could look across the hill-tops right down to the distant sea coast. On a clear night, the lights of Jaffa and Tel Aviv, Ramleh and Lydda could be seen twinkling, thirty and forty miles away. At that time, we had one small son (my wife was expecting a second) and a real old English nanny. We were the only Jews in the whole sub-district, apart from a Yemenite silversmith who kept his family in Jerusalem. He rode back every Friday on a donkey and left us in sole command over the week-end.

Our English nanny — Miss Alice Melinda Barker — stayed with us for many years. When the children were old enough to have a governess, Nanny went back to England. Each subsequent year, in December, she would write us a letter *a propos* of nothing at all, to serve as a gentle hint that Christmas was due. We would then send her a substantial (for me) cheque out of which she would send the boys postal orders of one tenth of the amount for their birthdays, out of which they in their turn would send her jointly one tenth of her gift back as their birthday present to her. This money had quite a velocity; and some of it crossed the Mediterranean three times.

Ramallah was really only a big village: its Christian inhabitants were likewise divided into *hamulehs* that jockeyed for position. I knew something about municipal administration after five years of handling the affairs of Jerusalem; and the town gave me little trouble. Christian Arabs were in any case better educated, more energetic and less violent than Moslems. By law, I had to nominate the mayor from among the elected councillors whenever a vacancy occured.

It was the Moslem countryside that provided most of my headaches. On paper, I had complete authority. All district commissioners and district officers were the King's representatives and flew a modified version of the Union Jack on their cars. As magistrates, we combined judicial functions with our executive duties. This involved largely trying peasants who carried firearms or who cut down trees without a licence — new offences which the old Ottoman magistracy, whom the Palestine Government had reappointed, refused to take seriously. I had at my disposal a police force of fourteen men, most of whom were engaged in escorting Government tax-collectors carrying money. I had a Moslem assistant district officer (who took bribes) and a Moslem police officer (ditto). The regular magistrate was also a Moslem and venal; while the Government doctor was a Christian Arab who told me about all the others.

As soon as I was appointed to Ramallah, I bought my first motor-car — one of the old original Ford 'tin lizzies'. It had been a British army car (in the Middle East, the 'jeep' of World War I) and was then second- or third-hand. But I could only get to a dozen of my villages by car. The rest

I had to visit on horseback and was provided with a Government mount for this purpose. For four or five days each week I was out on tour, usually accompanied by the assistant district officer, the police officer and the doctor, together with a policeman or two, including my own personal bodyguard. He was a grizzled, one-eyed ex-highwayman named Hamzeh who would stand up with his rifle in my car at night and shoot dead any leaping rabbit caught in the glare of the headlamps. We would ride horseback in single file for two or three days, up and down rocky hillside tracks, visiting two or three villages a day, staying the night on the way until we got back to our vehicles. These tours were planned well ahead and notices were sent by policeman to all the villages on the particular route. There were few places where I could stay the night with any pretence of comfort. The house and bedding of even the largest village landowner was sure to be verminous. The best bet was a hard iron bedstead in some local Catholic or Orthodox monastery or mission school. Most Arab visitors passing through a village of any size would stay at the *madafeh* or guest-house; but that meant sleeping on a mat on the floor. The guest-house was a simple, whitewashed room, with a hard earthen — or even tiled — floor, with window-glass if the village was wealthy. On the wall was pinned an Arabic list of some kind, arranged in three columns. It took me many months to discover that these columns showed the names of the heads of families — well off (by peasant standards), in-between, and poor. Whoever in the village sighted a visitor approaching in the distance roughly assessed his social position (if he walked, he was class C: if on a donkey, class B: if on a horse, class A: all Government employees, even a simple forest ranger, were class A.) The visitor would make his way to the *madafeh;* but the man who had spotted him would have got there first and seen who was next on the list. If the visitor was a poor man, the family next on the list of poor families would be notified and, in due course, along would come someone with bread and olives and perhaps cheese or an egg, and the inevitable coffee. A man in-between would get, an hour after arrival, a freshly killed or roasted chicken, with little plates of different kinds of vegetables. A well-to-do visitor would expect, several hours after arrival, a sheep stuffed with rice, many more plates of vegetables, many different sweetmeats and glasses of over-sweet lemonade. (Sugar-loaves hanging on the wall of a private house were a sign of wealth and generosity.) Moslems are extremely hospitable and, by custom, any guest in a village was housed and fed for three whole days, free of charge. (This, I assume, is the origin of the similar hospitality in the *kibbutz* in Israel today.)

While on tour, we had our midday meal in one of the better-off villages on our route. Even so, I was very unhappy at first to involve the peasantry in so much extra expenditure. But I felt somewhat better after a *mukhtar* had told me that, were it not for my visit, no one in the village would have any meat that month at all. For, when my official retinue and I had eaten, and the policemen had eaten, my host and his male kinsfolk would eat, ending with the women, children and, finally, the dogs. The *madafeh* with its lists on the wall was a beautiful worked-out system of socialised hospitality.

The villages in the hill country were mostly built of dressed stone: on the sandy coastal plain, far from a quarry, they were often of mud brick. Arab villages are built on no plan, and resemble rabbit warrens with narrow unpaved alleys between small walled courtyards. In the 1920's, for a village to have, at night, a single flickering oil-lamp in one alley was quite a distinction.

Most of the houses were really hovels, with a single living-room on a shelf above the stable where the cow, or a few goats, were kept safe at night. The hens scratched in the courtyard around the *tabun*, the clay oven where each family baked its own *pitta* — flat unleavened loaves of bread — in hot ashes. The women and children then went barefoot. There was no piped water, no water-borne sewage system: the fields were used as latrines. Animal dung, old bones, tins and rags, were piled in manure heaps in any open space in the middle of the village, topped, perhaps, with a dead dog. I fought a losing battle to get these manure heaps moved to the eastern edge of the villages (the prevailing wind is from the sea, to the west.) All I could do in the worst cases was to put on an act of violent indignation and refuse to sit down in the village, even for a cup of coffee. Sometimes there was an improvement on my next visit. The only sanitary measure that was enforced was the systematic and periodic governmental inspection of every cistern. Where possible, it was hermetically sealed to prevent malaria-carrying mosquitoes from breeding on the fresh, still water. Where this was not possible, a little oil was poured in to prevent the larvae from breathing. The eventual wiping-out of malaria in Palestine was one of the major successes of the Mandatory administration.★

As in India and elsewhere, the chief preoccupations of a district officer were to collect taxes and keep the peace.

★ This work was supplemented by an anti-malaria unit sent out as part of the American Zionist Medical Unit.

As the Ottoman Government did not police the rural areas, murders went unpunished and led to clan retaliation. The blood feuds that were thereby created lasted sometimes for generations. In such cases, the district officer and the police tried hard to persuade both clans to agree, first to a truce, then to a settlement. Someone well-versed in tribal law would be brought in, often a Beduin sheikh. He would sit in the village for weeks and months (being fed all the time at the expense of both parties jointly). He patiently totted up the number of killed on each side over the years. The side with an excess of victims would then claim compensation from the other side at the nominal rate of 333 gold Napoleons per head. The compensation payable would be announced at a great love-feast — or *sulha* — to which I came as principal guest. Even if there was only one excess victim to be paid for, everyone knew that there were nothing like 333 gold Napoleons in the whole clan. The sum available in cash was more likely to be 333 piasters — (£3-6-8 at the current rate of exchange). So an elaborate pretence was devised. The claimants remitted a quarter for the glory of *Allah* (loud clapping): another ten per cent for the sake of *Hadarat el Hakim* ('His Honour the Governor'—myself), ten per cent for the arbitrator and so on down the order of precedence until a minimal sum was reached. This was solemnly paid over. Only then could the two sides sit down to eat, a dozen or so round each large coloured straw platter, members of each clan alternately.

My most unpleasant task was trying to collect current taxes, and astronomic arrears, from heavily-indebted peasants who did not even have enough food to last them till the next harvest without further borrowing from usurers. I did manage, however, to get further large sums written off by the Treasury as uncollectable, as Pollock had done before me. The rest I tried to collect by fearsome threats in broken Arabic but on biblical models. 'If you pay now what I ask, oh, my children, I shall be as dew upon your fields, as honey on your lips. But if you do *not*, then I shall come as a wolf in your sheep-fold by night and you shall be consumed as by fire on your threshing-floor.' When I had got their eyes fairly popping out of their heads, I told them to scurry home and bring something on account. The tax collector sat by my side and kept the record.

I had only three demands from the villages — to maintain the peace, pay their taxes, and keep their alleys tolerably clean. Sometimes, shortly after I and my retinue had been spotted across the valley on some narrow winding track, I could see a cloud of dust rising from the next village. I knew that every man, woman and child had been conscripted by the apprehensive *mukhtar* to make the village a little more presentable before I arrived.

I used to keep a little black loose-leaf notebook in my pocket, in which I jotted down things that had to be seen to on my return to my office. In the end, I made the peasantry believe, or profess to believe, that, like a recording angel, I had *two* notebooks — a white one for their virtues and a black one for their sins. When I was particularly incensed and left the village in an artificial huff, writing their names in my black book, they would walk for miles at my stirrup, begging me to forgive them and restore them to grace. If I did, there was precious little I could do for them, except, perhaps, help to build them an access road, or to get the Department of Education to provide a teacher and schoolbooks, if they would build a school-room. There was an immense demand, even then, forty years ago, for education.

There were a few church schools here and there in the Christian villages, and excellent boarding schools for boys and girls in Ramallah, run by American Quakers. Many Moslem village children attended the Quaker schools, as there was no attempt at conversion. These children carried back the value of literacy to the remotest villages. But the Department of Education in Jerusalem was more interested in providing primary and secondary education for a few (who would become teachers and government clerks) whereas I was keen on a minimum level of literacy for all. We had many arguments: at the time I thought the department's attitude hard-hearted. Now I think that, taking the long view, they may well have been right.

Access roads were essential, first, to enable produce to be taken to market; secondly, for security. The Public Works Department was concerned only with main inter-urban highways. So the district administration made use of the old Ottoman system of the *corvée* — requiring every able-bodied man to give two weeks free labour a year after the harvest was in to improve the track to his village. When this was forbidden by a League of Nations anti-slavery convention, we had to rely on voluntary labour. Naturally, none was forthcoming, until one wise old *mukhtar* said to me: 'Oh Governor: if your Excellency will *order* us to volunteer, of course we will.' So I did, and they did too. The Government provided a few pounds for blasting powder and we got a lot of work done.

But such personal rule is heady stuff; and, after a year of it, in these holy mountains (Bethel, where the Ark of the Convenant had rested, was in my area) I began to get delusions of grandeur. Youth is an intoxicating time of life anyhow; and this was my first independent charge. A young naval officer, revelling in his first patrol boat, at least has men of his own generation under his command. I was someone from the twentieth century back in the eleventh century, with all the powers of a feudal baron. The peasants might be miserably poor and illiterate; but they were *mine*. I protected them against tyranny from my own liege lord and expected them to pay me homage accordingly.

I was, however, a city lad. I had never lived in the country except for summer holidays in Yorkshire with my parents when I was a school-boy. But, now, I spent a whole year riding a horse round a purely agricultural sub-district. I had known nothing about agriculture when I started and had had to learn fast. I asked innumerable questions everywhere I went and began to piece together the whole cycle of peasant life and of every crop and every rural occupation.

This joy of continuous discovery was itself exciting and I had the opportunity of putting it all immediately to use. I began to reform everything, to introduce new methods, new ideas. Some were disastrously wrong. Since time immemorial, Palestinian Arab peasants had used wooden ploughs, drawn by oxen. They ploughed the stony soil only a few inches deep. I got hold of some cheap iron ploughs from a German firm at Jaffa and arranged ploughing demonstrations. A few of the richer farmers were pressured into buying them; but the ploughs were soon abandoned. They were too heavy for oxen: mules had to be used, and mules required more to eat than oxen. When a plough caught on a submerged rock it broke. A wooden plough could be repaired in the village, but an iron plough had to be toted for miles to the nearest blacksmith. Even the deeper ploughing was a mistake: it opened up the soil so much that all its moisture was dried out by the hot sun. Heaven protect all peasants against well-meaning reformers from the city!

Or take the matter of rock clearance. I had a tidy mind and it distressed me to see mile after mile of fields covered with stones. 'Clear your lands!' I yelled at my lazy serfs. 'It will be so much easier to plough. Pile up the rocks into dry-stone walls around your fields and keep wandering beasts from grazing on your ripening crops!' It was all so beautifully logical — and so wrong. Soil experts have now discovered that, at night in summer, dew condenses on the cold surface of rocks and drips onto the surrounding soil. In England, even Stone-Age Man knew that cold clay beaten into a shallow pan would form a dew-pond. In the Middle East, small piles of stones served the same purpose, and the corn that grew around them was stronger and higher. Removing the stones actually damaged the crops.

The natural growth of crops enchanted me. To see the young and tender leaves bursting out of every fig-tree as I passed made me deeply conscious of the power of God. And I still remember galloping home to tell my amused wife of the revelation that had suddenly come to me: trees flowered first and *then* produced fruit; not, as I had always imagined, the other way round.

But this Garden of Eden was not for ever. I was just making my plans for a second year when I was recalled to Jerusalem, to work once more in an office. I was heartbroken. I took my wife and our two babies and our English nanny and our two Yemenite Jewish servants back to the city. My brief vision of Paradise had been ended.

CHAPTER 5

JERUSALEM AND JAFFA, 1926–27

The planning job I was recalled to undertake in Jerusalem was connected with naturalisation. At the time of the British occupation of Palestine, the Moslem majority had Ottoman citizenship: many Jews and Christian Arabs held foreign passports. Since 1920, Jewish immigrants had arrived in an ever-widening stream (30,000 in 1925 alone). They were desperately anxious to identify themselves completely with the Jewish National Home by becoming Palestinian citizens. But no Palestinian citizenship could be created by British order-in-council until a peace treaty with Turkey had been concluded. The original treaty, signed in 1920 at Sèvres, was torn up as a result of Mustapha Kemal's rebellion against Greek penetration of Anatolia. A new treaty was not signed (at Lausanne) until September, 1923. The Palestine citizenship order-in-council was only promulgated in 1925. In order to implement it, application forms had to be designed, procedures devised for handling them and the requisite staff trained. In March, 1926, I was temporarily seconded for that purpose to the Chief Immigration Officer's headquarters in Jerusalem.

The Chief Immigration Officer was then Albert Hyamson, another Anglo-Jewish civil servant. He had not only been an early Zionist sympathiser but had had many years administrative experience in the General Post Office in London, not a very exciting department. In consequence, Hyamson had developed a narrow outlook that eventually led, some eight years later, in 1934, to his being superseded by Eric Mills as Commissioner for Migration, with myself as Mills' deputy. Hyamson had a jaundiced view of his own staff: none, even the most senior, was allowed much discretion. Hyamson himself worked till late every night, examining all important immigration applications and deciding many of them personally: this ruined his own health. It was not a happy atmosphere for me to work in: luckily I had a specific job to do and was semi-independent.

Nor was I very happy outside the office. My planning job was estimated to take less than a year, at the end of which I hoped to escape again to an out-district. It was not worth while my taking a house again in Jerusalem. My parents had left Government House in July, 1925, and had gone back to England. They were thus unable to offer us temporary hospitality in Jerusalem. So, having stored all our furniture (including the Bechstein grand piano) we took rooms in a German Catholic convent in the German Colony — the quarter where most British officials in Jerusalem then still lived. The convent was an aseptic sort of place, chilly in winter, with meals that were monotonous in the extreme. To make matters worse, Hadassah had to go off to Europe to attend a conference of the Women's International Zionist Organization, and I was left with our two babies and their nanny. On top of all this, the senior British colonial civil servants who had frequently entertained us and whom we, in turn, had entertained when my father had been High Commissioner, now hardly recognised our existence. I was no longer the High Commissioner's son and could not, even indirectly, promote their careers: I had lost my usefulness. Their cold calculation was a bitter lesson. I was very naive in those days, and it took me years until I got accustomed to the fact that I was really very small fry indeed. We still had our Jewish friends, of course; and many Arab families welcomed us with cordiality.

But I found considerable consolation in setting up the naturalisation office. The new law accorded Palestinian citizenship automatically to the vast majority of the population — those Moslem Arabs who had previously been Ottoman citizens. For the others, who had foreign passports, I devised application forms and the procedure to deal with them — effectively, speedily and economically. Public administration, I find, is largely a matter of commonsense. It is neither a science nor an art but a very simple craft, something like carpentry. By intelligent design and competent workmanship, a carpenter makes a drawer that works well for a great many years without any adjustment. I have had to design or redesign many administrative units or undertakings in my life. I derive considerable satisfaction from the fact that they were all well-carpentered: some have lasted almost unaltered even till today. They all had built-in provisions for expansion and even change.

The end-product of the naturalisation system was a printed, numbered and signed certificate. To get it, the applicant had to show that he was legally in the country, had resided there for two years out of the preceding three, and had some acquaintance with English, or Arabic, or Hebrew — then the three official languages. On the strength of such a naturalisation certificate, the new citizen could obtain a Palestinian passport. But the 28 years of the Mandate was too short a period for the development of a Palestinian patriotism. Citizens still thought of themselves primarily as Jew or Arab, or Jew, Moslem or Christian, or Jew, Moslem or Catholic, Protestant, or Orthodox and so on. Nevertheless, to have a passport with the British royal arms on it (even if it was brown and not blue, as for British subjects) did confer a certain status on the holder. As a British protected person he was entitled to the help of British consuls throughout the world. In fact, on the outbreak of World War II, many Palestinian citizens — mostly Jewish — scattered about in Europe, were safely shepherded back to Palestine through British consular enterprise.

An unofficial requirement for naturalisation was a clean police record. Many years later, when I became deputy commissioner for migration myself, I supervised, among other units, the operations of the naturalisation branch. Applications were being referred to the C.I.D. special branch and many were returned marked 'not recommended'. The head of this branch at that time was a Mr Saigh who had an almost pathological hatred of Communism. I dislike Communism, too, and entirely approved the denial of naturalisation to Communist agents. But I was not satisfied with the methods of inquiry adopted by the C.I.D. After a prolonged struggle, I managed to secure their consent to their sending *us* the police file instead of the naturalisation application being referred to them. As I suspected, many police files contained nothing more than a typed slip of paper stating that, 'on such-and-such a date, the subject of the file was seen by police agent no. so-and-so talking in the bus to Communist suspect no. so-and-so.' In the absence of any more damning evidence, this casual association with a Communist suspect was overlooked and the applicant was granted citizenship.

★ ★ ★

By September, 1926, I had finished the organization of the new naturalisation branch and was allowed to return to the district administration. By a stroke of good luck, I was posted as a district officer to the headquarters of the Southern District at Jaffa. The district commissioner then was J.E.F. Campbell, a quietly able man and the most efficient chairman of a meeting I have ever met before or since. What little I know about running a committee meeting I learnt from Campbell. He always began on time, no matter how late any of the other committee members might arrive. A precise agenda and all the necessary documents had been distributed well beforehand. Campbell had gone over the files in advance with the secretary, knew exactly what points needed a decision and kept everyone to the point. In consequence, no meeting ever lasted for more than an hour; yet everything had been fully discussed and decisions reached on all points. I have tried ever since never to allow any meeting of which I am chairman to last longer.

Campbell also took the trouble to learn both Arabic *and* Hebrew and was one of the few British colonial civil servants in Palestine to pass the advanced Arabic examination. It was rare for any British official in the Administration to be able to write a letter in correct Arabic, much less in Hebrew.

A tall, good-looking man, Campbell early established amicable relations with the rapidly expanding city of Tel Aviv. Palestinian Jews did not take kindly to Government supervision and control. They found it irksome to have to apply for legal authority for every municipal by-law or tax. Campbell was wise and preferred to concentrate on the main issues, closing his eyes to a multitude of minor irregularities. As his voice carried great weight at Government offices in Jerusalem, he was allowed to run his district in his own way; it developed remarkably during his period of office, with the minimum of friction.

His deputy, Harold Crosbie, who eventually succeeded him as district commissioner, was equally restrained but much slower, at times exasperatingly so. He and his family lived in an airy Arab house in Jaffa on a cliff overlooking the beach. His wife Elsa was a superb housekeeper. Every meal prepared by her Arab cook for her children was brought on a tray by her man-servant the whole length of the central court, for her inspection, and was then returned to the nursery. The Crosbie children and ours were approximately the same age and the two families spent many afternoons together on the sands, then a haven of solitude, south of Jaffa.

In the local district hierarchy I was number three, and was given a fascinating job — the supervision of all local government throughout the whole of the Southern District. At that time, eight Arab towns had municipal status (Jaffa, Lydda, Ramleh, Majdal, Gaza, Khan Yunis, Beersheba and Hebron.) There were elected local councils in a further nine small towns, large villages or urban quarters (five Jewish, three Arab and one German Christian). My work involved the setting up or extension of new local authorities, revision of their boundaries and legal powers, supervision of their council elections and approval of their by-laws, budgets and senior staff appointments. This meant continual travelling and inspection, which I enjoyed. It also involved close liaison with the district officer in each sub-district and all the local departmental representatives in the Southern District—police, health, education, public works, agriculture, even the judiciary.

I still had my old Ford car from my time at Ramallah: in it I made my tours of inspection all over the Southern District. There were then few metalled roads. The coastal plain was largely sand which made good going, in winter, after rain; but in summer one got easily bogged down in deep, soft sand. Every driver in those days carried a shovel and even a roll of wire-netting with which to extricate his vehicle. Once, having been misled into following a track that ended in deep sand, I was manoeuvering my car slowly along a sandstone ledge a few feet above the track, when the ledge gently collapsed, completely overturning my car. In those early days, the jack, pump, tyre levers and other heavy equipment were housed in a tool-box on the running-board. As the car turned over, all these implements poured in through the open window on to my head. Luckily I was wearing a strong pith sun-helmet. Not realising the cause of the infernal clatter, I said to myself: 'Ha! So *this* is the noise of death.' But, when the car came to rest on its roof, I climbed out, found some labourers, uprooted a few wooden posts, levered the light car back onto its wheels and drove off, leaving nothing behind on the sand but a dark oil stain where my vehicle had bled almost to death. In those days of light cars, there was no damage save a slightly crumpled wooden and canvas hood.

My local government clients were many and varied: some were portly Arab mayors with whom I discussed budgets while we sat in ornate armchairs in the municipal offices over endless cups of Turkish coffee. Others were harassed Jewish local council chairmen in small cluttered rooms, always late in submitting their audited accounts. The most businesslike were the precise and pedantic German Templars, including the notorious enemy agent from

World War I—Fritz Frank—whom we had all tried so hard to catch. Apart from the Germans, the only Jewish authority that then had any inkling of good financial management was the orange-growing village of Rehovot (where the Weizmann Institute of Science is now situated). Their economy-minded council had discovered, all on their own, the English system of basing their flexible local rating on the fluctuating total of their expenditure, and not trying to reallocate annually the proceeds of a fixed charge.

My wife, our two children, their nanny and our two Yemenites lived in the orange groves outside Jaffa. We leased through the Government a typical large Arab villa, not wanting to be cooped up in Tel Aviv, by then becoming urbanised and noisy. As so many of my clients were Arab, it was preferable for me not to live in a wholly Jewish area. It was peaceful out in the groves, with the smell of the autumnal orange blossom for weeks on end. In the clearing round the villa there were two tall palm trees beneath which the children played. Although the Bible decries a 'house builded upon sand', it is decidedly safer than one builded upon rock. When an earthquake rocked Palestine in July, 1927, several towns and villages up in the mountains had heavy death rolls, whereas those on the coast (save for Lydda) were much less affected. Our house-boy had the presence of mind to pick up the two children from their room and dash out into the open. But the heaving earth, the rattle of everything in the kitchen, the subterranean roar, were unnerving, and I never want to be in an earthquake again.

We spent a happy year in Jaffa, living in two worlds—one Arab, the other Jewish. Jaffa was old-fashioned and dignified: Tel Aviv, its commercialised neighbour to the north, was bustling and uncouth. But it already had a rich cultural

85

life, having changed much since I had lived there during the war, nearly ten years earlier. The main expansion had been quite recent, in 1925 and 1926, as a result of a sudden wave of immigration of middle-class Jews from Poland. As a result of the flow of capital to Tel Aviv and the arrival there of dozens of big Jewish traders and manufacturers, quite a number of new factories were built in and around Tel Aviv, especially for the building and textile industries. Till then, much of the more commonly needed domestic goods and materials had to be imported. A determined Jewish drive to encourage local production — known in Hebrew as *totzeret ha'Aretz*—resulted in a Jewish demand for protective tariffs — against imported British textiles, for example. This demand, with only a limited support from the Palestine Government and the Colonial Office, illustrates one of the dilemmas of Mandatory rule. I remember, however, the excitement in Tel Aviv when a man paraded with a placard through the streets, dressed for the first time wholly in *totzeret ha'Aretz*—Palestinian-made shoes, socks, trousers, shirt, jacket, tie and hat.

The expansion of Tel Aviv was far too hectic and insecure. The rate of Jewish immigration — which had reached the unprecedented total of 30,000 (legally) in 1926 — began to decline and there was a sudden slump. With no new customers likely to arrive, building stopped abruptly, no new shops were opened, and some factories closed down. The Municipality, which had unwisely accepted unsecured bills of exchange in payment of rates, went bankrupt.

Our elder son David was now old enough to go to a Jewish kindergarten and I took him in to Tel Aviv every morning, fetching him at lunch-time. My parents-in-law, Yehuda and Rachel Grasovsky still lived in the house I had known during the war. The little garden around the house, with its clump of bamboo trees and pool, was where Asher Ginsberg (better known by his pen-name *Achad Ha'am*, 'One of the People'), the Jewish philosopher and friend of my father-in-law, came in his old age to sit in an arm-chair. There was plenty of room on the ground floor to accommodate all the children and grand-children on such family occasions as the Passover *Seder*. Asaph, the eldest son, had returned from California in one of the Jewish Battalions to become a horticultural officer in the Palestine Administration (and later chief horticultural officer in Israel). He had married and now had three children, all since grown up, with children of their own. Amihud, who had gone on to take a doctorate in forestry at Yale, had become a Palestine Government forestry officer, later the chief Israel Government forestry officer, and today a United Nations expert in arid zone afforestation. He also married and had two children, both now with children of their own. The third son, Shai (Isaiah) graduated at Edinburgh, became a Palestine Government veterinary officer and is now chief Israel Government veterinarian. My three brothers-in-law were among the first generation of *Sabras*★ to be educated abroad. It speaks for their father that they each rose to the top in their own country. I was also a Palestine Government official, which made four in my father-in-law's family. My wife's younger sister married a Czech Jewish engineer (who unfortunately died before his time) who became head of the Palestine (later Israel) Standards Institution at Tel Aviv. So the Goor sons and sons-in-law certainly played a full part in the public service.

★ Person born in Israel (Palestine).

CHAPTER 6

THE SECRETARIAT, 1927-30

After a year at Jaffa, I was again brought back to Jerusalem, much against my will. That meant four moves in two and a half years, each time with piano. On this occasion, I was due to replace Max Nurock — another British Jew — as an assistant secretary in the High Commissioner's Secretariat (there had to be at least one). Max, by now one of my oldest and closest friends, is, in fact, an Irish Jew. At Trinity College, Dublin, he had been a classics scholar who won a phenomenal number of prizes. Coming out to Palestine in 1919 as secretary to the Zionist Executive, he became my father's assistant private secretary and, in 1921, entered the Secretariat. He was a quick worker who could unravel instantly the most complex Colonial Office despatch and dictate an immediate reply. But, by 1927, having been in the Secretariat for five years with no district experience, it had been decided that he should do some field work in the newly-created Lands Commission. This, however, did not appeal to him at all: he was a born head-office man. So, after my own appointment had been announced, he managed to extricate himself from his new assignment. Hence, we two Jews worked in the Secretariat together, even sharing the same room, popularly called 'The Jewish National Home' — that is, small, but a hundred per cent . . .

Max was such a rapid draughtsman and so great a glutton for work that he would stay on late in the office and pick out unfinished business on the desks of his colleagues. When they arrived the next morning, they found all their problems solved. This infuriated some of them; but it suited me well. I still felt myself to be primarily a district man, happy only in the field, dealing with affairs face to face. Giving decisions by correspondence was, for me, life at second-hand. The work-load in the Secretariat was, in addition, very heavy. In the districts, I could spend four or five days a week out of the office on tour: on my return I found little paper-work to do: it was a gentlemanly existence. But, in the Secretariat, I felt that I was living at the bottom of a pillar-box, deluged every few hours with a new mass of letters. Try as I could, I never managed to catch up: it was a constant struggle. I became eternally grateful to Max for helping me out.

I never really succeeded in learning to use the baroque, eighteenth-century style vigorously insisted on for despatches to the Colonial Office. This demanded rotund sentences, stuffed with polysyllables. Max had the knack and could draft any kind of despatch almost in his sleep.

It was the baroque style required in drafting despatches to the Colonial Office that, in fact, impelled me to start writing on my own in order to preserve my personal, much simpler, style. Sir Harry Luke was then Chief Secretary and himself a writer of distinction. He not only gave me official permission to write a series of feature articles on Palestine, but personally encouraged me to persevere with the rigorous self-training required in any such undertaking. I am not a naturally gifted writer and whatever I have learned to do has been acquired the hard way—by trial and error.

My first efforts were terrible — each article a series of

purple patches, full of clichés, linked by commonplaces of exquisite dullness. I wrote on the religious ceremonies in Jerusalem at Christmas and Easter and on motor-trips across the countryside. A Russian-Jewish friend of ours, the late Joshua Gordon, then worked as liaison officer between the Jewish Agency and the Palestine Administration. He was a man of great literary and artistic sensibility, having worked on the stage in Berlin under Reinhardt. He read my first effusions and delicately pointed out my many errors of judgement. Gordon was an enchanting man, the quintessence of good manners. Once, when we were at Ramallah and had invited him to dinner, he came all the way out (then quite a journey) to apologise for not being able to be present owing to a pressing official engagement. (Of course, he eventually succumbed and stayed on to dine with us.)

But the man who really enabled me to get my first articles published was an American Jew, the late Henry Hurwitz. He had created in New York a literary quarterly — the *Menorah Journal* — and ran it almost single-handed until he died a few years ago. Many writers whom he discovered have risen to prominence later.

★ ★ ★

During the years that I was in the Secretariat, we lived in the Herod's Gate quarter, north of the Old City. This was the first suburb to be built outside the walls by Moslem Arabs, starting from the end of the nineteenth century. Some of the earlier houses were constructed in traditional style with vaulted rooms around an open central courtyard, where fountains played. Our neighbour, Mr. Justice Corrie, the British puisne judge in the Court of Appeal, lived in such a one. Ours had been built later, still vaulted but without a central court. It was roomy and had a walled enclosure, with rough grass, where our young children could safely play. Part of the day, they attended a Jewish kindergarten in a neighbouring quarter. Our own landlord was Hassan Sidki el Dajani, a good-looking, well-dressed and debonair young man-about-town and a member of one of the principal Moslem Arab families in Jerusalem. He would visit us from time to time and relate the most scandalous stories about his friends. One of the repeatable stories related to his boon companion — Fakhri bey el Nashashibi, a relative of the Mayor. Hassan and Fakhri used to go together to Cairo to gamble. Once they lost all their money and did not have even enough with which to get back to Jerusalem. They were staying together in a room at Shepheard's Hotel. In the middle of the night, Fakhri woke up Hassan with an idiotic suggestion how to raise some money for their return: 'Let's collect all the shoes outside the bedrooms and sell them!'

Hassan Sidki's devil-may-care attitude to life was his undoing. Although his family was in opposition to the dominant Husseinis, who led the Arab nationalist movement, he took no personal precautions and was, in due course, assassinated; as was, also, Fakhri.

When we first came to Herod's Gate, it was a pleasant place and there were many British and Jewish families living there as tenants of Moslem Arab landlords. But, after the Wailing Wall riots of August, 1929, it became somewhat unhealthy for Jews, and most left, including ourselves. The Jewish families who lived there earlier and became our friends included Siegfried van Vriesland, the genial Dutch treasurer of the Jewish Agency; Dr Israel Kligler, the American anti-malarial expert working in the Hadassah Organization; Dr Judah Magnes, the American rabbi and chancellor of the Hebrew University, of whom more later, and Dr Nelson Glueck, then head of the American School of Oriental Studies just round the corner from us. They had come to terms with Arab nationalism. They all knew where danger lay and escaped assassination. But Levi Billig, an inoffensive Anglo-Jewish Arabist at the Hebrew University, took no such precautions, sat by an open window at night, and was shot dead.

One of our friends at this time was George Antonius, a Lebanese Christian with a Cambridge University degree. He had become an assistant director of education but resigned when a British assistant director was promoted to deputy director instead of him. He was easily the most brilliant Arab then in Palestine and, with his Egyptian wife, Katy Nimr (daughter of the editor of the daily newspaper *El Mokattiam* in Cairo) developed a salon. There, British — both civil and military — met leading Palestinian Arabs. George was one of the observers then maintained in various parts of the world by Charles R. Crane, the millionaire American manufacturer of sanitary ware, and eventually produced *The Arab Awakening** — the first book in English to trace the early origins of Arab nationalism.

In the late 1920's, Jerusalem was still a cultural backwater. As the headquarters of the Palestinian Mandatory administration there were more British officials there than in any other town. But, in conformity with British colonial tradi-

* Hamish Hamilton, London, 1938.

tion, they kept to themselves. It was quite enough to mix daily in the office with Palestinian Arabs and Jews, always on guard lest an incautious word should cause offence. After office hours, the officials, with their wives and children, would congregate at the Sports Club in the German Colony for tennis, drinks, bridge and an occasional dance. There were one or two non-British honorary members, such as the Moslem Mayor of the city — Ragheb bey Nashashibi: he never appeared, of course.

My own relaxation was endlessly walking through the alleys of the Old City. From our house near Herod's Gate it was only a few minutes away and, every Saturday morning, I set off exploring. This constant contact with antiquity prompted me to read up as much as I could about Jerusalem's past. Its most interesting periods to me have always been those of previous European domination — by the Romans and by the Crusaders. Fortunately the excellent library of the nearby Dominican convent of St. Etienne was open to me and I found a wealth of material there on the Crusades. Even closer to hand were the libraries of the Government antiquities department in the Rockefeller Museum, and of the American School of Oriental Studies. There was no lack of source material. Our friend and neighbour, John Iliffe, was then curator of the Rockefeller Museum. One day, a large stone block was unearthed while a ditch was being dug in the Old City for main drainage. It bore part of a Greek inscription, ending with the word for 'death'. Iliffe was puzzled: Greek funerary inscriptions rarely ended with this word. In the middle of the night, he remembered that there was a similar inscription in the Louvre. He made his way to the Museum, unlocked the library and found the Louvre catalogue. His recollection was correct: the newly discovered stone was part of another Aramaic and Greek warning notice originally built into the outer wall of the Jewish courtyard of the Temple, warning Gentiles to keep out on pain of death. Jesus must have seen this notice many times as he visited the Temple. I found such discoveries wildly exciting.

★ ★ ★

The years 1927 and 1928 were years of apparent calm; but the underlying rift between Arab and Jew gradually deepened. The ultra-nationalist wing of the Zionist movement — the Revisionists — led by the fiery Russian-Jewish orator Vladimir Jabotinsky (with whom I had served in the Jewish Battalions) was demanding an immediate Jewish State on both sides of the Jordan. Even moderate Zionists hoped for an annual immigration that would lead to an eventual Jewish majority in Palestine and the establishment of an independent democratic state, preponderantly Zionist. These continually publicised aspirations led to an intensification of Arab nationalist activity. An Arab Executive was established under the aegis of the Husseinis and their allies to fight Zionism. The able organizer was Jamal eff el Husseini, while the Mufti of Jerusalem, Haj Amin el Husseini (later to flee to Germany and co-operate with the Nazis during World War II), gave it secret support and funds.

A few Jews in Jerusalem, mostly of German and Central European origin, became increasingly alarmed at the collision courses followed by the two movements. They formed a small society with a view to finding common ground and called it *Brit Shalom* ('The Covenant of Peace'). Some of my personal friends were members, including Hugo Bergmann and Gershon Scholem, both then professors at the Hebrew University. The spiritual leader of the society —though never actually a member of it—was Judah Magnes, the Chancellor of the University. A tall, good-looking American Reform rabbi, originally at Temple Emanuel in New York, he had been a pacifist in World War I, and was jailed for it. Few American Zionists had actually settled in Palestine, but he was one of them. A man of great moral courage, he advocated a bi-racial state in Palestine in which neither Jew nor Arab would dominate. Few Jews and fewer Arabs supported his plan. At the time, it looked attractive; but it is now obvious that such a built-in balance would soon have led to a constitutional deadlock as in Cyprus.

As a British colonial civil servant, I, personally, was not supposed to get involved in local politics. But Magnes' plan appealed to me very much, and I asked the Chief Secretary, Sir Harry Luke, for permission to join *Brit Shalom*. As reconciliation between Arab and Jew was Palestine Government policy, I was told that there was no official objection to my belonging.

Brit Shalom never had more than a couple of hundred members. But they included a number of able publicists, and the public believed that we had tens of thousands of supporters. One of my contributions was to help draft the society's programme. Another was to prevent it from putting forward any candidates for election to any Zionist or other Jewish organization that would merely serve to disclose its numerical weakness. I also helped to edit its Hebrew periodical *Sheifotenu* ('Our Aspirations').

Brit Shalom was violently attacked by almost every other

Zionist group in Palestine and abroad. The Revisionists, in particular, regarded its policy as little short of national treason. Nevertheless, it can, I think, be credited with one notable and hitherto little known success. Several members of *Brit Shalom*, including myself, had long talks with Harry Snell (later Lord Snell), the Labour Party member of the British Commission of Inquiry into the Wailing Wall riots of 1929. We succeeded in convincing him that the *Brit Shalom* policy provided at least a little hope that a peaceful solution to the Palestine problem could still be found. Some of the Commission's members were in favour of Britain's renouncing its Mandate then and there. But, in the end, they recommended that the Mandate should continue. It continued for a further eighteen years, by which time the foundations of the Jewish State had become far stronger than they had been in 1929.

★   ★   ★

Nineteen hundred and twenty-nine was a fateful year in my life. In May, Hadassah and I were shipwrecked on the Dead Sea: in August, the Wailing Wall riots broke out that resulted in the death of several hundred Jews and Arabs.

In 1930, Moshe Novomeysky, a Siberian Jewish mining engineer, had obtained a Government concession to extract potash and bromine from the Dead Sea. Its heavily impregnated waters were to be further concentrated by solar evaporation in shallow pans at the north end of the lake, and the resultant carnallite crystals processed in an adjacent factory. Several hundred Jewish and Arab workmen were employed at the north end of the lake. The heat in summer, at 1,200 feet below sea-level, was terrible: air-conditioning had not then been introduced into Palestine. The men lived in wooden bungalows, a few of which were reserved for the general manager and his guests from Jerusalem. Hadassah and I often used to go down for a few days during the cooler months. On Friday, the 13th May, 1929, we went there for the week-end, rather late in the year. On the Saturday, some of our friends from Jerusalem came down for the day. They included Harry Sacher (then a member of the Palestine Zionist Executive and now a director of Marks and Spencer in London) and his wife; her nephew Marcus Sieff (now himself a director of Marks and Spencer); Solomon Horowitz (the lawyer of the Palestine Potash Company); Louis Green (engineer to the Hebrew University) and his niece Elfie Graff. Arrangements had been made for them to use the company's motor-boat for a trip half-way down the east shore of the lake, to have a picnic lunch on the beach at Callirhoe (Wadi Zerka Maiin), to cross the lake and follow the western shore back again to the northern end. We were invited to join the party.

The motor-boat was light-shelled: it had formerly been in service in Portsmouth harbour and was quite unsuitable for the rocky shores of the Dead Sea. Its crew consisted of a Jewish mechanic and an Arab boatman: a surly Jewish potash company engineer also accompanied us. Together with two other passengers whose names I have forgotten we were thirteen persons in all, including three women: this may interest the superstitious.

After our picnic lunch, when we were about one third of the way westwards across the lake, the boat engine suddenly stopped. Lifting the floor-boards, the mechanic found that the hold was full of water. As the cause was not clear and no one seemed to know what to do, I stripped down to my shorts and lowered myself gingerly over the side, being careful not to get the brine into my eyes. By feeling along the wooden hull, I discovered that one arm of the metal propeller-bracket had been driven through the hull. We must have grazed an underwater rock while coming in to the beach at Callirhoe for lunch. The first thing was to stop the leak as far as possible, which I did, from the outside, with strips of my shirt. Clambering back on board, I set some of the men to bale out the water with any available utensil; but no matter how fast they baled, they could not lower its level appreciably, even when the rest all went forward in order to raise the stern as far as possible and reduce the water pressure from outside. We held a council of war during which it became clear that, if the water rose any higher, the boat, with its heavy racing engine, would sink to the bottom: we had no dinghy or life-belts. Even if we managed to lower the water-level and could restart the engine, we dared not use the propeller for fear of shaking the bracket loose and widening the leak. We found we had on board some wooden paddles and a rudimentary emergency sail. We were then already some four miles from the eastern shore and several of our party could not swim. The eastern shore was rocky, uninhabited and extremely hot. Even if we reached land, there was no way of walking either back to the north end of the lake or up the steep sides of the mountain. The nearest villages were about twenty miles away. We had no food or drink beyond the remnants of our picnic lunch and some unopened soda-water bottles. There were no other boats of any kind then on the lake. Most of the party would consequently die of thirst in the fierce summer heat before help came.

Having been a district officer for nine years, I had acquired the habit, before setting out on any trip by foot, horse, car or boat, of looking at a map. I had done so on this occasion and had mentally noted that there was a brackish spring on the *western* shore between the point we were making for and the northern end of the lake. If we took the longer course, about eight miles, and got to the western shore, we might be able to work our way along the shore northwards and reach this spring. There, we could lay in enough water to enable us to continue our journey back to the potash company's camp. I calculated that this would take us several days, considering the extreme heat and our lack of food. There was one other factor that I kept to myself: the eastern shore was Trans-Jordan territory: the western shore Palestinian. I felt I was better able to handle any wandering Arabs we might meet if they were Palestinians and not Trans-Jordanian Beduin. So, while some of us continued furiously to bale, others rigged up the emergency sail. There was, however, little wind, and we had to take turns at the paddles. Horowitz, a small man, who had coxed his university college boat, added some light relief by constantly urging us to pull together, until we managed to persuade him to desist. After some eight hours hard work (instead of the half hour we would have taken had the engine been working), we reached the western shore. It was already night, but the moon was up in a cloudless sky and the whole rocky beach was brilliantly lit.

Anyone who is in an accident while afloat and has faced the imminent possibility of drowning has an indescribable feeling of relief when his feet first touch solid ground again. The crunch of the gravel on the beach was music in my ears. We were all scorched by the sun and exhausted: lying down on the stones, we fell asleep. The night was warm. Each of us took turns to keep watch. The boat was securely anchored off the shore.

The next morning, before dawn, at about 4 a.m., we ate a little of the remaining food and water. I refused to allow anyone to try to make his way up the dry, hot, steep and rocky wadis to Hebron: it was all too easy to lose one's way. Only a short time before, two German students, trying to walk *down* the 4,000 feet from Bethlehem to the Dead Sea, had missed their way: one had died of thirst.

Nor was it possible for us all to walk northwards along the beach as, every few hundred yards or so, the steep cliffs came right down into the water. Hence, we decided to keep the women and the elder men on board and paddle the boat slowly northwards. But we found that there was a head wind from the north and we could make no headway. So we began to *tow* the boat along the shore, keeping it off the rocks with the boat-hook. Where the cliffs came down into the water, the towing party swam round the point with the end of the rope and then started towing again on the other side. We split up into two towing parties, each of three younger men. This meant that the three women and the four elder men were on board, together with the towing party of three that was resting, while the other towing party was on shore. It was very hard work and we could only tow for half an hour at a time, in the boiling sunshine, at 1,200 feet below sea-level, in the sub-tropics, in May. Our average speed was well under a mile an hour. We rigged up the little sail as an awning for those on board.

The worst feature of it, for the towing parties, was that, after swimming, our clothes dried on us and, owing to the salt, became as stiff as boards. All our limbs got chafed in consequence, apart from the cuts inflicted by the rocks. When we got back into the brine again, all the sores and cuts smarted agonisingly.

We towed all through the day from about 5 a.m. until we reached the brackish well late at night. The water was almost undrinkable, but we had no option, as our bodies had become badly dehydrated. It was cooler that night and a wind came up. We lay down to sleep, to find that the whole area around the well was a colossal dung-heap that had apparently been used for centuries by wandering Arab herdsmen watering their flocks. The flies and mosquitoes were intolerable: we had to muffle up our feet and hands and faces. Our noses, left exposed for breathing, were red and inflamed the next morning: we looked like a bunch of alcoholics.

That was Sunday night: our friends had been due back in Jerusalem before dusk on Saturday. On Saturday evening, when the Jerusalem party failed to return home, servants notified family friends, who informed the police, who asked the R.A.F. to search the shores of the lake from the air. We heard planes on Sunday night and lit a bonfire. But the R.A.F. were expecting to find us on the eastern shore and thought that *our* fires were the camp fires of nomadic Beduin.

Meanwhile, the press got hold of the story. Telegrams about our being lost on the Dead Sea were sent all over the world. One London newspaper office rang up my father in Wales, just before he was due to make a big political speech. They reported that our bodies had been found: he made the speech notwithstanding.

Monday morning, not having had any food for twenty-four hours and being rather the worse for wear, we set off northwards, still towing our crippled boat. The wind in the night had blown away the emergency awning and the party on board suffered badly from the sun.

Our progress on the third day grew slower and slower. Owing to the haze, we still could not even *see* distantly the potash company's camp on the north shore. Our spirits were low and our forces were almost exhausted. The Arab boatman here came into his own, encouraging us in Arabic: 'Just round the next headland: just beyond the next bay.' Without him, we would never have made it. (I am glad to say that, in gratitude, Harry Sacher, on his return to Jerusalem, set this boatman up for life, providing him with a little cottage at Lydda, and a pension.)

On the afternoon of the previous day, the Zionist Executive grew more and more anxious about the fate of one of their members. They knew that there were no other boats on the lake available for a rescue expedition. So, during Sunday night, they had some Arab boats and boatmen brought up on lorries from Jaffa over the mountains and down to the lake. As we eventually came within sight of the shore on Monday, we were surprised to see a couple of such boats approaching us, racing each other to be the first to reach us and claim the large reward that had been offered for our discovery, dead or alive. The winners boarded our fragile craft, pushed us aside and proceeded to tow us the last half mile or so. We were indignant, being justly proud of having brought ourselves back all alive and our boat, too.★

As we got closer, we were puzzled to see a dense long line of people skirting the shore. They included hospital nurses and ambulances: we had no idea that everyone would be

★ See photograph between pages 180 and 181.

so concerned. When we were eventually carried ashore, we were roundly scolded for having given our friends such a fright. We were all put to bed; but we recovered in a few days. I never want to be stranded again on the Dead Sea in May.

★ ★ ★

For me, the Wailing Wall riots in Jerusalem, three months later, were far more serious. They started on 23rd August with bloodthirsty Arab attacks on Jews in Jerusalem that spread to other towns with mixed populations, notably Hebron and Safad. In spite of the *Hagana* self-defence units, by the end, no less than 133 Jewish men, women and children were butchered and 339 wounded. The Arab police proved unreliable: the few British police and British troops then in Palestine were incapable of restoring order, and military units had to be brought up from Egypt and from as far afield as Malta. The number of Arabs killed by the *Hagana*, the police and the army in restoring order reached 116, making a total death roll of nearly 250, a disgraceful episode in a country under British administration.

I happened to be in the very middle of it all, as private secretary to Sir Harry Luke, then acting for the High Commissioner, Sir John Chancellor, away in England that summer on leave. It was a traumatic experience.

We were all aware of the underlying struggle between rival Arab and Jewish nationalisms for domination in Palestine. Few people, however, realised at the time that the decision taken by the Zionist Congress, held earlier that summer at Zurich to widen the Zionist Executive into a

Jewish Agency, would seem so threatening to the Arabs. The Jewish Agency, as envisaged in the Mandate, was to represent the World Zionist Organization on one side and non-Zionist Jewish bodies in various countries on the other. Some of them, especially in the United States, had access to great Jewish financial resources; and it was this increase in the capital now to become available for Zionist colonisation in Palestine that alarmed the Arab nationalist leaders.

The actual outburst of violence was caused by an absurd dispute over the exact rights of Jewish worshippers at the Wailing Wall. This wall, in the heart of a fanatically Moslem Arab quarter of the Old City, is the undoubted outer wall of the enclosure to Herod's Temple. The Jewish Temple itself was burnt and levelled by the Romans in 70 A.D. and the Jews exiled. Most of the outer wall was also destroyed: but a section of it, largely composed of huge, squared limestone blocks, is still standing. It now forms the outer wall of the *Haram esh Sherif* ('The Noble Sanctuary',) the broad precincts in which stand the mosque of el Aqsa and a particularly sacred Moslem shrine, the Dome of the Rock (often miscalled the Mosque of Omar), containing relics of the Prophet himself, and built over the actual site of the Temple.

Many Jewish pilgrims do not dare to enter the *Haram* for fear of treading on the sacred spot where the Holy of Holies had once stood. But, during the centuries, they had made their way through the adjacent Moslem quarter to pray and mourn for the destruction of the Temple; hence the Wailing Wall (in Hebrew it is called merely *Kotel HaMaaravi* — The Western Wall). The Moslems tolerated Jewish access to a narrow alley below the outer side of the Wall for the purpose of prayer. But they were particularly sensitive over any Jewish attempt to put up any structure in the alley which might give Jews proprietary rights in the Wall itself and possibly an eventual claim to be allowed to rebuild the Temple on its ancient site. In fact, some of the old-fashioned Jewish charities in Jerusalem had for decades depicted on their writing paper, used for sending begging letters to Jews abroad, a crude representation of the Moslem Dome of the Rock under a Zionist flag.

The trouble in August, 1929, arose over an attempt by Jews to put up a light screen in the alley to separate Jewish female worshippers from male worshippers, as in all Orthodox synagogues. The Moslems objected that this was an infringement of the *status quo ante* (that is, tradition) that was to govern all rights in the Holy Places. Disputes over the *status quo* were to be referred to a Holy Places Commission. But, owing to disagreement between France and Italy over who was to be chairman of this Commission, it had never been set up. There was consequently no body which could give an authoritative decision whether or not a screen should be allowed in the alley. The district commissioner himself tried to adjudicate, but found himself on weak legal ground. So did Sir Harry Luke, to whom the matter was referred.

I had previously served for several years under Luke when he had been deputy district commissioner for Jerusalem. Born Lukasch, of Hungarian origin (his first book was published under that name) he had been at Eton and Oxford. In 1922, he and Edward Keith-Roach (see page 136 below) produced *The Handbook of Palestine and Trans-Jordan*, a welcome addition to the then scanty documentation on those two countries. When, in the summer of 1929, Sir Harry became 'Officer Administering the Government' (the clumsy official title for anyone acting as high Commissioner or Colonial Governor), I was loaned by the Secretariat to be his private secretary. I lived not far away from his official residence. He had a great sense of history and, in the fateful weeks before the outburst over the Wailing Wall, I accompanied him on a tour of the Crusader castles in Galilee. As a man of taste and erudition, he would have made an admirable director of antiquities. As acting High Commisioner, with inadequate legal powers to deal with the situation in which he found himself, he was not prepared to act without suitable authority and a clash became inevitable.

Moslem suspicions over Jewish intentions at the Wailing Wall were fanned into flame by the Arab press. Here, too, the Government had, at that time, inadequate legal powers of control. The Ottoman press law, still in force, permitted the prosecution of a newspaper for incitement endangering the public peace. But prosecution takes time and, in the absence of any authority to close down a paper meanwhile, or to impose a censorship, the incitement continues. Some sections of the Jewish press were equally intemperate. There were also Jewish street demonstrations, and Arab counter-demonstrations, until the Moslems of Jerusalem boiled over after the noon-time prayers in the *Haram esh Sherif* on a Friday, when large crowds of Moslem villagers habitually came in to the city. Inflammatory sermons were preached against the Jews.

That afternoon, Friday, 23rd August, 1929, I was at the Government offices, just outside the Damascus Gate. The first that we knew of anything wrong was a faint and distant shouting, like the ominous buzz of bees. Looking out from the balcony, I could see small groups of men running out of the Old City through the next exit, the New Gate, and pouring down the hill towards the Damascus Gate. Other Arabs came running out of the Damascus Gate itself and attacked any Jewish passers-by they happened to meet. I could see in the sunshine the flash of the daggers that most peasants then carried. Some Jews ran and escaped: others took refuge in nearby Arab houses and were mostly saved; some were attacked indoors and killed. A few Arab mounted police with long staves arrived and tried to drive the crowds back into the Old City; but ten times their number could not have restrained the mob. Egged on by shouts from agitators, the crowd grew more excited by the minute: the noise of a crowd out for blood is truly frightening. The Commandant of the Palestine Police Force, Colonel Alan Saunders, arrived to take personal charge of the situation. But, by then, it was already out of hand and he came into the office, hot, dusty, spattered with blood, to telephone for reinforcements. Never once did he lose his composure during that whole week, even though he was almost dead from fatigue and lack of sleep.

As private secretary to Luke, I became one of the channels of communication between him, the Government departments, the army, the police, and the Jewish and Arab leaders. I stayed day and night at the telephone, either at Luke's office or his house, receiving reports of disturbances that broke out all over the country as wildly exaggerated rumours of the fighting in Jerusalem spread. The *Hagana* — the Jewish underground self-defence corps that had been secretly built up for just such an occasion — took up its positions and saved many of the Jewish colonies and outlying quarters of Jerusalem from slaughter. But isolated families were savagely wiped out, for example in the Jewish village of Motza, on the road from Jerusalem to Jaffa. Many Jewish theological students on the outskirts of the fanatically Moslem city of Hebron were butchered. The rest of the Jews in the Hebron ghetto were, however, saved by the personal gallantry of a British police officer, Raymond Cafferata. With a single Arab orderly as his loader, he kept the whole town at bay outside the ghetto gates until reinforcements arrived.

There were then few British troops or British police in Palestine. Most of the Arab police refused to open fire on Arab crowds, among whom might be some of their own relatives or friends. If someone of another Arab family is killed by an Arab, a blood feud results. In these circumstances, all British civil servants in Jerusalem and elsewhere were called up to act as special constables and were given arms. In view of my duties as private secretary to Luke, I was not released and was ashamed to find how relieved I was. I had acquitted myself satisfactorily during our stranding on the Dead Sea; but facing crazed Arab crowds who were armed with clubs, daggers and shotguns was a very different matter.

I was, however, spared the humiliation that overtook those British special constables who happened to be Jewish. As soon as the Arab nationalist leaders heard that Jews were being armed by the Government to fight Arabs, they brought such pressure to bear that the Jewish civil servants — most of whom, like myself, were ex-servicemen—were ordered to hand back their rifles.

That night, telephone reports came pouring in from all over Palestine, especially from exposed Jewish settlements, appealing for help. Luke, and the members of the Executive Council, were in almost continuous session in Luke's office or house. But, in the absence of military or police reinforcements, there was little that anyone could do.

The trouble lay in the fact that Palestine had been almost completely denuded of British troops and British police. In my father's time as High Commissioner, the large post-World War I garrison had been successively reduced to two battalions, one at Jerusalem, the other at Haifa. A British gendarmerie had been established, primarily to deal with inter-racial disputes in mixed areas. As a measure of economy, however, its number had been reduced from about 800 (a battalion) to less than 250, who were then incorporated in the Palestine Police as the British Section. Lord Plumer, the second High Commissioner, was a Field Marshal. His imperturbability alone was worth a brigade. Once, when he was told by the Mufti that he (the Mufti) could not accept responsibility for the results if some measure was adopted, the High Commissioner replied: 'No one asked you to. *I* take the responsibility for such decisions.' He further reduced, the British garrison however, for reasons of economy until, in August, 1923, it consisted of only 173 British police officers, N.C.O.'s and constables, and one company of R.A.F. armoured cars.

Plumer's successor, Sir John Chancellor, and Luke, who acted as High Commissioner in his absence, were men of lesser personality. Sir Harry was faced with the same dilemma that faces all colonial governors. If military reinforcements are called for in time, trouble often does not break out and the man who called for them gets a reputation of being 'windy'. If, on the other hand, as in Luke's case, he does *not* call for them until too late, he is blamed for the subsequent disorders. The latter was Luke's fate. As a result of the findings of the commission of inquiry into the cause

of the disturbances of August, 1929, Luke was transferred. without promotion, to be Lieutenant-Governor of Malta.*
I am still surprised that, having been present when many of the Government decisions on how to handle the violence were taken, I was never called either by the Government or by the Arab or Jewish representatives, as a witness on the exact sequence of disputed events.

When British military reinforcements eventually arrived in Palestine, they moved with disastrous slowness. The commander was Brigadier Dobbie with whom, as a member of Luke's staff, I had much to do. Although he was much older than I, we became personal friends. He was a man of the highest principles, one of those devout Cromwellian soldiers who prayed for guidance. He had had little previous experience of the use of troops in aid of the civil power. To him, the whole of Palestine was enemy territory that had to be reconquered. The police and the *Hagana* in Safad were holding on by the skin of their teeth; but, instead of rushing a lorry-load of infantry to Safad to stabilize the situation, Dobbie proceeded to 'occupy', first Nazareth and, later, Tiberias. By the time his men reached Safad, a day or two later, the balloon had gone up, with heavy loss of life.

Months after the riots, an *ad hoc* Holy Places Commission, set up by the League of Nations, arrived to determine Jewish and Arab rights at the Wailing Wall. By this time, everyone had lost interest in the matter. The ferocity of the disturbances did indicate, however, how deep was the rift between the two peoples in Palestine. There had been racial rioting in 1920 and 1921; but nothing more for eight years. We had all hoped

* In World War II he became Governor of Fiji and High Commissioner of the Western Pacific.

that the breach was being slowly healed. Now it was torn wide open. As a result of the recommendations of the Shaw commission of inquiry into the causes of the disturbances, the British garrison was restored permanently to two infantry battalions, one at Jerusalem, the other at Haifa. Seven years later, in 1936, even more serious Arab disturbances started, which developed into a two-year rebellion. No less than an additional division of British troops had to be brought to suppress it. After World War II, both Jews and Arabs increasingly resorted to the use of force to establish their political rights in Palestine. This ended in civil war and partition in 1948. It was against this background of recurrent violence that the remaining nineteen years of my administrative service in Palestine were spent.

★   ★   ★

It was in March, 1930, that George Bernard Shaw and his wife came to Palestine on a Hellenic Club cruise round the Mediterranean. My father knew him well and wrote to me from England to do what I could for him. What follows is based on detailed notes I made immediately after the conversation: direct quotations are thus permissible, I think.

G.B.S. and his wife were staying at the Hotel Fast and had been to the Dead Sea that afternoon. He was going on the next morning to Nazareth. Hadassah and I called at 7 p.m. and talked with him (or rather, listened to him talking) for an hour. We were joined at the end by Gene Tunney, the heavy-weight boxer (with whom he was dining) and Mrs G.B.S.

He came down, with his white hair combed smoothly

back, a bristling white beard and piercing pale blue eyes. He wore a plain dark suit. He refused to use an arm-chair, but sat at a little table, with his back to the crowd. I asked him what he thought of Palestine. He said he liked it very much, early in the morning, coming up in the train. But Jerusalem at first sight he found most unprepossessing, and quite unlike anything he had anticipated. The *Haram esh Sharif*, however, was marvellous. There one felt the magic of the place. None of the other buildings in Jerusalem was really the best of its kind. Even the Mosque was inferior to St Sophia. As for the Holy Sepulchre, 'you can have it for tuppence.'

I asked whether he didn't like the Church of the Nativity at Bethlehem. He said it was fine, except for the ridiculous limestone cave that they try and make you believe is where Christ was born. I asked whether he had noticed the Crusader *graffiti* on the columns. He said he had not seen 'those signs of man's restless striving for immortality'.

He was very derisory about the Holy Places. 'The Zionists ought to set up notices at every holy site saying "do not trouble to stop here: it isn't genuine".' He said that one of his friends, the abbess of a nunnery near Gloucester, had asked him to bring her back something from Calvary. 'Even if it were genuine, it would take a corps of engineers and a ton of nitrotoluene to blast away a souvenir. So I picked up a stone from outside the Church of the Nativity at Bethlehem to give her.'

He liked the Dead Sea. 'That is real and not a fake.' But he did not think the water was quite as salty as it ought to have been.

Hadassah asked him whether anyone had tried to make a Zionist of him. He said that several had had a try. 'It's a funny thing, how this country has been handled. Imagine a Crusader here today and you were trying to explain to him that this country, with all its Christian associations, having been captured by a great Christian Power from the Turks and heretics and infidels, is thereupon handed over to the Moslems and the Jews. The Crusader wouldn't know what to make of it all; he'd want to start another Crusade.

'When the leader of the Zionists (What's his name — oh, yes, Dr Weizmann) met Balfour (I think it was) and offered some invention,' (I, *sotto voce*—('acetone') 'oh, yes, acetone, Balfour asked him how much he wanted. Weizmann said, "Nothing." Balfour said, "That's strange, and you a Jew." Weizmann said, "All I want is Palestine." "Oh", said Balfour, "oh, *that* you can have straight away".'★

'That's the trouble with this country: during the war, England was ready to promise anyone anything. Lawrence promised Palestine to the Arabs as well.' (I had just been reading Ben Jonson's *Volpone*, in which the hero makes three different men his sole heir: the illustration is apt, but I thought it safer not to quote it.)

I then mentioned T.E. Lawrence whom I had met at G.B.S.'s house in London four months previously. G.B.S. replied: 'Now, did you notice the jury's rider on that Air Force crash?' ('Meopham' I murmered). 'Well, when I read that, I saw at once, it was "Shaw". (T.E. Lawrence's assumed name) No one else at Portsmouth could write like that. "Shaw" is in the bottom rank of the Air Force. The rank above requires a knowledge of reading and writing: but, whenever an exam comes along, "Shaw" has become illiterate. Nevertheless, whenever a specially difficult order

★ This story is apocryphal.

113

has to be issued, they always call in "Shaw" to draft it. He has all the power and none of the responsibility. He commands his unit from the bottom.' I said that must be awkward for his military superiors. G.B.S. then said that 'Shaw' deliberately set out to mock his superiors. 'He's rather a rogue. He attended, day after day, a corporal's class to learn English spelling. He bought a racing motor-cycle, which does eighty miles an hour. He made a "property" carrot and, when the colonel comes past in his Rolls Royce, "Shaw" just lets the motor-cycle out and dangles the carrot behind. A rich American had a motor boat "that did a thousand miles an hour". He brought it to Portsmouth and "Shaw" used to drive it for him. Then he got bored with it and gave it to "Shaw", who now dashes about in it. He gets his sergeant to give orders to his squad to have it painted.

'Lawrence's official superiors were very upset about the distinguished friends Lawrence cultivated and told him he mustn't associate with people so much above his station. Lawrence said, "very good", and asked whom he might meet. "Lady Astor?" "Oh, no." "Lord someone else?" "Certainly not!" "Bernard Shaw?" "Oh, well, you can meet Bernard Shaw".'

Hadassah asked why Lawrence went into the Air Force. G.B.S. said: 'I think he regarded it as a kind of monastery. His nerves were all done up after his experience in Arabia. Lawrence has a tremendously sensitive conscience and poisoning wells upset him. He was, of course, in the Colonial Office at a £1,000 a year, but he got tired of giving orders. He hadn't a penny. He used to stand in York Place as being the most likely spot to meet a friend who could give him lunch. I tried to get him a pension of £300 a year. David Hogarth said Lawrence would never take it, but I spoke to him and found he was ready to take it.' After Lawrence had been turned out of the Air Force the first time, he joined the Tank Corps, 'but that's an awful regiment', said G.B.S.

Hadassah asked why Lawrence didn't write for a living. G.B.S. said that he didn't know if Lawrence *could* write. His *Seven Pillars of Wisdom* was not a test. Anyone with war experience like Lawrence should be able to write a great book. 'When someone showed me *Journey's End* before it was produced and asked me if the author had talent, all I could say was that I didn't know. You can't have a European war every time someone wants to write a great book.'

G.B.S. said that, when Lawrence brought the *Seven Pillars of Wisdom* to him, he found it full of the most violent abuse. "Why", I said, "that's libellous", so I rewrote all these sentences for him. But I found later he had taken my version as well as his original text, and showed them to all the people about whom they were written.'

Lawrence did try once to write a book. 'He went on some training course which was awful. He reproduced the whole thing with all the obscene language of the soldiers. It couldn't possibly be printed: he's still got it locked up somewhere.'*

G.B.S. then looked at his watch and said that he must soon go to fetch his wife as Gene Tunney was coming to take them to dinner at the King David. I asked about Tunney. G.B.S. said: 'He's got the finest eyes of any man living.' He then said that Tunney was an Irishman, a railway clerk before the war on £3.10.0 a week. He served in the Royal Marines during the war and, although he couldn't box well, gradually became their champion. After the war, he couldn't go back and become a railway clerk again at £3.10.0: he

---

* Published after World War II as 'The Mint'.

couldn't do anything else except box. So he became a boxer. I asked whether Tunney had ever been beaten. 'Only once', said G.B.S. 'by a man called Greb who had squared the referee and began by charging Tunney with his head and broke his nose. But Greb knew Tunney was a coming man and, when he next fought him, whispered to Tunney before they began "Don't put me down, Gene". So Tunney didn't and everyone thought he hadn't a knockout blow in him. When Tunney met Dempsey, everyone backed Dempsey, but Greb put everything he had on Tunney, made a fortune and retired. When I saw a film of the fight between Tunney and Carpentier, Carpentier seemed to be getting all his blows home, but Tunney never stirred a muscle. I said to myself that man must be made of ferro-concrete.'

'I know Tunney well', G.B.S. continued. 'The last time I met him was on the island of Brioni in the Adriatic when his wife nearly died of some trouble in the appendix. I prevented Tunney from going distracted by walking him round the island and talking to him about everything imaginable. At the last moment, as if by a miracle, a German doctor and a German surgeon landed on the island and saved her life. The German doctor was very rich and travelling for pleasure and had taken the surgeon with him in case anything went wrong with his own insides during the voyage.'

'I once asked Tunney to what he owed his becoming a champion. Tunney answered: "I have great objection to being hit on the head." I told this story once to an Italian captain on board ship. He corrected my Italian and said, "What you mean, of course, is that Tunney said 'I am indifferent to being hit on the head"'.'

Turney always refused to fight anyone whom he had

not previously watched in another fight. He always used to say that no one could ever learn to box until he had seen game-cocks fighting.

'Tunney is very interested in literature. It's funny how one finds unexpected traits in people. The greatest mystic I ever met was Hackenschmidt, the wrestler.* He would make an Indian fakir climb down. After he became world-famous, he followed in the steps of all these champions and decided to open a gymnasium. He made all his preparations but, at the last moment, decided that real strength must come from some other source. He gave up the plan and spent three years in writing a book on mysticism. He took it to a friend and asked him if he understood it and liked it. The friend said he didn't understand it, so the second question didn't arise. Hackenschmidt then threw the book in the river and sat down for five years and wrote a second one explaining the first. Where do you think Hackenschmidt lived? Not in the Himalayas, as one might suppose, but at Nice.'

Gene Tunney then arrived and the conversation stopped.

Later, we met G.B.S. at the Villa Melchett on the shore of the Sea of Galilee as guests of Eva Reading, daughter of Alfred Mond, later Lord Melchett, who had built the villa but had never lived in it. Eva (now the Dowager Marchioness of Reading) had inherited the villa and came out for short periods to stay in it. I took G.B.S. swimming: he swam powerfully on his back, his white beard sticking up like a periscope. When he had got out about a quarter of a mile, I began to be worried, as he was not a young man. I had visions of the London papers next day: 'G.B.S. drowned

* Who died only in 1968.

117

in the Sea of Galilee: Edwin Samuel makes gallant effort to save him.' I suggested that we should return: he paid not the slightest attention but struck out even more boldly into the centre of the lake, where sudden squalls are frequent. After half a mile, I had visions of another headline: 'Edwin Samuel drowned in the Sea of Galilee: G.B.S. makes gallant effort to save him.' So I said 'I don't know about you, Sir, but I'm going back.' He then did the same. Subsequently I took a snapshot of him on the shore (wearing my swimsuit), looking like a mixture of Tolstoy, Homer and Rabindranath Tagore.* I sent it (with G.B.S.'s permission) to the weekly illustrated London *Sketch:* they printed it full-page and sent me a cheque for three guineas. I sent it back, saying it was not enough: so they sent me five guineas, with which Hadassah bought a hat.

★   ★   ★

I was not happy in the Secretariat. My immediate superior was Eric Mills, a remarkable man under whom I served later for five years in the Department of Immigration, completely content. But, in the Secretariat, he 'rode' me mercilessly and I never seemed able to do the right thing. The senior of the eleven assistant secretaries at that time was Sidney Moody, a cautious Yorkshireman.** His motto was: 'Never allow a particular instance to develop into a general prin-

---

* See photograph between pages 180 and 181.
** He had been district officer at Safad and ended his colonial career as Chief Secretary in Mauritius, later to do extremely well as, of all things, a raspberry-grower in Scotland.

ciple.' At that time, I was dealing with staff questions. Again and again I would have to argue identical cases of, say, pensions, without being able ever to establish a precedent which would have saved me, and everyone else, a great deal of time and effort. Eventually, Moody was instructed to break the news to me: 'Nebi, you don't seem suited for the Secretariat.' 'I couldn't agree more,' I replied.

So, in December, 1930, I found myself back in the headquarters of the Jerusalem District, this time as deputy to a new district commissioner — Edward Keith-Roach. He was a fantastic extrovert who, before World War I, had been, I think, a bank clerk in Khartoum. Whenever he referred to this period of his career, he would begin. 'When I was Financial Secretary in the Sudan . . .' He found it difficult to express himself succinctly and I had to write many of his letters for him. He once said to me: 'The trouble with me, Nebi, is that I'm illiterate!' I had great difficult in restraining myself from saying: 'Yes, Sir'. But he had a heart of gold and did many acts of private kindness which he kept wholly secret, with becoming modesty. He even invited British police constables to his house. In the eyes of high caste British colonial civil servants in Palestine, British police constables were untouchables. A man of imposing bulk, Keith-Roach was popularly called 'The Pasha', a title in which he revelled. I worked again under him later when he was district commissioner at Haifa and I his assistant district commissioner in Nazareth (see Chapter 8).

I stayed in Jerusalem as his deputy until I went to the United States in the summer of 1931 for a year on a Commonwealth Fund fellowship. I returned to the same post on my return for a few months until I moved up to Galilee.

CHAPTER 7

U.S.A., 1931–32

As a young man, like many others, I had been intrigued by the Americans. When I got to Balliol College at Oxford, in 1919, the war was over, but the Rhodes scholars had not yet begun to come again from the United States, or elsewhere. Some imaginative corps commander had nevertheless allowed hundreds of graduate officers from the American Army of the Rhine to spend a year at Oxford. Some became my friends and urged me to visit the United States. However, I hurried back to Palestine instead and got married in December, 1920. Two children later, as a permanent colonial civil servant with no money, I was further away from America than ever.

My chance did not come until I was in the Secretariat. In 1929, a Colonial Office circular happened to pass my desk, notifying all Colonial administrations that applications might be submitted for Commonwealth Fund fellowships in the United States for 1930–31. This Fund had been established by Stephen Harkness, an American millionaire, to enable twenty young British graduates a year to spend fifteen to twenty-four months attached to an American university. They could study the subject of their choice without having necessarily to take another degree. Three additional fellowships were allotted to the British Colonial Service. Having distributed the circular to all Palestine Government departments and districts, I set about trying to get a fellowship for myself. I rightly guessed that everything depended on my selecting a subject of study that no American selection board could possibly reject. After consulting Dr Judah Magnes, the American-born Chancellor of the Hebrew University and a personal friend, I came up with the American administration of the Philippines as my subject. No British colonial civil servant had *ever* wanted to study this effort to be imperial by a non-imperial Power. I was interviewed in London while on leave for one of the three 1930-31 Colonial Service fellowships and was placed fifth. Advised to apply again the following year, I was then nominated. The Palestine Government gave me a year's study leave on half-pay: no one else from Palestine ever managed to get such treatment, so I was indeed lucky. I parked my wife and children with my parents in London and set off for the Promised Land.

The fellowship was munificent for those days and included payment of my fare to and from the U.S.A., all university fees, an ample monthly food and lodging allowance, a one-time book allowance and a considerable clothing allowance (which enabled me to invest in a new dinner-jacket). I had asked to go to Columbia University for the sole reason that I wanted to live in New York. I found myself a room in International House on Riverside Drive, not far from the University. International House was all washable tiles and olive-green metal furniture, thoroughly antiseptic and chill.

When I called at the Columbia Graduate School, they said: 'Of course, you don't *really* want to study the American administration of the Philippines, do you? Looking at your subjects of study at Oxford, what you ought to do here is economics,' which I did. I had the good fortune to be guided in this by Edwin Seligman, the former Columbia University economic historian, recently retired and professor emeritus. He was also a bibliophile and had a wonderful collection of rare early economic books and pamphlets, all beautifully encased in new leather bindings.

So I spent the next twelve months making up for my lost third year at Oxford. I was thirty-three, with eleven years of experience of colonial administration in Palestine. There I had lived on the edge of civilisation: a few miles to the east the great deserts of Asia began. Now I was in the very centre of development and I was determined to make the most of it. I knew — or at least thought I knew — what I wanted. It was a miraculous year.

I attended a few graduate economic discussion groups and seminars: I followed a course on statistics. The rest of my time I spent in the libraries reading, chiefly theoretical economics and economic history, as well as American history, institutions and literature. But, on top of all this, I dived headlong into anything and everything that took my fancy. I visited almost every museum and gallery in New York, Washington, Philadelphia and Boston, as well as dozens of university departments, specialist libraries and institutions that had the remotest connection with my own interests. On my first visit to Washington, D.C., I presented a number of letters of introduction and was admitted immediately to some of the centres of power — including Congress and the Supreme Court. At the end of an exhausting day, I sat in a venerable club of which I had been given temporary membership and wrote to my father an 84-page letter on that day's doings. In spite of the current economic depression, America was like champagne to me. The crisp winter air of New York was the elixir of youth. I worked all day and danced all night with never a care for the future.

In the spring of 1932, Hadassah arrived to spend three months with me in New York, with the assistance of the Commonwealth Fund. We were invited to stay for the whole period with Felix and Frieda Warburg, friends of my parents, who lived at the corner of Fifth Avenue and 92nd Street. From the upper floors of their baronial mansion, we looked across Central Park to the skyline of Central Park West.

The Warburg mansion was one of the last to survive in Millionaires' Row: it is now the Jewish Museum. Felix, the German-Jewish immigrant, had married the daughter of the banker Otto Schiff and had become a partner in his banking firm of Kuhn, Loeb & Co. They all had, of course, to cut down their expenditure somewhat during the depression: so Felix and Frieda reduced the crew of their private yacht from eight to six. They had a butler, a footman, two chauffeurs, and a houseful of cooks and maid-servants. Although Frieda was not a Zionist, she decorated our bedroom with little blue-and-white flags to avert our homesickness. Hospitality could go no further.

The Warburgs mixed almost entirely with other well-established German-Jewish families whose ancestors had come over after the abortive 1848 revolution in Germany (described by Stephen Birmingham in *Our Crowd: The Great Jewish Families of New York*).★ After offices hours, even Felix felt ill at ease among Gentiles. Nor had Felix and Frieda anything to do with the more recent East European immigrant families, among whom was Hadassah's uncle in

★ Harper & Row, New York, 1967.

Brooklyn, and others of her acquaintances. When the Warburgs gave a reception for their friends and ours, theirs kept at one end of the room and ours at the other: it was almost impossible for the Warburgs to mix them.

To add to our pleasure, their eldest son Freddie lent us one of his automobiles in which Hadassah and I drove through Virginia to Charleston in South Carolina which then still preserved much of the flavour of the Old South. For example, admission to the annual ball of the local St Cecilia Society was refused to anyone who was in trade or had been divorced.

After Hadassah returned in June to London and our children, I set off with Edward 'the youngest son' in *his* car across the United States to California. He was going anyhow and let me go with him. This was regarded by the Commonwealth Fund as a suitable form of the summer travel that each Fellow was required to undertake. Edward was then 23, a wealthy young man in his own right ($75,000 a year). I was ten years older and went as a combined companion, bodyguard and relief driver. He had an open Chrysler sports car and we spent six weeks together in it. We drove first through the cities of the Great Lakes — Buffalo, Detroit and Chicago — where Eddie knew the curators of all the art galleries.

From Chicago, we motored westward a thousand miles across the plains to Denver. In those days, there were no paved roads west of Chicago until one reached California. But the dirt roads were scraped periodically and kept level and well-drained. After rain, however, they became impassable for a few days; but we were lucky, and covered the thousand miles in three days, eating at little cross-roads 'diners.' We managed to spend each night — this was before motels were invented — in a little fireproof brick hotel in some small rural town. (Eddie would not sleep in any wooden building.) From Denver we turned north through the national parks (then not at all crowded) as far as the Canadian frontier. There we went for a steamer cruise on Glacier Lake, which eventually empties into the Mississippi. I was surprised to see on the bridge 'Regulations for Pilots of Craft on Waters Flowing into the Mexican Gulf', nearly 2,000 miles away. Then we turned westward again, over the Rockies, to hit the Pacific coast at Portland, Oregon, the city with rose bushes all along the streets. It is still one of my favourite American cities, perhaps because I was so relieved, after a month's driving, to find that the Pacific really did exist. From Portland we drove southward through the giant redwoods to San Francisco and Los Angeles.

In San Francisco, Eddie had family and friends with whom we stayed and who fêted us royally. As Kuhn, Loeb & Co. helped to finance Hollywood, he had the entrée there, too. It was while I was dancing with some film star that I received an urgent cable recalling me to Palestine to replace Archer Cust who was to accompany Ronald Storrs to Northern Rhodesia. This was a severe blow: it meant not only that I could not continue for a second year; but I had to leave unfinished my thesis on the economic factors determining the expansion of the citrus industry in Palestine. I never did finish it; nor did I ever obtain a master's degree, much less a doctorate. This mattered little as long as I was merely a British colonial civil servant. But it mattered a great deal when I became a university teacher. I realise only too well now that I have not been adequately trained as an academic. Like much else in my life, I am still trying to catch up.

It was while I was in New York that I gave a series of seminars to a group of Zionist youth leaders under the auspices of Mrs Rose Jacobs, then a Hadassah Organization leader. As a result of the questions put to me, I wrote my first book, in the form of a catechism, entitled *A Primer on Palestine*. I asked myself the most fundamental questions on Zionism and Palestine and tried to give honest answers. The book was subsequently published as a training manual by the Junior Hadassah movement with the help of a grant from Edward Warburg. As I was a British colonial servant, I could not attach my name: even its publication anonymously was strictly a breach of regulations.

★ ★ ★

Six years later, in 1938, just before World War II, I managed to return to the United States on a coast-to-coast United Jewish Appeal fund-raising tour, at Edward Warburg's invitation. I have been back many times since and have criss-crossed the North American continent from Vancouver to Miami and Montreal to Houston. Sometimes I went for the Israel Bond drive; sometimes for the Friends of the Hebrew University. Every April, since 1963, I have gone on a lecture tour, in part for B'nai B'rith. Now I work through a Jewish lecture bureau. This takes me into Jewish communities, congretations and Hillel Houses on university campuses as well as to non-Jewish audiences in small colleges on my route. One whole year — 1948-1949 — I spent at Dropsie College, Philadelphia, on a visiting professorship in modern Middle East studies. In 1963, I spent a semester in the graduate school for public affairs of the State University of New York at Albany, again as a visiting professor. I gave there two seminars — one on Britain, the other on Israel and the Middle East

I find my periodical tours of the United States and Canada immensely stimulating, especially when I am 'on the road'. The pattern is fairly regular. I am met at the airport by my local Jewish sponsors and conducted to an unnecessary suite at a hotel (often that owned by a 'Big Giver' — a generous Jewish benefactor to local causes). The communities, especially in the smaller centres where they have but few visitors from Israel, are apt to kill me with kindness. They leave no moment for repose, unless I absolutely insist. I am happy to see one or two local Jewish institutions — a school, a synagogue, a community centre, an aged home — but not necessarily all of them. I am equally happy to see the local university, art gallery and museum. I am less enthusiastic when I have to receive *separately* half a dozen newspaper reporters, and radio and television interviewers. It seems, however, vital for the sponsors to get *themselves* advertised in this way, however superficially.

Although I try to limit my public appearances to one a day, with week-ends off, I find that few sponsors can resist the temptation of taking me to local businessmen's lunches — Rotary, the Kiwanis, Lions, Elks, and what have you. These appearances also help to advertise the sponsors through whose kindness I am present. The main event is, however, still the community centre, or synagogue hall, or Hillel House. Some of these buildings are magnificent, with heavy mortgage payments still outstanding. Usually, the smaller the Jewish community, the larger the attendance: they are not as surfeited as in the larger cities with speakers from Israel.

There was a time when speakers from Israel were expected to give an inspirational oration. This gave way to the factual talk. Nowadays, there is little one can say that most of the audience do not already know. Many have visited Israel: some have relatives there: much of the news from the Middle East is reported fully by the press, radio and television. I try more and more to persuade sponsors to let me answer questions from the floor after a talk that I do not give. This method has many advantages: as I reply only to questions asked, it makes the audience believe that I am not giving them a prepared and 'slanted' talk. (This, however, is an illusion, as I could equally well 'slant' the answers; but, in fact, I do not.) Then, such a method induces audience participation and breaks the monotony of a single voice. It is, however, essential to have someone in the audience ready with the first question: otherwise, when I ask for questions, there is an awkward pause. But questions should not be invited in writing beforehand: that prevents spontaneity. The method requires a good chairman who knows the audience and can spot and head off the *nudniks* anxious to make long speeches themselves in the guise of questions. Even so, there is always the risk of malevolent or — what is even worse — stupid questions. I have, of course, to know the answers — or frankly to admit that I do not. This involves a great deal of continuous reading — books, articles and news bulletins; and, in critical times, listening to the radio. There is nothing worse than having a questioner start: 'I heard on the radio this afternoon . . .' and go on to mention something important that I have not yet heard of. But, if the evening goes well, I find that, by the end, I have supplied in my answers most of what I would have said had I given a set talk in a more logical form. This kind of one-man's

brain-trust is equally suitable for non-Jewish audiences —
for example, a class of university students or even a Rotary
Club lunch, once they have got over the strangeness of it all.

The creation of the new State of Israel has given a tre-
mendous feeling of pride to Jewish communities all over
the world. A few assimilated Jews may have taken this
opportunity to move right out of the Jewish community,
feeling that individual Jews in the Diaspora no longer have
an equal responsibility for preserving the Jewish people.
They say: 'Let the Israelis do it.' But, generally speaking,
whole Jewish communities are now being kept alive largely
by their contacts with Israel. Fund-raising for Israel has
become a form of community life. Many members of the
community visit Israel, and more than once. (They buy
Israel Bonds in their home town and cash them when they
arrive in Israel — a novel travel savings scheme.) In most
towns, there will be at least one or two proud families whose
children have settled in Israel.

In consequence, I feel much at home in these distant Jewish
communities. I feel much at home in the United States
generally, and much excited by it. To me, it is the centre
of the modern world; and I have to keep in direct touch
with it, or I fall behind. There is so much anti-Americanism
about that, unless I go every year to America, I feel I might
become slightly anti-American myself. When in Jerusalem
and London I read several American magazines regularly
— *Time*, *Life*, the *New Yorker* — as well as many Jewish
magazines, such as *Commentary*. But nothing can replace
personal visits.

It is not easy for some Americans — Jews and non-Jews
alike — to cope with the pressure of modern civilisation.
For example, in the United States, affluence is a problem,

especially when bringing up children. They are apt to have everything, and become blasé very young. Americans are also burdened by their international responsibilities. As a whole, they are kindly people: it is not easy for them to maintain the peace of the world. Hence, while I am glad to come every spring to the centre, I am happy to live for most of the year on the rim, in Jerusalem, where the pressures of modern civilisation are felt much less.

CHAPTER 8

GALILEE, 1933–34

On my return from the United States in 1932, I resumed my post as deputy to the district commissioner in Jerusalem: but I soon escaped to Nazareth. A new grade of British assistant district commissioner had been created, between the British district commissioners and the district officers, nearly all of whom were by now Palestinian. In the Northern District, for example, there were three British A.D.C.'s — one in Haifa (Morris Bailey) to look after the Haifa and Acre sub-districts and act as deputy to the D.C. (by now Keith-Roach); a second at Nablus was Hugh Foot* to supervise Samaria, consisting of the sub-districts of Nablus, Tulkarm and Jenin. I was in charge of the Galilee division, with the four sub-districts of Nazareth, Beisan, Tiberias and Safad.

Galilee was the largest division in Palestine and the most beautiful. For an administrator, it had a special advantage: it was a long way from Jerusalem. In those days of poor communications, one could do unorthodox things there

---

* His father and two brothers all entered the House of Commons. Hugh himself made a brilliant career and is now Lord Caradon, a Minister of State and chief British representative at the U.N. He was commemorated in the Jewish coastal town of Netanya in the Samaria Division by 'Foot Square'.

on one's own without fear of word getting back immediately to headquarters.

My first sub-district, eight years earlier, had had sixty hill villages, all Arab. Now, I was responsible for about 300 villages, of which some two-thirds were Arab and one third Jewish. At Safad, I had an experienced Jewish district officer — Yaaqov Bergmann, bullet-headed and indestructible. Born in Galilee in 1897, he had served as an officer in the Turkish Army and started his career in the Palestine administration in 1920 as a police officer. (He has recently retired as district commissioner of Haifa, under the State of Israel.) At Nazareth — the 'home farm' — there was a Christian Arab district officer — Wadie Issawi, rather a weak personality. That did not matter much, as he worked under my direct supervision. The least satisfactory of the four was an elderly Christian Arab named Awad Sifri at Beisan. He was a failure who, I assume, had been sent in disgrace to that small and very hot sub-district where he could do little harm. In charge of the Tiberias sub-district, with the most progressive town in my division, was an unusual man named Tewfik Yazdi. He belonged to that strange sect — the Bahais — originally from Persia where they had broken away from Islam and were severely persecuted in consequence: a section had settled at Acre. Yazdi was intelligent, energetic and got on well with Moslems, Christians and Jews, all of whom regarded him as neutral. He helped me a great deal to carry out my plans for the development of his area.

A British A.D.C. in those days was responsible for as much, or as little, as he wished. He was really a co-ordinator and inspector of departmental activities in his division, and, on occasion, the initiator. There was a Palestinian medical officer of health in each sub-district of the Galilee and Samaria

The author's father, Sir Herbert Samuel, as High Commissioner

Dr. Chaim Weizmann and the Zionist Commission, Tel Aviv, Spring, 1918

Front row: the author; Captain Eric Waley; Major William Ormsby-Gore (Later Lord Harlech); Dr. Weizmann; Major James de Rothschild. Second row: Israel (now Lord) Sieff (in light suit); Sylvain Levi (France); Joseph Cowen; Walter Meyer (US). Behind Mr. Sieff and M. Levi, Dr. Montagu Eder; behind M. Levi, Leon Simon; behind Dr. Weizmann, Aaron Aaronsohn.

Divisions responsible to a British senior medical officer at Nablus. There was a Moslem Arab assistant district engineer for Galilee as a whole, responsible to (an American) Jewish district engineer at Haifa. Similarly there were Palestinian education, agricultural, veterinary and forestry officers stationed in various parts of the Galilee Division. Ultimately they were all responsible, in technical matters, to their British head of department in Jerusalem, but they had instructions to keep me informed of their plans, to accept my proposals for priorities, and to call on my help when they got into difficulty.

By far the most important role of the British A.D.C. was to maintain law and order. That was why the new grade had been created, now that nearly all the posts of district officer had been 'Palestinised'. Hence I maintained constant contact with the British police officers in my area. The police were organized on the model of Great Britain, with police stations in the larger towns, each under the supervision of a British inspector. There were police posts in some of the larger villages, under a sergeant. Most of the N.C.O.'s and constables were Arab, but, in view of the number of Jewish villages in Galilee, a proportion of the police there was Jewish.

It was not easy to get Jews to join the police. The pay was low; the work arduous. Jewish policemen (outside Tel Aviv) had to wear an 'Arab' headdress (actually, the Circassian *kalpak*). They served largely under Arab officers and N.C.O.'s, which they disliked. Being a policeman in Eastern Europe had never been a 'Jewish' occupation: it meant reporting other Jews to hostile authorities.

For administrative purposes, Galilee was divided into two police divisions, each under a British assistant district superintendent, with headquarters in Nazareth and Safad respectively. Safad was under the aegis of Eric James; while Nazareth was managed by a burly Yorkshireman, completely unflappable, named Patrick Hackett, both responsible to the district superintendent at Haifa. I saw James about every two weeks and Hackett several times a week.

There was in Palestine as a whole an ever-present risk of political, racial and religious friction, which could easily escalate into riots and even massacres. Every district, division, and even sub-district, had its own secret plans for the prevention and rapid suppression of such 'disturbances', as they were euphemistically called. The prime responsibility for the maintenance of law and order rested on the police. But, if the situation seemed likely to get out of hand, they could ask the district administration to call on the nearest British military unit for support 'in aid of the civil power.' After the disastrous Wailing Wall riots of 1929, Palestine had been supplied once more, as I have already related, with a permanent garrison of two battalions of British infantry, one based on Jerusalem, the other on Haifa. In my day the Haifa garrison consisted of the Seaforth Highlanders. In an emergency, one company was designated for Nazareth and another for Safad. There were also some R.A.F. armoured cars available for Galilee. A special cavalry regiment called the Trans-Jordan Frontier Forces (T.J.F.F.) had also been created, as far back as 1926, primarily for the defence of both Palestine and Trans-Jordan from Beduin raids from the east. It was composed of Trans-Jordanian and Palestinian troopers, N.C.O.'s and junior officers, with British senior officers. All ranks wore a distinctive khaki uniform, based on an Indian model, with broad red cummerbunds (sashes round the waist), chain-mail epaulettes and a Circassian black fur or woollen astrakhan *kalpak*. Some of the recruits were themselves Circassians, noted for their martial qualities. Others were warlike Moslem Arabs from the Nablus and Hebron hill villages. There were a few Jewish specialists as veterinary officers, radio operators, and so on. The T.J.F.F. had its headquarters at Zerka, near Amman. There were detachments in southern Trans-Jordan and at places along the eastern edge of Galilee — at Beisan, Jisr el-Mejamie (covering the Rutenberg hydro-electric power station), Semakh, Rosh Pina and Metulla. Most of the cost of this force came from the Palestine Government budget, with a small titular participation by the Trans-Jordan Government (in fact, covered by a grant-in-aid from the British Government). It was a well-disciplined force, largely because its units were not stationed in centres of urban political activity. In 1929, for example, a small detachment of T.J.F.F. Arab troopers, under an Arab sergeant, had gallantly helped to defend the *kibbutz* of Ein Harod against Arab attack; whereas, elsewhere, Moslem Arab police constables had refused to fire on their co-religionists.

These five T.J.F.F. detachments were a welcome addition to our armed forces in Galilee. They were incorporated in our secret defence scheme, for activation should trouble break out. But I was still rather worried about Safad, with its large, fanatical Arab majority and a small Jewish minority, largely hidden away in a ghetto of its own, down the hillside. It consisted of a maze of narrow alleys in which troops were at a disadvantage. I knew that the *Hagana* were equally worried about the Jewish quarter. So I let them know, through Bergmann, that, if they would take full responsibility for the Jewish quarter, they could use their (illegal) arms openly, in case of attack, without fear of arrest. The Palestine

Police and the army in Safad would then be free to protect outlying Jewish institutions and to form a mobile reserve. To this the *Hagana* agreed.

I worked hard for six months to perfect my defence scheme, travelling all over the division to guess where the trouble spots were likely to be. In October, 1933, there were Arab demonstrations in Jaffa to protest against the rising tide of Jewish immigration. British police with steel helmets and shields intervened and several Arabs were killed. Excited Arab motor-drivers leaving Jaffa spread exaggerated reports of the numbers of Arabs killed by Jews. The next day, there were Arab demonstrations in Jerusalem; the day after in Haifa and Nablus. I sat in Nazareth holding my breath. Eventually, in the afternoon, I rang up Keith-Roach in Haifa and asked for troops as a preventive measure. The two Seaforth companies moved out at once and were billetted in Nazareth and Safad. Putting the defence scheme into operation, Captain Barclay, the company commander, Hackett, the A.S.P. and I formed a joint central control point. I was particularly worried about Beisan, where the district officer was weak. There was a violent Arab nationalist lawyer in Beisan who could be counted on to whip up the crowds to march on the neighbouring Jewish settlements, no matter *what* the district officer might do. So I asked for R.A.F. armoured cars to go down to Beisan at dawn the next day: they arrived just as the crowd was beginning to move. But, at this show of force, it dispersed without the need for a shot to be fired. Galilee was the only area in the whole country where, on this occasion, there were no deaths. This was just as well: being Jewish, I was closely watched by everyone to see how I would handle racial riots. If there had been an appreciable death-roll, I would have been removed from my independent post and returned to some head office as a 'number two'.

★ ★ ★

But now came a more serious threat, from a totally un-expected direction. Bergmann rang me up one day to say he had something to tell me which he did not like to say over the telephone. I asked him to come down and see me. He then told me that a Jewish newspaper vendor in Safad, a Revisionist, to whom apparently I had once done some favour (I could not remember what, where or when) had dropped a hint to Bergmann: 'Tell Mr Samuel to watch his step!' I had learnt enough in fourteen years' service never to disregard a hint, especially if it was one that Bergmann also took seriously. But it was first essential to find out what this warning implied. I had three possible official channels of intelligence — the Police C.I.D., the Army intelligence service, and M.I.5, the so-called British Secret Service concerned solely with movements and people likely to be hostile to Britain and her imperial interests. M.I.5 then had an office in Jerusalem headed by a man masquerad-ing as an R.A.F. squadron leader. So I motored down through Nablus to Jerusalem and told him the story: he said he would put some of his agents on to the job. A week or so later he phoned me to come to Jerusalem: there, he gave me somewhat disturbing news. A group of Jewish right-wing terrorists had been formed, calling themselves *HaBiryonim* (after a Jewish terrorist group during the Roman occupation, nineteen centuries earlier). They had decided to liquidate prominent Jews suspected of being insufficiently

137

nationalist or anti-Arab. At the top of the list were three names — Dr Chaim Arlosorov, a well-educated and highly intelligent man, then head of the political department of the Jewish Agency, who had been trying to make contact with Arab leaders; Dr Judah Magnes, Chancellor of the Hebrew University, who had been outspoken in promulgating his plan for a bi-national State; and myself, presumably only because of my earlier participation in the society *Brit Shalom*.

This was the first time I had known of any personal threat, beyond that which every civil servant, every Englishman and every Jew in Palestine expected to meet, in general. I went to see Arlosorov and Magnes, both personal friends of mine, and told them what I had heard. Magnes refused to take any steps whatever to protect his own life (he was a pacifist by conviction). But he lived in an Arab quarter and I suspect that some of his Arab friends arranged for a discreet cordon to be thrown round his house. Arlosorov did not believe the whole story: his answer was: 'No Jew would kill *me*.'

On return to Galilee, I took elaborate evasive action, believing that it is the first duty of a civil servant to keep alive. I did not consider that any arrangements made by the Palestine Police would be efficient. Besides, if they had to detail a whole squad of men to protect me, I should become such a burden that I would again be in danger of removal by the Government from my post. So I hired a Jewish bodyguard at my own expense — a *Hagana* man from Binyamina. Having read over the years quite a number of reports on court cases involving assassination, I realised that, to keep alive, one had no option but to follow vigorously the following rules:

Never go anywhere regularly (e.g., to one's office or house) by the same route or at the same time each day;* never sleep two nights running in the same place; and never telephone one's movements.

I followed these rules, at considerable inconvenience, for about six weeks. By that time, the *Biryonim* presumably came to the conclusion that I was too elusive. So they turned on someone easier to catch. On 17th June, 1933, Arlosorov was shot dead while walking with his wife on Tel Aviv beach after dark. Two men, Zvi Rosenblatt and Avraham Stavsky** were charged with the murder. They were identified by Mrs Arlosorov; but, in the absence of the corroborative evidence required by the then Palestine law, they were acquitted. The Revisionist Party has always maintained that Arlosorov was killed by Arabs. As he was head of the Jewish Agency's political department, such an attack is conceivable. But no evidence of any Arab plot was ever revealed. Bergmann and I were not called as witnesses because our information was hearsay: Bergmann's informant would certainly not have testified.

As soon as Arlosorov was murdered and some of the *Biryonim* suspects were arrested, M.I.5 notified me that the heat was off as far as I was concerned. So I discontinued my own precautions and went back to normal life. But

* Lewis Andrews, my successor in Nazareth, was under Palestine Police protection. In September, 1937, an Arab terrorist assassinated him, with his police escort, while they were walking to church in Nazareth on a Sunday.
** Stavsky was one of the men killed on the Tel Aviv beach in 1948 when the Revisionist arms ship *Altalena* was prevented, on Ben-Gurion's orders, from unloading arms during the truce.

not before some of my well-meaning friends in Jerusalem who knew what was happening had tried to persuade the High Commissioner to withdraw me for my own safety. That, again, would have been fatal to my future career.

★ ★ ★

As our two sons were by now of school age, and had to go to a Hebrew school, they obviously could not live with me in the then wholly Arab town of Nazareth. So we took a charming furnished villa on the nose of Mount Carmel, overlooking the Bay of Acre. The view was so beautiful at times that it positively hurt. The boys went to the *Beth Sefer Reali* lower down the mountain. I spent my week-ends with Hadassah and our children: the rest of the week I was either at my office in Nazareth about an hour away, or touring my division. I had a permanent room at the German-owned Galilee Hotel in Nazareth. Occasionally, my district commissioner, Keith-Roach, would call me in during the week for a talk or a meeting. Sometimes I would drive to Jerusalem, with his consent, to settle outstanding matters direct with departments there.

In my Nazareth office I had only an Arab chief clerk, a Hebrew translator and a typist. Any further staff I needed for special jobs I borrowed from the office of the district officer, Issawi, whom I saw almost daily. I also accompanied him on occasion for talks with the Mayor of Nazareth. Then there were local leaders to see, both Arab and Jewish, in order to get the general trend of opinion in the division. I have already mentioned the departmental representatives — police, education, health, agricultural, veterinary, forestry and public works — all of whom I saw at regular intervals in their offices or in mine.

One of my hobbies was the preservation of the traditional handicrafts — works in copper, silver, wood, pottery, glass, wool and straw. To that end, I leased an old vaulted Arab house on the main road through Nazareth, so that tourists could easily find it. There, all kinds of locally-made artifacts were on sale — domestic vessels, jewellery, mats, rugs, horse-trappings and so on. The rent of the house, and the monthly salary of the salesman in charge, were paid by the Municipality. The money received for each article sold went back in full to the craftsman. To provide a congenial background, I borrowed from some of the leading Arab families in Nazareth wooden chairs, chests and screens, and olive-wood coffee-mortars and pestles, Frieda Warburg in New York sent me a few hundred dollars with which I acquired a dozen Arab peasant costumes, even then rapidly disappearing. (Later, I presented them to the Folk Museum in Jerusalem, of which I was one of the founders.) I invited Rubin, an old friend of mine in Tel Aviv and a well-known painter, to come up and arrange 'The Peasant House', as we called it. It became a permanent exhibition and lasted until I left Nazareth.

Most of each week, however, I was on tour. I had my own car again — a new Ford — in which I would take my police escort and go to the Jezreel Valley, visiting Arab and Jewish villages on the way. In the *kibbutz* at Geva, near Afula, some of my former soldiers from the 40th Battalion of the Royal Fusiliers had become farmers and I was always warmly welcomed by them whenever I passed through. From my contacts with this and other *kibbutzim*, I became fascinated with the whole *kibbutz* movement and eventually wrote a *Handbook of the Jewish Communal Villages*, the first ever to be published. I gave the manuscript as a present to the Jewish Agency. Their Youth Department published it in English in 1938, with a German edition as well. Revised editions in English and French came out in 1945. It is now hopelessly out-of-date.

Later, I became interested in the *kibbutz* of Mishmar HaEmek, on the north-eastern slopes of Mount Carmel. During World War II, when home leave to England was impossible, I spent several short holidays there. In thanks for their hospitality, I wrote a short monograph on their excellent secondary school. This they published in English in 1942 as *The Children's Community of Hashomer Hatzair* ('The Young Watchman', a left-wing Socialist movement) *at Mishmar HaEmek*.

However, when I was still at Nazareth, there was little I could do for — or against — any *kibbutz* in my division. Each was devised with a central command, the more easily to withstand pressure, either from the Arabs or from the Government. Financing, stock and technical advice they obtained almost entirely from non-government sources. As the only Jewish assistant district commissioner they had ever had, I established happy personal relations with all of them. Several members of different *kibbutzim* became close friends and we were on a first-name basis. With the Arab villages, things were much more formal. They awaited with awe my state visits. Accompanied by my staff and a big police escort, we would have long meetings about their non-payment of taxes, their Government school, their sanitary conditions, a new road, or what have you, followed by a huge banquet. I always visited a *kibbutz* alone: no one met me; there were no complaints or requests; and I was lucky if I got a glass of milk and some bread and cheese.

Going from Arab village to *kibbutz* to Arab village involved quite a lot of mental gymnastics, from the 11th century to the 20th and back again, several times a day.

My year in Galilee passed swiftly. Every week I was in Haifa and Tiberias: every two weeks in Beisan and Safad: about once a month in Jerusalem. I again held a magistrate's warrant with power to impose prison sentences up to six months and/or fines up to P£ 50. I would often sit as magistrate in a village while on tour and dispense justice on the spot. I was always accompanied by the local district officer and police officer, and by several departmental officials. We would go as far as we could by car, which was then quite a lot: the rest we did on horseback, for which I borrowed a police mount. I spent the night with some leading Arab landowner, or in an Arab village resthouse, or a monastery, or a *kibbutz*, or a Trans-Jordan Frontier Force camp. I visited every single one of my 300 towns and villages, most of them many times. I constructed schools, reafforested barren hill-sides and built village roads. I got to know Galilee like the back of my hand and much of its two thousand years of history. In one village, near the northern frontier, called Jish (from which John of Gishala got his name) Josephus, when Governor of Galilee, started a road to the village well. I am proud to have completed it, nineteen hundred years later.

Of all the towns in Galilee, Tiberias was my favourite, and still is. Much of my weekly visit was spent in trying to promote its development. I managed to get a little money from friends in America to plant an avenue of trees along the lake: all have since disappeared in the course of road widening. To strengthen the sense of local government, I invited the municipal council to name the streets. After much prodding, they supplied a list, including their own names. I sent it back saying that no living person could be thus commemorated. They returned it with a pained note, claiming that I had misunderstood: those particular names on the list were of their grandfathers. So I named the streets myself after ancient towns in the neighbourhood — Gadara (of the Gadarene Swine), Gamala, Hamat — and after famous figures in local history. I named one the 'Street of the Redeemer', explaining to the Jewish mayor (Tiberias was the only mixed Arab-Jewish town in Palestine with a majority of Jewish voters) that this did not imply which redeemer was intended. For the Christians it might mean Christ; for the Jews he had still to come.

During World War II, we built a small cottage at Migdal (the birthplace of Mary Magdalene), a few miles north of Tiberias along the Lake shore, and still own it. For some years we went there week-ends: but, after the direct route via Nablus was closed in 1948 through the partition of Palestine, it became more difficult to get there. So we went only during the Hebrew University winter recess. We still go to Tiberias every winter; but it is now too hard for Hadassah to manage the cottage and we stay at the *Galei Kinneret* ('Waves of Kinneret') hotel. The cottage itself is leased to a doctor from Tel Aviv who comes up with his family week-ends for water-skiing.

In 1933-34 — my golden year in Galilee — I was frequently visited by the High Commissioner, that extraordinary Scottish soldier, Sir Arthur Wauchope, formerly commanding the Black Watch. He was a bachelor, of independent means, and outwardly very frail: he ate very little and looked like an Egyptian mummy. But he was the most dynamic man ever to govern Palestine under the Mandate, not excepting my own father. Wauchope came up to Galilee every week or so. He was his own director of agriculture, of education, of health and of public works. He knew no Arabic but asked through an interpreter the same questions of everyone he met, from wealthy landowner down to the poorest camel-driver. By some strange mental process of his own, he came up at the end with a completely clear and accurate picture of the rural situation. I had been warned, before I ever met him, that the one thing he hated was bluff. I had hardly been in Nazareth for a week when he came and literally took me for a ride in his car. As we passed along one of the valleys, he pointed to some fields, away up the hill-side, and asked 'Is that wheat or barley?' I was still only a town boy and said: 'I can't see from here, Sir.' 'Would you know if you were closer?' he asked. 'No, Sir', I replied. 'I can see we shall get on well', he concluded. So I accompanied him everywhere, even when he inspected village latrines about which he was most particular. I stayed with him at his favourite places — the Franciscan monastery on top of Mount Tabor, and in the German Catholic hospice at Tabgha on the Sea of Galilee, next door to the traditional site of the miracle of the loaves and fishes. Every few months I would be invited for a rest at Government House. His encouragement of my efforts in Galilee was invaluable.

I had a big blackboard in my office in Nazareth on which all my several projects were chalked up, with the current position of each. I looked forward to several more years of productive activity when, after only twelve months in Galilee, I was suddenly recalled once more to Jerusalem — my usual fate. This time I was to become deputy commissioner for immigration under Eric Mills, the new commissioner, who had specially asked for me. I was heartbroken.

But there was nothing to be done about it and, after fourteen years in the political service (District Administration and Secretariat) — exactly half my colonial career, as it turned out to be — I became a departmental headquarters officer in Jerusalem, where I spent the remaining fourteen years.

CHAPTER 9

IMMIGRATION, 1934-39

Having been recalled once more to Jerusalem in the spring of 1934, I found myself involved at once in the reorganization of the Department of Immigration and Travel. For the previous fourteen years it had been an appendage of the Secretariat, controlled for most of the time by Albert Hyamson, under whom I had worked briefly in 1926. Mistrusting all his staff, he still insisted on doing as much as possible himself, which was just possible prior to 1933. Then, Hitler came to power in Germany. German Jewry had largely disregarded the writing on the wall: now, they panicked and deluged the Immigration Department with requests for visas. Hyamson was completely overwhelmed by the flood of applications and, by 1934, the department was nine months in arrears. As decisions were a matter of life and death, criticism mounted. The Palestine Government then decided to pension Hyamson off and to replace him with one of the ablest men in the Administration — Eric Mills. They also replaced Hyamson's deputy — Richard Badcock. As Hyamson, a British Jew, was replaced by a non-Jew, it was decided to replace Badcock, a non-Jew, by a Jew. Mills was asked to nominate his own deputy and asked for me. This surprised me, because, when I had served under him from 1927 to 1930 in the Secretariat, he had ridden me mercilessly. But, apparently, he had been impressed by the effect on me of my year at the graduate school at Columbia University — not so much the added economic knowledge, perhaps, but the greater maturity and self-confidence. Whatever it was, he thought I would be useful to him in handling the Jewish communities, both in Palestine and abroad. So, for the next five years, I worked very closely with him. He was a most remarkable man, even among the several remarkable men who served in Palestine during the thirty years of British administration. Considering the small size of Palestine, the Colonial Office would not normally have sent to it some of their ablest administrators; but, to their credit, they did, largely owing to Palestine's political complications. Mills was a Cambridge University graduate and a first-class mathematician. Like so many other members of the Administration, he had served in the Egyptian Expeditionary Force and had been detailed by the Army to take over the administration of Gaza, shortly after its capture in 1917. After working as deputy commissioner in Haifa, his exceptional abilities were recognised and he was brought to the High Commissioner's secretariat in 1925 as an Assistant Chief Secretary. He had a very clear mind and should himself have become a Chief Secretary, and even a Colonial Governor in some part of the Commonwealth. But, having been gassed in France in World War I (which resulted in his being sent out to Egypt for light duty), he was a sick man, subject to blinding headaches. His wife, too, was very deaf and unable to take on the onerous social duties required of a Chief Secretary's or Colonial Governor's wife. He was so useful in Palestine that no High Commissioner was willing to release him, not even when he had a chance of becoming the secretary in London of an

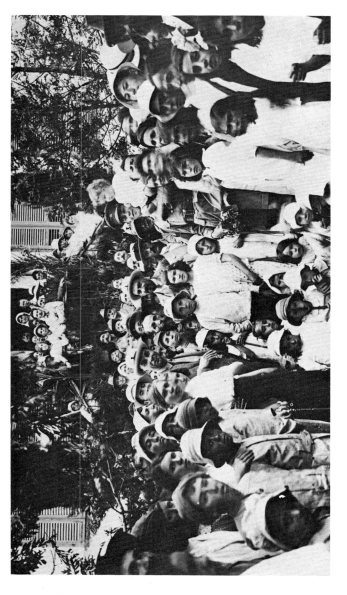

Dr. Chaim Weizmann and the Zionist Commission tour the Jewish settlements in Judaea, Spring, 1918

At Nes Ziona. Dr. Weizmann (with beard and panama hat); Joseph Cowen (also with panama hat); the author (with bouquet presented to Dr. Weizmann).

Dr. Chaim Weizmann and the Zionist Commission at Rishon LeZion, Spring, 1918

To right of Dr. Weizmann, Joseph Cowen, the author and Mr. Rosenheck: to his left, Sylvain Levi and Walter Meyer.

Presentation to General Edmund Allenby by the Jewish community of Jerusalem, Spring, 1918

(From the left): Colonal Ronald Storrs; Colonal Lord Dalmeny; Dr. Weizmann (in panama hat); General Allenby; Chief Sephardi Rabbi (reading speech of welcome); Brigadier Gilbert Clayton (looking down); behind him, Major James de Rothschild; further along, Captain Eric Waley; the author; Aaron Aaronsohn; Walter Meyer. Below, in front of crowd (with panama hat), Leon Simon.

The author's wedding

After the marriage ceremony of Edwin Samuel (having been dressed in Sheikh's robes) and Hadassah Grasovsky, Government House, Mount of Olives, Jerusalem, December 6, 1920. (From the left): Lady Samuel; behind her, Godfrey Samuel (groom's brother); Sir Herbert Samuel; behind him, Nancy Samuel (groom's sister); Hadassah; behind her, Asaph Grasovsky (her eldest brother); the author; Rachel Grasovsky (bride's mother); behind her, Yehuda Grasovsky (bride's father); behind him, 'Shai' Grasovsky (bride's youngest brother); Major Kenny Levick, Governor of Beersheba (in uniform) with several of the Sheikhs of Beersheba who had presented the robes.

eminent scientific body for which post he had all the requisite qualifications. He was never one to promote his own interests; Palestine was the gainer. To overcome his and his wife's physical disabilities and his own secret disappointments, he developed a powerful will. I have never met a more strong-minded man or one more willing to assume responsibility. He was one of the few British Colonial civil servants in Palestine — or in the Colonial Office to which he was seconded for a time — who had an intellectual understanding of what Zionism implied. Although, at times, he appeared to be a sympathiser, some of his less guarded remarks were definitely anti-Zionist, if not anti-Semitic. Still, he was an inspiring man to work for, and I learned from him how to manage a medium-sized administrative unit.

One of his chief claims to fame is, I think, the graphs he prepared for the Royal Commission that came out to Palestine in November, 1936, to investigate the causes of the Arab Rebellion. These graphs indicated precisely what would be the eventual racial composition of Palestine according to several different annual rates of Jewish immigration, taking into consideration the relative Arab and Jewish fertility and mortality rates. These graphs had a decisive effect on all subsequent British, Arab and Jewish political, economic and social attitudes. As a matter of fact, Jewish immigration was *the* central problem through all the thirty years of British rule. And it was primarily the Jewish fight after World War II to win the right to immigrate that led to the War of Independence and the creation of the State of Israel.

★　★　★

In 1934, European Jews were caught between a blind fear of Hitler and the Nazi domination of Europe on one side; and the British policy of restricting Jewish immigration to Palestine on the other. When I became deputy commissioner of migration, the limitation was still only economic. Only after I had left the department in 1939 was a political limitation added to the economic one.

Prior to 1938, immigration to Palestine had waxed and waned. Before World War I, it was prohibited by the Ottoman Government. Nevertheless, many Jews managed to get in somehow and to remain with false papers. The size of the Jewish population increased from 24,000 in 1882 to 85,000 in 1914. Numbers of energetic young Christian Arabs, however, emigrated *from* Palestine because of the harshness and incompetence of the backward Ottoman Moslem administration. Those who were Protestants went largely to North America: those who were Catholics went largely to Latin America. But the rate of natural increase of the Moslem Arab population of Palestine was high.

During World War I, nearly all Jews in Palestine with Russian, Rumanian, British, French and, ultimately, Greek and American passports, became enemy subjects and had to leave. Many Arabs died of starvation, disease, or as soldiers in the Turkish army. Some civilian Jews died, too; and the Jewish population fell to 60,000. Only when the civil administration of Palestine had taken over from the military administration in July, 1920, was Jewish immigration permitted. Those who then came in were largely from Eastern Europe and included many *halutzim* ('pioneers'). Most had left Russia before the Bolshevik revolution in October, 1917, or had managed to get out of Russia illegally even after the exit gates were officially closed. From July, 1920, until

1922, there were *no* restrictions, either economic or political, on Jewish immigration into Palestine. Jewish immigration figures during those years were as follows:

1919	1,800
1920	8,200
1921	9,100
1922	7,800
Total	26,900

According to the Government census of 1922, the total Jewish population had risen again to 84,000, compared with 590,000 Moslem Arabs and 71,000 Christian Arabs — a total population of 752,000, of which Jews formed eleven per cent. Nearly all these Jewish immigrants were, however, penniless. There were then few factories that could absorb them and no capital available to construct such factories. Nor was capital available to buy the land needed for the establishment of new Jewish settlements, for the construction of farm buildings and for the purchase of stock.

The Zionist leaders who had negotiated the Balfour Declaration had assumed that not only Jewish *halutzim* would come to Palestine from Russia but also Jewish capital. After the October 1917 revolution, however, Russian Jewish capitalists were either liquidated or in exile themselves and penniless. Only one, Michael Pollak, managed to bring a considerable amount of his oil capital to Palestine. He used some of it to build the *Nesher* ('Eagle') cement works near Haifa. At the same time, the wealthy Jews of the West, in particular of Germany, France, Britain and the United

States (excepting, of course, the Rothschild family) refused to have anything to do with Zionism. They were largely assimilated and viewed Jewish nationalism with horror; they were sure it would lead to accusations against themselves of 'dual loyalty' and would undermine their own hard-won positions. Weizmann had hoped to raise £ 10,000,000 sterling a year for investment in Palestine — a fraction of what is raised nowadays each year abroad for investment in Israel. In fact, it took him ten years to raise the first million. It must now be admitted that, although the Zionist Organization spoke in the name of the Jewish people, it then had only 100,000 members throughout the world, out of a total Jewish population of 12,500,000. It was not able on its own to raise enough funds to support the unemployed *halutzim* in Palestine. So it made what eventually proved to be the fatal step of pressing the Palestine Government to provide relief works for the Jewish unemployed. Sir Wyndham Deedes (with my father's approval) allocated money from the Government's scanty budget — then less than £ 2,000,000 a year for all purposes — for the construction and repair of certain roads in Galilee by *halutzim*. This decision was considered to be a great Zionist triumph; but it led the Colonial Secretary, then Winston Churchill, to insist on the Zionist Organization's agreeing to limit Jewish immigration for each six months in future to the estimated number of new jobs that would be created during that period — the so-called economic limitation of immigration. The Zionist Organization strongly resisted this demand; but the British Government refused to approve the country's constitution —the Palestine Order-in-Council of 1922— until they had capitulated. The British Government had no intention of allowing Palestinian tax-money to be spent on Jewish settle ment, even though, in the long run, Jewish settlement would vastly increase the Government's revenues. So the golden moment of free Jewish immigration was lost, largely through lack of Jewish capital for the settlement of the immigrants. Jewish immigration in subsequent years was as follows:

1923	7,400
1924	12,900
1925	33,800
1926	13,100
1927	2,700
1928	2,200
1929	5,200
1930	4,900
1931	4,100
1932	9,600

The high immigration figure for 1925 was largely due to a change of government in Poland and the accession to power of a finance minister with the appropriate name of Grabski. He imposed a confiscatory income tax that bore heavily on many Jewish businessmen. Some consequently came to Palestine, with much of their capital, and helped to develop Tel Aviv. But the following year, when Grabski fell, many of these Polish Jews returned, with their money, to Poland. There was an excess of Jewish emigration over immigration (for example, in 1927, only 2,700 Jews arrived while 5,100 left). Immigration certificates, later to be worth their weight in diamonds, went begging. There was again unemployment in Palestine and no applications for admission.

Immigration began to revive in 1929; but the Wailing

Wall riots in that year (with 133 Jews killed and 332 wounded) deterred many prospective immigrants. It was not until Hitler came to power in 1933 that the flow increased again. During the five years that I served in the Department of Immigration, no less than a quarter of a million Jews entered Palestine, of whom 184,000 were there legally. But the high figure of 62,000 for 1936 produced an Arab rebellion which lasted for two years. This led to the White Paper of 1939 that imposed *political* (in addition to economic) limitations on the volume of Jewish immigration. That was a deliberate decision, calculated never to allow a Jewish majority in Palestine to be reached.

To project the story ahead, there was a truce over the White Paper policy during the first part of World War II. But, once the German and Italian threat in North Africa had been disposed of by British and American armies, Jewish resistance to the White Paper policy began in earnest. The British Government, largely on Ernest Bevin's insistence, refused to yield. Commission after Commission — British, Anglo-American and international — failed to find any peaceful solution. Britain refused to impose partition by force. Faced with armed attack by either Jews or Arabs whatever it did, Britain gave up the Mandate. In the ensuing civil war, the country partitioned itself and the State of Israel was born in 1948. Nineteen years later, as a result of a threat by several Arab States in combination and their somewhat unexpected defeat, Israel, without much premeditation, reunited Palestine.

★ ★ ★

I began to play my modest part in the central problem of immigration in 1934. At that time, there was no overall maximum figure of Jews permitted to enter in any one year, based on political considerations calculated to prevent an eventual Jewish majority. The immigration ordinance of 1933, which I had to help operate, provided for a six-monthly 'labour schedule' specifying the number of working-men and women allowed to come in during that period. The certificates approved under the labour schedule were distributed largely by the Jewish Agency. The remainder were allotted either by the immigration department in Jerusalem or by our agents abroad — the British passport control officers in major centres and the consuls-general or consuls elsewhere.

The six months' labour schedules were fixed by the Palestine Government with the approval of the Colonial Office in London. They were based on the Jewish Agency's assessment of Palestine's economic absorptive capacity, as revised by the department. Until a separate department of statistics was set up — also under Mills as commissioner of migration and statistics — one of my jobs was to make a periodic analysis of Palestine's economy. I devised my own series of economic indicators and then checked my conclusions by consulting several Jewish leaders. Among these were the late Dr Werner Senator, a member of the Jewish Agency Executive; Dr David Horowitz, then a Jewish Agency economist (and now Governor of the Bank of Israel) and, above all, the late Eliahu Golomb, the (secret) head of the *Hagana*. He was not only well-informed about all Jewish development plans, but also remarkably frank in his comments on them. Over the years, all three of them became personal friends.

Once the total number of labour schedule immigration certificates for the following six months was decided by the Government and announced, their distribution among the several countries of Jewish emigration to Palestine was decided by the Jewish Agency. There was a small reserve for non-Jewish immigrants, mainly for staff coming out to work in foreign banks, mission schools and other enterprises. These were individually allocated direct by the department. Otherwise, non-Jewish immigration into Palestine was prohibited: it was a Jewish preserve. We then distributed the certificates to the P.C.O.'s (British passport control officers) in Berlin, Warsaw, Prague, etc. and to the consuls-general and consuls elsewhere. In each major centre of emigration, the Jewish Agency maintained a local 'Palestine Office'. It received and processed all applications for visas for Palestine to be granted by the P.C.O.'s, not only under the labour schedule but under all other categories of the immigrants arriving, all bachelor *halutzim* were. required, Jewish Agency in Jerusalem to each country were then further subdivided by the local Palestine Office among the several *halutz* organizations in that country: we had nothing to do with that further distribution. It was, however, an open secret that, in order to increase the number of Jewish immigrants arriving, all bachelor *halutzim* were required, if nominated by the Palestine Office for a certificate, to take along with him a young unmarried woman *halutza* as his 'wife'. They went through a legal marriage ceremony before a rabbi in their country of former residence and got legally divorced by a rabbinical court on arrival in Palestine, without ever having consummated the marriage. The rabbis, both abroad and in Palestine, connived at this evasion of the law as a national duty. There was nothing that the

Palestine Government could do about it, in the absence of any provision in the law for limiting some immigration certificates for issue to unmarried men only. The Jewish Agency which, under the terms of the Mandate, had to be consulted about changes in the law, would have violently resisted any such proposal.

There were several other categories of immigrants for which, at that time, the total number to be admitted in any one year was unlimited, provided that they were fully qualified for their particular category. For example, there were special categories for rabbis and for university students, nominated by the body that needed their services or was willing to enrol them. Some 'rabbis' were not really qualified for their particular category. For example, there were were: nor were all the offers of employment in Palestine genuine. It was equally impossible to determine who really intended to study at the Hebrew University in Jerusalem or the Technion in Haifa. Many, in fact, did study; but some enrolled on arrival and then immediately went off to a job. Others never even bothered to enrol but quietly disappeared in order to avoid arrest, prosecution and possible deportation.

Another category was provided by law for highly skilled workmen abroad nominated by reputable employers in Palestine. Such nominations were made to our immigration offices in Jerusalem, Jaffa, Tel Aviv, Haifa and Tiberias. The *bona fides* of the employer and his need for additional skilled labour, unobtainable in Palestine, were investigated by our own immigration officers in each town. At the same time, the *bona fides* of the prospective immigrant was investigated by the P.C.O. abroad and his staff. Many of the skilled workmen were not, in fact skilled at all: others were skilled but were never employed after arrival by the firm that had applied for their admission. During my inspections, I stumbled on an application made on notepaper with the printed letter-head of a firm that did not, in fact, exist. The notepaper had been specially printed for that sole purpose by a firm of ingenious but unscrupulous immigration agents in Palestine. The immigration officer who was supposed to have investigated the *bona fides* of the applicant was George Msarsa, of mixed Arab and Abyssinian parentage. He had been bribed to accept such applications at their face value without visiting the employer's place of business. The police looked into this racket and unearthed dozens of such fictiaous applications that had been approved by Msarsa. It was estimated that, through these bribes, he had amassed a fortune of some £40,000, all of which he eventually lost through gambling. I was personally in charge of the prosecution and was more interested in getting Msarsa out of Government service than in sending him — or any of the applicants — to gaol. I brought him up before a disciplinary committee (headed by the Attorney-General) of the High Commissioner's Executive Council — a procedure never used in Palestine before or subsequently. A few applicants had turned King's evidence: most were German Jews and essentially law-abiding. Out of twenty-five specific charges, Msarsa was found guilty on twenty-three and was duly dismissed. This operation took much of my time for about six months.

One of the most useful immigration categories was that devised for so-called 'capitalists' — persons with not less than the equivalent of £1,000 'at free disposal'. Arrangements were made by the Jewish Agency with the Government of Nazi Germany to allow Jewish emigrants to buy, with their own capital, £1,000 worth of German goods which were then exported to Palestine. A company set up for this purpose was called *Ha'Avara* ('Transfer') and many thousands of middle-class German Jews were rescued by this device. 'Capitalists' in other countries — such as Poland — had to prove to the P.C.O. that the £1,000 was their own. There were undoubtedly several such sums that were passed from hand to hand.

Every married male immigrant in any category was allowed to bring with him, then or later, his wife and minor children. Many Jews abroad habitually supported their elderly parents or an infirm mother or adult sister. The restricted definition of a family in the Palestine immigration ordinance caused much hardship.

Some of the birth certificates produced for children were forged. Either the child was not a minor or was in fact not really the child of the adults who applied for the visa; it was the child of some far-sighted friend who could not get out of Eastern or Central Europe, but was desperately anxious to save his children from the impending holocaust.

One of the most successful schemes for the rescue of Jewish children was devised by Mrs Recha Fryer in Germany, but forever associated with the name of Miss Henrietta Szold, a member of the Jewish Agency and the veteran founder of the Hadassah (American Zionist Women's) Organization. Under that scheme, thousands of children, then in the 16-17 age group, were brought to Palestine under Jewish Agency Youth *Aliya* ('Immigration') auspices, educated in special schools set up mainly in the *kibbutzim* and, on graduation, put to work. The scheme still continues today, largely with Middle Eastern and North African children of any age group. Over 120,000 children have come to Palestine and Israel under Youth *Aliyah* auspices.

Miss Szold was a remarkable woman, with a ferocious sense of public duty. Even when she was over eighty, she would never allow herself the luxury of an easy chair. She would offer me something comfortable to sit on whenever I called on her; but she herself would sit bolt upright on a chair with a straight wooden back. She was a woman with the greatest sense of self-discipline I have ever met outside a convent.

To cope with this flood of applications, Mills was immediately given authority to employ many more Palestinian inspectors, both Jewish and Arab. British assistant commissioners were appointed to take charge of our Tel Aviv and Haifa offices, which were the busiest. We inherited from Hyamson's regime several very experienced immigration officers, including the late Nathan Mindel, a British Jew who became the senior assistant commissioner at headquarters for Jerusalem and my own deputy. At Tel Aviv we had Cecil Arnott; at Haifa, Ernest Stafford. In the Jerusalem district offices, there was an able Moslem Arab, Najati Nashashibi; after 1948, he became a senior district official on the Jordan side of the frontier in Jerusalem. Shortly before he died, I went to meet him at the Mandelbaum Gate where he was supervising the entry of Christian Arab Easter pilgrims from Israel. I had to train all these new officers and devise administrative procedures for them. By superhuman effort over the first six months, we cleared the nine months backlog left by Hyamson and reduced to two weeks the time required to decide on a normal application.

There was a further section of the department, under another English Jew — Abraham Tattenbaum — to deal with naturalisation and the issue of Palestinian passports.

He also supervised our own frontier control offices at every point of entry and exit, by land, sea and air, from Metullah and Ras en Naqura (now Rosh Hanikra) on the Syrian and Lebanese frontiers, to Kantara, the railway station on the Suez Canal on Egyptian territory, through which all train passengers across the Sinai Desert to Palestine had to pass.

I became the chief mechanic responsible for keeping the whole department running smoothly. Mills was a superb administrator himself and maintained that authority began at the bottom and not at the top. He encouraged all officials of the department to take as much responsibility as they felt they legally could. They referred to a higher authority in the department only those cases about which they were not quite sure. Mills had very broad shoulders and a generous character. If a junior official did something well, he could take the credit: if he made a mistake, Mills would take the blame. Who would not work happily in such circumstances?

As a result of this system of wide decentralisation of power, Mills had few papers on his own desk. I estimated that he only did about four hours of paper work a day. The rest of the time he received V.I.P.'s or went to see the High Commissioner, or just sat and thought.

I spent much of my time touring Palestine to inspect our immigration offices and frontier controls. (Later, during the Arab rebellion, the frontier controls were taken over by the British section of the Palestine Police.) In my office in Jerusalem, I dealt with some of the more tragic cases for which no one else had been able to find a legal solution. By interviewing the local applicant once more myself and often discovering new facts, I was able to rescue a number of people from what later was seen to have been certain death. Even today, at public lectures in Israel or abroad, I occasionally meet Israelis who come up to thank me for having saved their parents or grandparents. This is some compensation for the efforts I had constantly to make to block every new loophole ingeniously devised to facilitate 'illegal' immigration.

Apart from the various types of 'illegal' immigrants I have already mentioned, there were many thousands of Jews who entered Palestine legally as 'tourists', having convinced the P.C.O.'s that they had legitimate business or other reasons to visit the country. Once they arrived, some went to ground and remained as 'illegals', cheerfully forfeiting the £60 deposit they had had to make at the British consulate abroad when getting their visa.

There were, in addition, tens of thousands of Jews escaping from Europe and other parts of the Middle East who were smuggled in. Some came by sea, others over the northern frontier from Syria or the Lebanon, guided by experienced Arab smugglers for a high fee. To combat this type of flouting the immigration law was a police duty and luckily not mine.

One of my jobs was writing Mills' monthly reports to the Government on the work of the department. I also devised and wrote a periodic and confidential letter to all our British P.C.O.'s and consular 'agents' abroad to keep them in touch.

When Mills was away in Britain on long leave, I acted as commissioner, with a seat on the purely British, *ex-officio* Advisory Council that rubber-stamped legislation already approved by the High Commissioner in Executive Council and the Colonial Office. Its meetings were a farce: the short title of the new ordinance would be read out by the clerk to the Council — an assistant secretary in the Secretariat. The High Commissioner then said: 'Any comments?' There never were any. The heads of departments all worked on the principle: 'You keep quiet about the laws for my department and I'll keep quiet about those for yours'. The only time when I ever remember an animated discussion was on a proposal to raise the customs duties on motor-cars imported into Palestine, including those bought by British colonial civil servants. At no time during the twenty-eight years of the Mandate was there a legislature containing a single Palestinian citizen, either elected or even nominated. This was another victim of the Arab-Jewish conflict: they could never agree on its composition.

★   ★   ★

After six months in the department, it was decided that I should make an extended tour of eastern Europe to establish direct personal contact with our 'agents' there—the P.C.O.'s, consuls-general and consuls — with whom I was in constant correspondence. A secondary object of the tour was to speed up still further the handling of immigration applications. I took this opportunity to study the situation of the Jews in all the countries through which I passed and was warmly welcomed by the Palestine Offices and the representatives of the local Jewish communities. My tour took me briefly to Salonika and Istanbul and then to Constanza, Galatz and Bucharest in Rumania; to Crakow, Warsaw, Bialystok Lodz and Vilna in Poland; and finally to Berlin, Prague, Paris, The Hague and London. I had previously been on holiday in Greece, Turkey, Germany, Czechoslovakia, France, Belgium and Holland; but Rumania and Poland, with their teeming Jewish communities, were new to me.

Palestine was very lucky in being able to call on the British P.C.O.'s and British consular staff to handle Jewish emigration to Palestine without any payment from us. It was frequently proposed that Palestine Government immigration officials should be stationed abroad and, in fact, one had been posted in Hyamson's time to Trieste. But supervision of such officials would have been difficult. Some British P.C.O.'s, paid for wholly by the Foreign Offices in London and supervised by them, had large staffs almost exclusively engaged in dealing with emigration to Palestine. We were also very lucky in the calibre of the P.C.O.'s principally concerned — Gibson at Prague, Hamilton-Stokes at Warsaw and, above all, Major Foley in Berlin. They had wide authority from Jerusalem and displayed a concern and a humanity that were instrumental in saving hundreds of Jewish families from certain death.

My visit to Germany under Hitler was unpleasant. As a British civil servant, I was in no personal danger. On the contrary, the Nazi officials whom I had to meet, knowing my position in Palestine, were particularly 'correct' in their behaviour. But Hitler had already been in power for over a year and several stages of his anti-Semitic programme had already been introduced. The evening of my arrival in Berlin, Foley had arranged for me to meet the London *Times* correspondent, a remarkably brave man named Ebbutt, then a voice crying in the wilderness. I sat up all night listening with growing horror to his description of the anti-Semitic legislation and practices already in force, and his unfortunately accurate prediction of what was still to come. On arrival in London, I wrote two reports — one to the department in Jerusalem on technical migration matters, the other on the situation of the Jews in Eastern

Sir Herbert Samuel with the heads of the Christian religious communities of Jerusalem

Visit of General Allenby to Jerusalem, 1921

Front row (from the left): Rikabi Pasha; H. St. John Philby; Sir Wyndham Deedes; the Amir Abdallah; Lady Samuel; Sir Herbert Samuel; General Allenby; Gilbert Clayton; Mrs Deedes; Sir Thomas Haycraft. Second row: Peake Pasha; Colonel Bramley; unknown; Captain Abramson; Colonel Cox; Sir Ronald Storrs; Norman Bentwich. Behind him, the author; Sir Spencer Davis. Behind him, Captain Archer Cust; Sir Stewart Symes; Colonel Bewsher; Colonel Stirling.

Visit of Winston Churchill to Jerusalem, April, 1921

Above left, the author; next to him, Mr. James de Rothschild; in front of him, Hadassah Samuel, Sir Herbert Samuel; behind him, Mrs. Deedes (mother of Sir Wyndham); Mr. Winston Churchill; behind him (blurred) Sir Ronald Storrs; next to him, Nancy Samuel; next to her, Godfrey Samuel; Mrs Winston Churchill; Sir Wyndham Deedes.

Family Group in Tel Aviv

Front row (from the left): Mr. and Mrs. Yehuda Grasovsky; Edwin and Hadassah Samuel; Sir Herbert and Lady Samuel; second row: Asaph Grasovsky; Nancy Samuel; 'Shai' Grasovsky; Nechama Grasovsky (Hadassah's younger sister); Godfrey Samuel. (Amihud Grasovsky and Philip Samuel were not then in Palestine.)

Europe. The former had quite an effect on speeding up immigration. Copies of the latter went to the Foreign Office and I was closely cross-examined on it by Sir Ivone Fitzpatrick, then the Foreign Office expert on German affairs. I was told in the Foreign Office, the Colonial Office and in Jerusalem that, till then, no-one had quite realised the full monstrosity of Nazi anti-Semitism. All this, however, has since been fully documented by several writers, in particular by Gerald Reitlinger in *The Final Solution* (Vallentine, Mitchell, London 1953) and by William L. Shirer in *The Rise and Fall of the Third Reich* (Simon and Schuster, New York, 1960).

Immigration reached its peak in 1936 with 65,000 legal entrants and, possibly, an additional 35,000 'illegals'. This flow, accompanied by considerable amounts of capital, produced a boom. Sir Arthur Wauchope, the High Commissioner, made a second attempt, in 1936, to establish a largely elected Legislative Assembly, with a complicated racial and religious composition. One of the main provisions was that Arab consent would be needed for further Jewish immigration. Whereas, in 1922, my father's offer of an elected legislature had been refused (foolishly, in my opinion) by the Arab leaders, Sir Arthur's offer was now refused by the Jewish leaders. The Arab nationalists viewed with alarm the increasing flood of Jewish immigrants which seemed likely to rise even higher with Nazi pressure on Jews in Germany and continued prosperity in Palestine. In the summer of 1936 they declared a general strike with which Sir Arthur failed to cope. The strike rapidly degenerated into a rebellion. The High Commissioner even then was loath to take strong action against the leaders. With all his qualities, he was no politician and privately confessed to me that he was completely out of his depth. Large British forces eventually had to be imported, reaching a peak figure of two divisions in November, 1936. Even then, the rebellion only came to an end with British capitulation to Arab demands. A political limit to Jewish immigration was imposed, so calculated as to prevent any possibility ever of a Jewish majority in Palestine.

It was at the beginning of the general strike that I received a warning from a friendly Moslem in Hebron, through an Arab member of my staff, that I was high up on an assassination list, this time one composed by Arab nationalists. To them, I was an obvious target, both as deputy commissioner for immigration and as a Jew. The Police posted an armed sentry outside my office door. I preferred to provide my own bodyguard for the inevitable daily journeys between my flat in the (Arab) Talbia quarter and the department of immigration. I hired another *Hagana* man from Jerusalem — Yona Ettinger: he came to Talbia at a different hour each morning and searched the neighbourhood before I emerged. We normally used two cars: sometimes I drove in front, sometimes he, using a different route each day. This lasted for two years. Many other British officials were assassinated; but, again, I proved to be too elusive and escaped any direct attempt on my life at that time. But my daily existence became somewhat restricted. I could never use the telephone to make plans: I never went to a cinema or concert, or even walked in the street outside a Jewish quarter. Our front door was of iron: our back door had to be reinforced to prevent anyone breaking in. I could never answer either of the doorbells in person or even look out of the window, especially after dark, unless I first dowsed the light. I devoted a disproportionate amount of time to the mere process of keeping alive. My pride was also at stake: I had no intention of being outwitted by any Arab gunman. I had constantly to use my imagination and, to me, the game was full of interest. But Hadassah found the strain somewhat tiring.

Life in Jerusalem in general was somewhat precarious and one never knew where terrorists would strike next. Although our two sons were only thirteen and eleven when the Arab general strike was declared in 1936, I insisted on their learning to use the old World War I rifle that I had retained. I also showed them what to do if they were ever on a road when a bomb was thrown — dive instantaneously into the nearest ditch, without waiting to see what else was happening. They never had to do this at the time; but it became part of their training when both of them went into the British Army in World War II.

It was about this time, on May 19th, 1936, that Hadassah and I were involved in a serious motor accident. We had gone down, in a hired car, with her brother Asaph's wife Devorah, and my bodyguard, to the opening of the new Tel Aviv jetty. There had been torrential rain and, on the way back, we found the road east of Ramleh under water. Our driver proceeded gingerly, at about ten miles an hour, along the flooded road. The driver of a heavily-loaded lorry, coming towards us at about the same speed, suddenly panicked as we drew near. He jammed on his brakes; the lorry skidded and swung round, crushing the near side of our taxi and so injuring our driver that he died. Devorah was thrown out of the car and was taken to hospital: Hadassah hurt her hand. My bodyguard, sitting next to the driver, was badly cut about the face by the broken glass. I was thrown against the roof, cut my scalp and got concussion. We were taken to the Ramleh Government clinic where all I could think about was the fact that I was due to broadcast that evening in Jerusalem. So, leaving the dead and injured, I hired another car and, propped up with pillows, had myself driven to Jerusalem, in spite of Hadassah's protests at being left stranded in Ramleh. At the door of our flat, I was greeted by David, who was alarmed to see me with bloody bandages around my head. I then apparently fainted and was put to bed for several days. This only goes to show what a disadvantage a powerful sense of duty can be when one has concussion. It took me many years to get over my nervousness when being driven in a car by anyone else. And I am inclined still to be overcautious when driving myself.

In spite of almost two divisions of British troops in Palestine, rebel Arab nationalists managed to establish control over large areas of the country. Hired Arab guerrillas and gun-runners from Syria slipped over the border with impunity. Few were ever caught, even when it was discovered in which mountain cave they were holed up at night. If a police informer reported the whereabouts of such a band, the information would be transmitted from office to office by telephone or telegram, during which process, more often than not, it would pass through the hands of some Arab telephone operator or telegraphist who was himself a secret nationalist supporter. He would pass on the message but, simultaneously, inform the nationalists that the hide-out had been discovered. Even if this did not happen, the movements of British troops leaving camp by lorry at night to surround the hide-out would be reported by pro-nationalist Arab peasant look-outs. They would signal with electric pocket torches from hill-top to hill-top, first, the direction the lorries took on leaving camp; secondly, where the lorries stopped to debus the troops (who made an infernal clatter in the process); and up which hill they were climbing in the dark. It was not surprising that, by the time they surrounded the hide-out, the band had moved elsewhere. Hence, few guerillas were ever rounded up.

Such was the position when Orde Wingate came on the scene. At that time, he was serving as a captain in the intelligence section at G.H.Q. He was our neighbour in Jerusalem and we got to know him well. His father had been a Plymouth Brother, and Orde had more than his share of fanaticism and intolerance. (I once said to Orde: 'I imagine that your father's religious outlook has had quite an influence on your own views.' He was very angry and said: 'That's got nothing to do with it at all!') He became an extreme pro-Jewish nationalist and soon learned a little Hebrew. His young and beautiful wife was as imperious as he was intolerant; so it was not surprising that they were thoroughly unpopular with the British community in Jerusalem. But he was a man of rare originality of mind, with an unbending will. On one occasion, he was sent by G.H.Q. to the Lebanese frontier to try to discover the route used by Arab arms smugglers. Having got some information about the route, he proceeded to test it by laying an ambush for the smugglers. For this, he used Jews from the nearest *kibbutz*: these were all *Hagana* men, using unlicensed weapons. The ambush was successful: a whole party of smugglers was seized, together with their mules laden with arms and ammunition. But then all hell broke loose: for Wingate had committed the unforgivable offence of pitting Jews against Arabs. He was summoned to a stormy interview with the G.O.C., then Sir Archibald Wavell, and officially reprimanded. But Wavell knew a military genius when he saw one and placed fifty British infantrymen at Wingate's disposal for counter-guerrilla operations in the north-eastern corner of Palestine. He ordered Wingate never to return to the north-western corner, whose irate Brigadier in charge Wingate had not even bothered to notify of his previous operation. Together with about a hundred picked *Hagana* men, these British infantrymen, under Wingate, formed the famous Night Squads. By day they holed up in their laager in the *kibbutz* of Ein Harod, in the Valley of Jezreel, near Beisan.

Wingate gradually developed a series of basic propositions for counter-guerilla work in Palestine which he expounded to me in the following terms:

a. Always use your own intelligence agents who report orally to you alone, and never by phone.
b. To confuse the Arab look-outs on the hill-tops, have empty army lorries leave the laager every night by every road.
c. Never go by the most direct route to the area to be searched. Make for the next valley and cross the ridge silently on foot in the dark.

Wingate himself was a superb map-reader and never failed to reach his destination on time. He and his column would arrive before dawn at the cave where the Arab guerrillas were sleeping. They were totally unaware that any British forces were within twenty miles of them. Even if they had a man outside the cave on guard, he was silently garotted. Wingate then posted machine-guns covering the cave entrance, with a cordon of riflemen further down the hill. As it grew light enough to see, a grenade was tossed into the cave. The startled guerrillas seized their rifles and dashed out of the cave, some to be mown down and the rest to be taken prisoner.

In these operations Wingate never lost a man. Once he himself was wounded in the arm when he got in the way of one of his own machine-guns. Life became so unhealthy for the guerrillas—all mercenaries from Syria—that they began to filter back over the northern frontier. It became harder and harder for the Arab nationalists in Palestine to recruit new mercenaries. To help keep Syrian guerrillas and arms smugglers permanently out of Palestine, a barbed wire fence, continually patrolled by British motorised troops—the so-called Teggart Wall—was built all along the northern and north-eastern frontiers.

But all this was insufficient to suppress the Arab Rebellion. A Royal Commission, headed by Lord Peel, was sent out from Britain, but could find no solution acceptable to all sides. Their main proposal was partition, which the Arabs rejected out of hand.

After Munich, in September, 1938, it became increasingly clear that Hitler meant war. The British Cabinet was desperately anxious to quieten down the Middle East. Otherwise when hostilities began, many troops would be tied up to protect its communications by land, sea, air and cable with India and the Far East. So the Cabinet eventually accepted the main Arab nationalist demand — the limitation of further Jewish immigration to such a low figure that a Jewish majority would never be achieved. This was announced in the 1939 White Paper and the Arab Rebellion petered out.

★ ★ ★

During these years—1934-39—we lived on the upper floor of a new two-storey villa in the Christian Arab quarter of Talbia, owned by a tough Armenian named Vartan Matossian. Our two sons were now teenagers and went to school at the Hebrew *Gymnasia* in the adjacent Jewish quarter of Rehavia. We had an English governess for the boys and, in addition, we still employed a Yemenite woman cook and a man-servant

I then realised that, having to deal primarily with Jews after fourteen years of dealing principally with Arabs, a proper knowledge of Hebrew was essential. I do not know exactly why, but I have had a life-long struggle with that language. In part, this is possibly psychological. First, my father-in-law was a noted Hebraist; so, if I could not speak Hebrew correctly I preferred not to speak it at all in order not to expose myself to his expert criticism. Secondly, under the Mandate, English was the master-tongue: to know Hebrew too well would make me a 'native' instead of a member of the ruling caste. Nevertheless, I have dutifully studied Hebrew in Jerusalem for the past thirty years and more, with some of the best teachers available — the late Professor Eliezer Sukenik, the archaeologist (and father of Professor Yigael Yadin); the late Professor Moshe Schwabe, once Principal of a Hebrew *Gymnasium* in Kovno; the late Avraham Yaari, head of the rare books department of the Hebrew University library and a noted writer on medieval Jewish history; and, today, Dr Mordechai Kamrat, inventor of the *ulpan* (the residential whole-time Hebrew institutes for adult immigrants) and a senior official of the Ministry of Education and Culture. I can now lecture in passable Hebrew at the Hebrew University and am collaborating with Kamrat in producing a small English-Hebrew lexicon and an English dictionary of Hebrew first names in use in Israel today.

English remains the language in which I think, dream, count and write. Shortly after the Palestine Broadcasting Service was set up by the Government in 1936, I proposed its use for teaching English to Palestinian listeners. I suggested that Adam Mendilow (now head of the Hebrew University's English department) should give these lessons. He agreed, but, at the last moment, could not undertake the job owing to more urgent work. I was asked by Mrs Ruth Belkine, the talented Anglo-Jewish radio producer, to do it myself. I had never given any English lessons in my life; so I bought some grammars and worked out a few specimen scripts. They were instantly rejected. Ruth Belkine said: 'These talks to Palestinians will be given in the English Hour, primarily intended for British officials, police and troops. So you must make these talks entertaining for them as well.' So, in each fifteen minute talk, I made a few jokes and then used them as a basis for instruction in English pronunciation, vocabulary, idiom or grammar. Although Ruth was still very doubtful about the proposal, and refused to commission more than four talks, they were an instant success, ran to twenty-four in all and were subsequently printed. They were given anonymously by 'The President of the Brighter English League'; but everyone knew who it was. Listeners were invited to enrol as members of the League and received weekly (in an O.H.M.S. envelope) a list of the words to be discussed in the next broadcast. The British listeners laughed at the jokes; the Palestinians — especially the new German-Jewish immigrants — took them very seriously. The name I coined for bad Palestinian English — Pinglish — entered the country's vocabulary and is still in use in Israel today.

Our younger son Dan had not done too well at school in Palestine, in part because of despair at being unable to emulate his elder brother. So, in 1936, we sent him, at eleven, to a residential preparatory school in England till the age of thirteen. Then, after considering a number of other public schools, we decided then to try to get him accepted at Rugby. Dan, however, was very homesick in England. During his school holidays he could only go to my parents in London. In 1938, Hadassah and I went to England to see him; David also went at that time to Balliol straight from the *Gymnasia* in Jerusalem. But, instead of their being able to come out and see us, or our going to England to see them in alternate years as we had planned, we were cut off by the war. Hadassah managed to go again to England in 1939: but she did not see the boys again for four years: I for five. The Mediterranean was closed to Allied shipping; and it was only in 1943 that we both managed to get to England again on leave. This was hard on all of us.

It was in 1938 that, while in England, I attended a Colonial Service seminar at Oxford during the University vacation. It was not only an opportunity to meet colleagues from British dependencies all over the world; but the opportunity was taken to bring us up-to-date on contemporary political developments in Europe. Living all our lives abroad we were woefully ignorant about the Spanish Civil War, the rise of Fascism and of the Nazis. I had seen something of Germany at the beginning of Hitler's regime in 1934: but this was four years later. The University professors who lectured to us provided a picture that was truly frightening.

CHAPTER 10

IMPERIAL CENSORSHIP, 1939–45

Britain is always prepared for war — more or less. In time of peace each Ministry prepares its war-time regulations, its printed forms and instructional handbooks. When the warning bell is sounded, they are taken out of the safes and distributed to the staffs who will use them.

Among the many war-time services for which such detailed plans were prepared by the Home Office was the Imperial Censorship. Main offices were to be set up in huge requisitioned buildings in Liverpool and London, with local branch offices in every self-governing Commonwealth country and in each crown colony, protectorate and mandated territory. The purpose of the Imperial Censorship was: a) to prevent useful information reaching the enemy in outgoing mail; b) to keep a constant watch on incoming, outgoing and transit mail for changes of morale in allied, neutral and enemy territories; c) to collect information about enemy and neutral countries useful to British and Allied intelligence and propaganda services; d) to detect offences against laws relating to trading with the enemy, foreign exchange control and so on; and e) to keep a constant watch on trade between neutral and enemy countries in order to assist in the economic strangulation of the enemy. During World War II, some 10,000 people were engaged on censorship throughout the Commonwealth. Close liaison and interchange of information was maintained between the Imperial Censorship and other Allied censorships. Russia, however, was very secretive.

After Munich, in 1938, it was clear that war with Hitler could hardly be avoided, Steps were taken to nominate a cadre of Imperial Censorship administrators in Britain and abroad. Sir Edwin Herbert (now Lord Tangley), an able London solicitor with a genius for administration, became head of the network. In most dependencies, the chief censor was, *ex officio*, the local deputy postmaster-general. By virtue of his daily work, he had an extensive knowledge of land, sea and air postal routes; and of wireless telegraphy and telephony links, all of which, in wartime, had to be controlled. Under each chief censor, a small cadre of permanent senior civil servants and clerical officers (including some linguists) was designated. As soon as wartime operations began, these would be supplemented by temporary staff. Among them would be many with expert knowledge of common and uncommon languages. Provision was made for direct liaison between each overseas censorship and the London head office, with the local Cabinet offices or Colonial Secretariat, with all the local intelligence bureaus, and the propaganda, economic warfare and other wartime departments that could make use of the information derived from censorship.

In Palestine, it was assumed at the time of Munich that, when war broke out, immigration would cease. Although this cessation was not in fact complete, a number of immigration department staff were designated for the Imperial censorship. I was told, confidentially, that, in the event of hostilities, I would myself become postal censor in Jerusalem.

Other British civil servants stationed in Jerusalem, belonging to other departments, were appointed telegraph censor in Jerusalem and censor of the Palestine broadcasting service. Similar postal censors and telegraph censors were appointed at Tel Aviv and Haifa. British police N.C.O.'s at every place of exit from Palestine — by road, rail, sea or air — were authorised to check the documents taken out by travellers. The censorship of the mail of British and Allied soldiers, sailors and airmen's mail was, however, in the hands of military censors.★ The censorship of the Palestine press — which was practised in peace-time — was considered to be primarily an internal *political* matter. It remained almost to the end of the war with the public information officer in Jerusalem (see page 199). He was also in charge of all war-time propaganda services in Palestine, acting on instructions from London, transmitted through a Middle East centre in Cairo.

Shortly after Munich, I was shown a short list of the staff to be allotted on the outbreak of war to the Jerusalem postal censorship (J.P.C.), mostly Government clerks, both Jews and Arabs. About ten days before World War II actually did break out, a warning message — actually a false alarm — was received in Palestine and we all reported for duty. The J.P.C. was accommodated in the G.P.O. building and provided with all the necessary office equipment, specially printed forms and confidential manuals. Having had some experience in organizing offices, I immediately began to work out the additional staff likely to be needed for the

★ Professor Geoffrey Driver, Regius Professor of Hebrew at Oxford, was sent to Jerusalem as a captain to censor British tommies' letters—in English.

amount of mail that the local post office staff was then handling. Using the authority I had been given, I proceeded to recruit them.

Jerusalem, linguistically, was in a unique position. It had four sources of linguists from which to draw: a) British colonial civil servants and others who had served in various parts of the Commonwealth and had acquired a working knowledge of the local languages, some of which were uncommon (for example, Kurdish): b) Moslems who had come on pilgrimage to the Holy City from other parts of the Islamic world and who had stayed on, knowing such languages as Bokharan and Javanese which they could translate into Arabic, from which others could translate, if necessary, into English; c) Catholic priests, missionaries and monks, especially the White Fathers who had served in Central Africa and knew many African languages; and, lastly, d) Jews who had come to Palestine from all over the world. One, for example, was a German physicist who had taught in Kyoto University and became the only Japanese linguist in the whole Middle East.★ Some of these linguists were appointed whole-time. Others were part-time and were called to the censorship to read letters whenever a few in their particular language had accumulated. I checked personally the list of monthly payments to the part-time

★ I remembered from the department of immigration having had great difficulty with his application for an immigration certificate which was valid for only six months. As he had to give six months' notice to his university, which he would not do until his certificate was actually in his hands, its validity would have expired before he could use it. I bent the law and extended the validity as a special case. I got his address from a factory near Tel Aviv where he was working and engaged him. His wartime services to us were invaluable.

examiners, at so much per letter. A year or so after the war began I discovered a curious fact: to one of our examiners—in Finnish — the monthly sum paid was almost exactly the same, month by month. Fearing some racket, I called the examiner, a highly respected Finnish woman missionary, living on the Mount of Olives, and cross-examined her. She said: 'I was wondering when you would question me about this. You see, I'm the only person in Jerusalem who knows Finnish. I write a weekly letter to my organization through Sweden, and post it. You then call me and ask me to read it for you. I say it's all right and put the censorship impression on it. You then let it go forward and pay me my fee. I get nothing now from Finland and every little helps, so I hope you'll let this system continue.' I was, however, not able to do that, and allowed her to frank her own letters and we passed them unopened, save for spot checks. Any information of military value she might accidentally have slipped in would have been out of date by the time the letter had gone round the Cape in a neutral ship and was intercepted by Germans in the Baltic several months later.

We were eventually able to cope with every European language, including Albanian, Catalan and Basque. We could also decipher such combinations as Low German written in Hebrew letters (Yiddish); Castilian written in Hebrew letters (Ladino); Hebrew written in Arabic characters and Arabic written in Hebrew letters. In all, we could do 120 languages, whereas even the London censorship could manage only seventy. We frequently received letters in languages undecipherable in London marked on the envelope in pencil 'Try Jerusalem'. In such cases, the first thing was to try to identify the group to which the language belonged and then to find someone to puzzle it out. For that purpose, on the outbreak of the war, I had bought up the whole of the Jerusalem stock of booklets published by the British and Foreign Bible Society. Each contained examples of the more than 600 languages and dialects which the New Testament had been translated.

The J.P.C. was organized basically in language sections — for example: English, West European, East European, Middle Eastern—each with a group of examiners under a chief examiner. There was a special section dealing with business correspondence, staffed by examiners who had previously worked in banks or similar firms. Another section examined parcels; and yet another went carefully through the private papers of everyone leaving Palestine on business or leave. Most of the chief examiners and examiners, as well as my own deputy, were women, some being wives of Hebrew University professors or of British civil servants or army officers, anxious to undertake useful war-work. Many of these slaved away all through the war, long after the work had become tedious in the extreme. Few of the British women were linguists; but, at the beginning of the war, when one European country after another was invaded, mail with Palestine was suspended, and British defeats followed thick and fast, these British women kept a stiff upper lip and helped to maintain the morale of the whole office. The relations between many of the British women and their Palestinian-Jewish women colleagues inside the censorship were far closer than between their British or Palestinian husbands outside. To many of the British women who were paid at the princely rate of £8 a month (the salary of a junior clerk in the Civil Service); this was the first money they had ever earned. On pay-day at the end of the first month, the haberdashers in Jerusalem were packed with

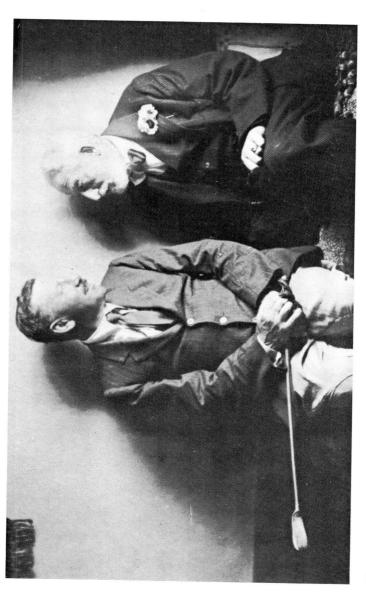

Sir Herbert Samuel and Baron Edmond de Rothschild, at Zikhron Yaaqov, 1925

The author, Ragheb bey Nashashibi, and Hadassah Samuel at the Jerusalem 1914–18 War Cemetery

The motor-launch which nearly sank in the Dead Sea, May, 1929

The author standing, on the left.

George Bernard Shaw at the Sea of Galilee, March, 1930 (photograph by the author)

British censorship wives buying ties for their husbands with 'their own money', the first they had ever earned in most cases.

As I have already said, we were all mobilized on a false alarm, ten days before the war actually broke out. After a day or so, we were told to stand down. However, I kept all my staff together and began a course of intensive training. The basic circular instructions needed in any new office were issued. The limits of authority of staff at each level were prescribed. In consequence, when hostilities actually did break out, it took weeks before Tel Aviv and Haifa got themselves organized. In Jerusalem, censored letters were being returned to the G.P.O. within half-an-hour of the declaration of war. We kept this lead all the way through; and, in consequence, were given all the more interesting work — for example, mailbags seized at sea by the British navy.

Within a few weeks, it was decided that the telegraph censorship in each city should be merged with the postal censorship: this meant that I took over the staff of the telegraph censorship who worked in shifts all round the clock. I was also charged with radio censorship. As the news-casts themselves were drafted by the public information office throughout the war, all I had to do was to provide reliable men in the studios who switched off the broadcast if the announcer deviated in any way from the approved script. This involved no exercise of judgement but only continuous concentration, which was extremely exhausting. The radio switch censors also had to prevent any particular tune being broadcast to carry a hint (say, of troop movements) to listeners abroad. Musical request programmes were, therefore, prohibited till the end of the war. Even a mispronunciation of a word, or a stammer, or merely a cough, had to be considered as a possible means of instant communication with enemy monitors in the Balkans, or in neutral countries such as Turkey.

★ ★ ★

We were lucky in Palestine to have as chief censor H.C. Willbourn. He had originally gone out to East Africa in World War I as a private soldier in one of the British regiments that chased the German colonial troops under Von Lettow all round German East Africa without ever catching up with them. At the end of that war, he became postmaster in Nairobi and, for years, never received promotion until, shortly before World War II, he became deputy postmaster-general in Palestine. He was a bluff man who liked his pipe and his glass of beer. But, not only did he have a remarkable knowledge of all the lines of communication in the Middle East and throughout the world, he also possessed a great fund of commonsense. He used to visit us almost daily. Whenever I had some insoluble problem, I consulted him. 'I can do A or B. If I do A, there will be this result. If I do B, there will be that result. Either will be equally disagreeable. What shall I do?' He would think for a long time, walking up and down my office, tap out his pipe on my window-sill and say: 'What about C?' I could kick myself for not having myself thought of this before. He also had a lively imagination and a corresponding sense of initiative, rare in so stolid a character. For example, we never interfered with airmail in transit through Palestine from one friendly country to another: it was censored either in the country of despatch or of receipt. But, from the morning that Hitler invaded Holland, it became enemy-occupied territory. Willbourn quickly got into his car and motored down to Lydda airport. There he held up the K.L.M. plane from the Dutch East Indies to Rome and Amsterdam, and took off all the mail-bags in spite of violent objections by the captain and crew. He sent up the mail-bags to us for examination and return in time for the next K.L.M. plane. I am still bound to my wartime secrecy pledge and may not divulge any information obtained through censorship. But I can safely say that Willbourn's quick reaction took a great many enemy agents in the Dutch East Indies by surprise; and they were all rounded up as a result of the information we supplied.

Similarly, when the British and Free French forces in Palestine pushed the Vichy French out of the Lebanon and Syria, Willbourn and I drove up to Damascus and on to Aleppo behind the advancing troops. (We narrowly missed being caught by an enemy counter-attack to recover Damascus.) Willbourn knew, by a careful examination of large-scale maps of the Turkish frontier that, at one point, the Berlin-Baghdad railway-line passed, for a few miles, through Syrian territory, by now under Allied occupation. Taking a few British military police with him from Aleppo to this stretch of track, he held up the train from Berlin at pistol point and had all the mail-bags removed from the postal van. He then searched the whole train and found further sacks of German mail hidden in the *wagon lits*. When this mail was read at the new British censorship unit at Aleppo (that had been trained by us in advance in Jerusalem), the information obtained was enough to send to gaol numbers of Axis agents and sympathisers in Iraq.

Jerusalem was the centre for the training of censors-in-charge and chief examiners for postal and telegraph censor-ships in other territories in the Middle East. The censors-in-charge were usually middle-aged British army officers; the chief examiners were selected Palestinian Jews and Arabs. As soon as they took over their new posts, they recruited examiners locally and trained them in British censorship methods. By the end of the war, I had Palestinian staff in Aleppo, Baghdad, Khartoum, Eritrea and even Teheran where, believe it or not, there was a joint Anglo-Russian-Persian censorship.

The Russians, for all their suspicions, had little under-standing of the use of enemy mail as a source of intelligence. During the Russian reoccupation of Eastern Europe towards the end of the war, we heard that they had captured a large quantity of enemy mail in which they were not in the slightest interested. After much prompting they sent it on to us unopened: we found a wealth of information in it.

It was highly desirable that all our examiners should have as wide a knowledge as possible of the countries and people whose mail they were reading. For that reason, we built up a comprehensive reference library. It included all pub-lished material available on censorship in World War I, on espionage and on cryptography. While we were not equipped to crack high-grade cyphers, we had several expert mathematicians on our staff, or available at the Hebrew University, who decyphered for us low-grade codes on several occasions. Some of our examiners in German, who went through intercepted mail from Germany to neutral countries, developed an uncanny power of reading between the lines. They managed to pick up deliberate allusions that had escaped excision by the German censorship. We began to get hints of the incineration of Jews in Nazi concentration camps in Germany and Poland long before anyone (including myself) was prepared to believe the awful truth.

We also took every opportunity of trying to keep our staff, especially British, in touch with what was going on in Britain. Palestine was effectively cut off from Britain for several years during which Germany and Italy succeeded in closing the Mediterranean to Allied shipping, even in convoy. Hence, I took pains to persuade every British civil servant, officer and personality out from Britain to come to the Jerusalem censorship and give a talk to our staff on the progress of the war. Among them was my father, returning from a wartime visit to India. These talks were a wonderful tonic for the morale of the whole office.

One of the problems I faced as an administrator was the continuous expansion of our censorship records. On the outbreak of war, I devised a simple cross-reference system. The name of the sender and addressee of every suspect communication was card-indexed, together with the names and nicknames of every person named in the communication. By the end of the war, there were over a quarter of a million names on our index. Every name in a subsequent suspect communication was checked with this index and all kinds of clandestine links between suspects were discovered. By contrast, in the Cairo censorship, which dealt with twice the volume of mail that we had, they opened a separate file for each suspect. A full hand-written copy or translation of every suspect communication was made for inclusion in the file. By the end of the war, they employed some sixty people on this work: we managed it with two. It meant that, with us, the examiner concerned had to look for previous mentions of the same name in different files instead of having all the information in the same file. But the smaller number of staff engaged in copying enabled us to employ a few more examiners and analysts and still show a considerable saving in manpower.

Most other Imperial censorships passed the transcripts of interesting or suspect letters to the civil departments or intelligence bureaus concerned. There, someone had to collate all the raw material pouring in and produce a connected story. I suspected that, in some offices, through shortage of staff, pressure of work or lack of interest, our reports were merely being filed away. So, in addition to sending copies of individual reports as they were made, we sent, from time to time, our own summaries with the conclusions *we* drew from the evidence. Each examiner wrote her own summaries, as only she really had the intimate knowledge required — whether it be 'German attempts to purchase wolfram from Spain' or 'the activities of Mr X in Brazil'. Some of these summaries received high praise from other civil departments or intelligence bureaus in the Middle East and London and helped to maintain our reputation. Every case where a particularly good piece of summarising had received such praise, it was mentioned, together with the name of the examiner concerned, in an internal bulletin that we circulated monthly to all our staff.

The third unusual thing that we did was to publish monthly reports on positive intelligence we had derived through perusal of incoming foreign newspapers addressed to residents of Jerusalem district. We divided up the information into sections: for example, 'Morale in a) allied countries; b) neutral countries; c) enemy countries': or 'Economic warfare', with each section further subdivided by country. Every newspaper was assessed A, B and C according to its veracity and estimated circulation, based on our knowledge and research. We gave this foreign press review wide circulation among official bodies in the Middle East. There was a similar review emanating from a British listening-post in Switzerland: but it was intended primarily for London; few copies reached the Middle East. Another British press review was issued in Istanbul but also failed to reach a wide British official audience in Palestine and Egypt. I was instructed several times to stop issuing *my* review: it was not my business. But I always got some British intelligence bureau to certify that it was valuable, and it came out to the very end of the war. At least, it helped many people to get a picture of what was going on, apart from the information provided by British war propaganda units.

One of our difficulties was to prevent our women examiners from getting emotionally involved with the persons whose letters they were reading. There was a madman in Jerusalem who kept on writing begging-letters to God, always asking for ten (Palestinian) pounds to save him from starvation. After censorship, the letters went back to the G.P.O. and were put in the 'dead letter office' as undeliverable. These piteous pleas always went to the same examiner and eventually got her down. She took a five pound note out of her purse and sent it anonymously to the writer of the letters. By the next post came the following:

'Dear God,
Thank you so much for the ten pounds; but those bastards in the censorship stole half of it.'
So much for good intentions.

★ ★ ★

After a year or two, the number of separate countries in the Middle East with censorship units had grown considerably: each country depended direct on London. With the difficulty in communicating with London after the Mediterranean had been closed by the enemy, it was decided to establish a new post in Cairo of Director of Middle East Censorship. Willbourn was selected to fill the post, to the dismay of the British head of the much larger censorship in Egypt who expected the nomination for himself. Similar Middle East directorates had been created in Cairo for supplies (the Middle East Supply Centre) and for war propaganda. To fill Willbourn's post in Palestine, W.G. Foster, a former deputy postmaster-general for Palestine, was brought back from retirement in Britain. But he died a few months later after a minor operation in a not-very-good convent hospital in Jerusalem (he was a Catholic). I was accordingly promoted (without change in my official peacetime salary) to succeed him. There was some feeling that the post should have gone to one of the retired British army officers then in Cairo; but none of the candidates apparently had the censorship knowledge that I had meanwhile acquired. I fancy Millbourn made the final choice, and I was grateful to him. So at last I became head of a department in Jerusalem, if only a wartime department. This meant that I did not become *ex officio* a member of the Advisory Council, which was no great deprivation.

Being head of the Imperial Censorship in Palestine gave me great freedom of action. Although our salaries were being paid by the Palestine Government, we operated under instructions from London and Cairo and had direct communication with pretty well anyone we liked in the Middle East. We had British military liaison officers attached to our units in Jerusalem, Tel Aviv and Haifa. After the United States entered the war, an American army intelligence officer was attached to my own office. We passed to him any information we obtained of possible interest to the United States.

The total number of Imperial censorship staff in Palestine was about three hundred. The Haifa office was under Ernest Stafford, formerly head of the immigration office there. At the head of the Tel Aviv office was Witold Hulanicki, the former Polish consul-general in Palestine who had been stranded when Poland was overrun by Germany and Russia. He was especially valuable as a linguist himself in half-a-dozen languages. He also became resident representative of the Polish Red Cross when General Anders and his Polish army came out of Russia through Persia to Palestine. Unfortunately, towards the end of the Mandate, when he still lived in Tel Aviv, his frequent journeys for the Red Cross gave the impression to one of the Jewish dissident underground forces that he was spying for the Arabs and he was assassinated.

My new duties as Chief Censor for the whole of Palestine involved frequent inspections of the Tel Aviv and Haifa offices, as well as of all the frontier controls. I also paid friendly visits to the heads of neighbouring censorships, both British and French, in Amman, Baghdad, Damascus, Beirut, Aleppo and Cairo — and, of course, to Willbourn at G.H.Q. in the same city. While I was away, Harry Carter acted for me as Chief Censor. He had been brought from the London censorship to be deputy chief censor in Palestine. He was a sensitive, bearded man, who, in private life, had a wide knowledge of typography. After the war, he worked in this field at the Oxford University Press. Unlike most British colonial officials, he was without pretensions and saw nothing wrong in making his own furniture or in visiting the families of ordinary British police constables in Jerusalem. Both of these actions scandalised the regular British civil servants and military officers and their wives.

At the end of the war, I asked the British section of the Allied Control Commission in Germany to find out from the German intelligence files whether any important information about Palestine had got through the Imperial Censorship to the German intelligence staff. There was no record of such news getting out to the Axis powers by letter, cable or radio, which was a welcome reassurance.

★ ★ ★

When the war started in 1939, I was already too old for active military service. Even British Colonial civil servants in Palestine in their twenties were not allowed to volunteer. But, after the fall of France and the entry of Italy into the war against Britain, the threat to Palestine from the Italian Empire in Tripolitania, Tunisia, Libya, Eritrea and Ethiopia became much more real. A local civil defence force was consequently formed in the three main cities in Palestine and I was one of the first to sign up. We were called the P.V.F. — the Palestine Volunteer Force (I maintained that P.V.F. stood for Purely Voluntary Fatigue). We wore a simple khaki uniform with a sun helmet in summer and a forage cap in winter. Meeting two afternoons a week at the British military base in Jerusalem — the Allenby Barracks — we trained in musketry and squad drill, and did field operations up and down the hills to the south of the City.

There were two platoons of volunteers in Jerusalem, partly British civil servants and other resident British employees: the rest were Jewish. Few Arabs joined, as they wanted to avoid having been too much involved with Britain when Hitler and Mussolini won the war.

Our commander was Captain Mason, of the Department of Agriculture, with Michael Hogan, then Crown Advocate (now Sir Michael and Chief Justice in Hong Kong) as second-in-command. I started in the ranks, worked my way up to platoon sergeant and eventually commanded one of the two platoons, with my brother-in-law, Asaph Goor, as platoon sergeant. The other platoon was run by A.E. Mulford, a local British importer and insurance agent.

We were armed with British service rifles and had a couple of old and heavy Hotchkiss machine-guns. As a fighting force we were useless. Once we went down the railway line to Artuf station for night operations and had to 'defend' the station against a squad of tough Australian commandos. We were adjudged by the umpires to have all been wiped out in the first five minutes. By the time we were disbanded, in 1943, I think we might have been able to withstand an attack by any unit of the Italian army women's service corps.

★ ★ ★

During World War I, Palestine was ravaged. Its population suffered from conscription, bombardment, exile, starvation, disease, locusts and disruption of foreign trade. But, in World War II, it was a haven of tranquility. It was never bombed: the Vichy French once got in to the Metullah

191

police station in the extreme north for half-an-hour but were chased out. Many small war-industries were developed in Palestine, working on contracts for the enormous British Middle East forces, manufacturing such things as land-mines and jerry-cans. Although no oranges could be exported to Europe during the war, large quantities were bought for army consumption as fruit juice. The Middle East Supply Centre in Cairo arranged for interchange of products throughout the whole area. Even though raw materials had to be rationed, there was full employment in Palestine all through the war. Many thousands of Palestinians, mostly Jews, served in the British army, first in British units, then in special Palestinian units and eventually in the Jewish Brigade. Much money was spent in Palestine by British soldiers on leave: there were vast recreation camps on the coast as well as many military hospitals. A great deal of constructional work was also done in widening and resoling roads to be used as convoy routes between Egypt on one side and Syria and the Lebanon on the other, and in strengthening the bridges. The main railway line from the Suez Canal to Haifa was extended to Beirut to provide a second link with the Hejaz railway. Many military air fields were developed, still in use by the Israel Air Force today. Lydda airport was taken over as a base for long-distance heavy bombers operating in North Africa.

By 1943, the German and Italian forces had been cleared from North Africa, and air cover could again be provided for convoys through the Mediterranean. Once more it became possible for members of the armed forces and civilian officials to go in turn to Britain on leave. I had had no home leave for five years (instead of the normal two), and was one of those selected to go on the first convoy, for men only.

Hadassah followed a month later in the second convoy, on which army nurses and other women were included.

My convoy assembled at Suez: we waited off Algiers for a week to pick up wounded from the invasion of Sicily. No-one was allowed to land at Algiers except myself: I persuaded the port authorities to let me visit the French censorship. Somehow or other, wearing a macintosh and pulling my felt hat over my eyes, I was known by the military police at the foot of the gangway as 'The man from Scotland Yard'. We then steamed half way to South America, half way to Greenland and north of Ireland to Glasgow, taking six weeks in all, instead of the usual ten days in peace-time. I went at once by train, across country, to Newcastle to see my elder son, David, then an artillery officer, before he left for India and Burma. Next I went to London and stayed in the cellar of my parents' house: they themselves had moved to Oxford during the blitz.

England after four years of war was strange. There was little bombing during the months I was there: the 1940 blitz was over and the rockets had not yet begun. But large sections of many cities were in rubble: the railway coaches were decrepit and trains moved at a snail's pace. Blackout was everywhere, so different from the normal life I had led in Palestine.

I reported to the Colonial Office and then called on the Imperial Censorship headquarters in London, comparing their methods with ours: there was little I could learn. What was more interesting was a tour arranged for me by the Ministry of Information to enable me to see something of Britain at war. It included visits to civil defence and fire-fighting control centres in London, steel works in Sheffield and aircraft repair shops at Oxford.

When I arrived at Oxford railway station, my father met me in a broken-down taxi. He was carrying a string-bag, containing some old copies of *The Times*. On the way to his temporary lodgings in North Oxford, he stopped the taxi outside a fish-monger's. We stood in the queue, inching forward until my father received a slab of fish. He wrapped the fish up in *The Times*, put it in the string bag and got back into the taxi.

I mentioned this in a talk I gave on the B.B.C., beamed to the Middle East, describing Britain at war. When I got back to Palestine, I was told that nothing had brought the war home to listeners more vividly than the fact that their former High Commissioner, who had lived in such pomp and state at Government House, was now reduced to standing in a queue outside an Oxford fish-shop.

★ ★ ★

By the time I returned to duty in Palestine, the struggle had restarted between Jew and Arab for the repeal or maintenance of the White Paper restrictions on Jewish immigration and land purchase. It grew worse and worse as time went on. At the beginning of 1945, my friend and colleague, Christopher Holme — then public information officer and press censor — was thoroughly exhausted by his war service. He seems to have made an error of judgement in allowing a piece of inflammatory news to be published. The Chief Secretary Sir John Shaw, who had an exaggerated opinion of my political wisdom, asked me to take over the duties of press censor in addition to those of the Imperial Censorship, although there was really nothing in common between the two. So, for the last six months of the war, I assumed this responsibility, too. It had at least one good result: it left me with a whole-hearted dislike of press censorship. This was not so much because it interfered with one of the basic liberties (which had to be curtailed in Palestine, anyhow, in the interest of maintaining inter-racial peace) but because of its futility. Material that I had painstakingly kept out of the local press could be picked up a few days later by Palestinian listeners to foreign broadcasts or read a few weeks later in imported foreign newspapers, which were not censored on entry.

During the previous 25 years of the Mandate, press censorship in Palestine had gone through three stages. Under Ottoman law, an editor could be prosecuted for publishing inflammatory news; but he could go on publishing it until the case was heard in court. After the 1929 Wailing Wall riots, the law was strengthened to allow inflammatory newspapers to be suspended by administrative order. But editors got round this by having a whole series of alternative titles registered, each one of which had to be separately suspended, each supervision taking several days. Finally, *pre*-censorship was introduced, which required the editor to submit to the press censorship all political news in galley-proof. A Jewish or Arab representative of the press censor sat in the office of each Jewish or Arab newspaper, passing or rejecting galleys for publication. They referred to an assistant press censor any items about which they were in doubt. From time to time, the press censor received Government notices of matters on which a 'stop' had been imposed. It was this system that served well in wartime to prevent the publication of information that might be of interest to the enemy. Only about one third of a newspaper was, however, censorable. Another third was normally exempted; for example, literary reviews and sports articles. The rest was advertisements, also not liable to censorship.

As press censor, I had two British assistants — one an elderly water-colourist named H.C. Gray who controlled the daily *Palestine Post* in Jerusalem. Most of the daily newspapers and other periodicals, however, appeared in Tel Aviv where a former British police officer, J.K. Hutchens, was in charge. He was assisted by a Jewish and an Arab chief examiner, who were available till midnight to give decisions on questions referred to them by examiners sitting in individual newspaper offices. After midnight, if Hutchens himself was not available, night editors were authorised, when later news came in, to ring me up personally. This they did, once or twice a week. It is rather nerve-racking to be woken at 2 a.m. out of a deep sleep, and be asked to give an immediate decision whether a particular item of political news was publishable or not. I knew very well that, if I slipped up, there could well be rioting the next day. I often spent the rest of the night wide awake, worrying whether my decision had been right.

I introduced a system of weekly conferences in Tel Aviv where I personally met the editors of all the Jewish newspapers and, at Jaffa, those of the Arabic press. This enabled all grievances to be thrashed out orally and allowed me to induce the more responsible editors to practice self-censorship. This meant taking them much more into the confidence of the Government and letting them know confidentially what were the restrictions actually in force and the exact purpose and wording of each 'stop'.

I also introduced a revolutionary principle for the guidance of my press censorship staff. The first question to be asked,

Lord and Lady Samuel on a cruise to Scandinavia, August, 1965

The author as a Victorian child

when an item of news came up for consideration was: 'Is it true?' If it was, they were to pass it, if possible: if it was false, then to have no compunction in killing it, if it was on the borderline of news to be stopped.

Ever since that time, I have always had most friendly personal relations with the whole of the Jewish press and, up to the end of the Mandate, with the Arabic press as well.

CHAPTER II

THE PALESTINE
BROADCASTING SERVICE, 1945–48

The P.B.S. was founded in 1936 with a single medium-wave transmitter at Ramallah, some ten miles north of Jerusalem. The studios were situated in the city, first in the G.P.O., later in a building owned by the Abyssinian Church off a steep and narrow lane then named after Melisande, a Crusader queen.

The main programmes were in Hebrew and Arabic, broadcast in turn at different times of the day. Although a strict balance in broadcasting hours was kept, the great majority of listeners were Jewish. There were shorter programmes in English, primarily for British officials, police and troops. But Jews and Arabs listened to the English programmes as well, either for pleasure or to improve their knowledge of that language.

From 1936 to 1945, the P.B.S. was part of the Department of Posts and Telegraphs, under the administrative direction of the deputy P.M.G., who also supervised the radio engineering services. The program director, in the earlier years, had been seconded from the B.B.C. in London. These directors included Randall, Fry and McNair. On his return to London, Stephen Fry subsequently rose to high office in the B.B.C. itself. The P.B.S. was thus very much a B.B.C. creation, as in other British overseas dependencies.

The P.B.S. was divided into a number of sections, three of which were determined by the language used — English, Hebrew and Arabic (including Arabic music). Two more dealt with the nature of the programmes, regardless of languages: news (in English, Hebrew and Arabic) and music (for both the Hebrew and English programmes). There were two further common services — engineering (under the G.P.O.) and administration, making seven sections in all.

During World War II, both the news section and the Arabic section had been taken over by the public information officer as part of British efforts to influence Arab opinion in the Middle East. Whereas the listeners to the Hebrew programmes were known to be anti-Hitler and anti-Mussolini, many Arabs were impressed by German and Italian flamboyance and were convinced that the Axis would win the war. A second radio broadcasting transmitter, wholly for Arabic transmissions from Jerusalem, had been ordered from Britain to offset enemy transmissions in Arabic from Bari and elsewhere. But the second transmitter had been sunk on the way out, as had a replacement. A second replacement was ordered but it arrived only after the war was over. Its installation at Ramallah would enable the daily hours of broadcasting to be doubled, with Hebrew on one wave length and Arabic on another.

It was in these circumstances that the Palestine Government ment decided to separate the P.B.S. (save for its engineering services) from the G.P.O. and to create a new Department of Broadcasting under a separate director. As chief censor, in close touch with the G.P.O., I had heard of this proposal and asked the Chief Secretary if I might be considered for the new job. I did not want to go back to my substantive post as deputy director of immigration, especially under the political restrictions imposed by the White Paper of 1939, still in force. I had by now some 25 years' service and would normally have been eligible for appointment as a district commissioner. But this was now impossible. From 1943, with the expulsion of the Axis troops from North Africa, and the German surrender at Stalingrad, all enemy threats to the Middle East had vanished. The violent racial, religious and nationalist struggle for the domination of Palestine, suspended during the critical years from 1939 to 1943, was resumed. Even wider powers of suppression were given to district commissioners, and I realised that it would have been doubly difficult for the Government to support measures against Arab nationalists taken by a district commissioner who was himself Jewish. The Chief Secretary did not quite know what to do with me, now that the wartime Imperial Censorship was being closed down. I had had some scientific training at school and had been interested, before the war, in the use of the P.B.S. for teaching English (see page 173). Running the P.B.S. was something I thought I could do. To manage men and machinery and to mould public opinion in three languages looked interesting. I hoped that I knew enough about Palestine to recognise a political problem when I saw one and to keep the P.B.S. out of undue controversy. So I was appointed. Looking back, I think my optimism was justified. At last I had an opportunity to put into practice all the administrative techniques I had learned so laboriously from my succession of departmental chiefs — Sir Harry Luke in the Jerusalem district, J.E.F. Campbell at Jaffa, Eric Mills in the department of migration and H.C. Willbourn in the censorship. Anything I managed to achieve during my three years of office, I owe largely to them.

As head of a substantive peace-time department, I was now brought into close personal touch with the High Commissioner and the Chief Secretary. With the Chief Secretary, then John Shaw, I had a weekly interview. He was an immensely tall and rugged man, of great integrity, who had earned his sobriquet of 'Honest John'. In a service where senior officials were well-provided with stenographers, he struck a discordant note by typing his own minutes. We got on very well together. Shaw had not had a university education himself and took, I think, a rather exaggerated view of my own intellectual ability. But I had already managed to keep the press censorship out of trouble for six months and perhaps that was the touchstone. I am inclined to think that it was Shaw who pressed for my being made a Companion of the Order of St Michael and St George two years later.

Having Shaw as my patron at the centre of government was a great advantage. He gave instructions that all my requests for the additional staff needed to build up a new well-rounded department were to be met. He also supported my insistent demand for the return to the P.B.S. of the news section and the Arabic section that had been managed by the public information officer for the six years of the war.

I had a fortnightly interview, too, with the High Commissioner at Government House. The primary purpose was to enable me to be briefed on the general lines of Government policy. For most of my three years of office, the High Commissioner was Sir Alan Cunningham, who was friendly and helpful. At the beginning, however, in 1945, Field Marshal Lord Gort held that office. He was a man of legendary valour, holder of the Victoria Cross and defender of Gibraltar and Malta all through the war. He had a strange ability to open and close his mind at will. If something I asked did not interest him, he could be utterly bone-headed about it. But, if a question touched his imagination, he would anticipate the end of my question and think out a complete reply to it at lightning speed, long before I had finished the sentence. It was a great misfortune for Palestine when he resigned through ill-health only a year after assuming office, and died shortly after from cancer.

★   ★   ★

I came to the P.B.S. at a propitious moment, when planning for the use of the second transmitter was about to begin. It was clear that one transmitter could now be used for Arabic and the other for Hebrew; but on which wave-length should English programmes be broadcast? There were fewer Arab listeners than Jewish listeners; but the Arabs were determined to maintain the principle of equality and not to allow any of 'their' time to be used for programmes in any other language. I ruled that the English programmes should be broadcast simultaneously on both wave-lengths, ostensibly because I did not want to deprive any Arab or Jew of the chance to listen to English programmes on 'his own' wave-length. As the Hebrew press mildly objected to the use of 'their' wave-length for English programmes, the Arabs were satisfied that my decision must be in their favour. I had no further trouble with Arab nationalism for the whole three years of office.

Having 'taken away' the P.B.S. from the deputy P.M.G., and the news section and Arabic section from the P.I.O., I was naturally concerned with retaining their goodwill.

After all, I was still dependent on the G.P.O. for all engineering services and on the P.I.O. for our official Government news communiques. The P.I.O. also published separate weekly magazines in English, Arabic and Hebrew in which the P.B.S. was accorded half the space for its programmes and other radio material. So I personally paid a weekly call on the P.I.O. and a fortnightly call on the deputy P.M.G. This enabled all friction at lower levels to be removed before it could do much damage.

I was equally concerned with the maintenance of proper control over the several sections of the P.B.S.: yet, at the same time, I wanted to give them enough leeway for the development of their own programme plans on which a good broadcasting service depends. Luckily, there were some able and experienced section controllers available. The controller of Arabic programmes was Azmi Nashashibi, a relative of Ragheb bey Nashashibi, the former Moslem Mayor of Jerusalem. He was somewhat of a playboy; but his social status, his personality and his interest in broadcasting enabled him to manage his team well. They provided very good programmes.

The Hebrew section, in whose programmes the majority of the listeners were interested, was ably managed and developed by Mordechai Zlotnik (now Avida). Shortly after I took over the P.B.S., the gifted head of the English section — Reggie Smith, formerly with the British Council in Egypt — left to become one of the B.B.C.'s leading producers in London. His place was taken by Robert Finnegan, now also with the B.B.C. The music section was run by an elderly but hardworking German-Jewish composer, Karl Salomon.

I managed to persuade a friend of mine, Roy Elston, to

accept the all-important post of controller of news and to train staff how to compose really good news bulletins. Elston had come out to Jerusalem during World War II, as director of the British Political Warfare Executive's radio stations in Cairo, Jerusalem and Bari. As Chief Censor, I had worked closely with him and had acquired a high regard for his professional competence as a journalist. Before the war, he had represented the *Christian Science Monitor* in the Rhine Valley (I always assumed that this was a cover for some additional British intelligence duties). I also admired his political sagacity as far as Palestine politics were concerned. Later, he became the London *Times* correspondent in Jerusalem. As the administrator of the news-room, however, he proved to be hopeless.

The P.B.S. administrative section was managed by an able Christian Arab — Nimr Ghanem. To be my deputy director, Rex Keating came up from the Egyptian Broadcasting Service in Cairo. He was the son of a British Suez Canal pilot, and both Rex and his wife had become highly skilled professional broadcasters. It was he who supervised our programme co-ordination and trained our broadcasters in the finer points of production. He and I, however, did not see eye to eye on the political implications involved in Palestine.

★   ★   ★

Of the 120 permanent members of the P.B.S. (apart from a further sixty G.P.O. transmitter and studio engineering staff), many had other professions of their own, as writers, journalists, teachers, musicians and so on. Their service in the P.B.S. often gave them much well-deserved personal publicity: some of them were in great demand whenever there were vacancies in important positions in their own profession outside. Previously, the deputy P.M.G. had raised strenuous objections whenever any member of the P.B.S. staff wanted to leave, because of the extra trouble involved in having to train his or her successor. I took the opposite view and made the most of our inability to retain all our staff. Broadcasting, by its very nature, needs a constant stream of new ideas. After a few years, even the most imaginative producer is apt to run out of originality. Hence a rapid turnover of production staff becomes a positive asset, provided that there is enough new talent willing to come in at the bottom to be trained. But, by my allowing people at the top to leave freely, promotion in the P.B.S. was rapid. Hence, there was a constant line of bright young Jewish and Arab university graduates waiting for admission; we had our pick of the rising generation. I threw every vacancy, even at the upper levels, open to competition between newcomers and the old-timers who often made up with experience what they lacked in brilliance. A selection board, on which I often sat myself, chose the best qualified candidate to fill each vacancy. There was no promotion by seniority: age and length of service were only two of the factors to be considered. Even those on the staff who were passed over agreed that their claims had been fairly considered. By the end of my three years' direction of the P.B.S., I calculated that half the new posts and the vacancies in old posts had been filled by promotion and half by appointment from outside. So sure was I that a rapid turnover of staff was to our advantage that I even went out my way to *look* for better employment as a reward for some of our outstanding broadcasters. The fact that it was easy to get out of the P.B.S. into a first class job, naturally led to an even better field of candidates for appointment at the bottom. By the time the Mandate was wound up, it was, I think, generally agreed, both inside and outside Palestine, that the P.B.S. was one of the best broadcasting stations in the Middle East. Many of our staff went on to further success in Israel, Jordan, Cyprus and even Britain.

The successful operation of such a system depended, of course, on the immediate availability of educated men and women capable of filling every possible vacancy. We embarked on continuous professional training of existing and potential staff at all levels and for all sections — producers, announcers, studio actors and, above all, script writers. As, even then, we were broadcasting some fourteen hours a day on the two transmitters, the amount of new radio material needed every week was enormous, assuming that we were not going merely to play old gramophone records over and over again. Many of our listening audience, especially the Jewish listeners of European origin, took broadcasting very seriously and demanded a far higher standard than that. It was as if we were promoters of a variety theatre playing from early morning till midnight (with occasional breaks) every day of the week, month by month, year after year, without ever repeating the same turn more than once or twice.

★　★　★

Broadcasting in three languages on two transmitters, with British, Jewish and Arab staff, made it essential to have a closely welded department, with the minimum of personal friction. I secured this, first, through a collective weekly meeting of heads of sections where all differences would be thrashed out in my presence. By adhering to a carefully prepared agenda, and only dealing with questions ripe for general discussion, these weekly 'Cabinet meetings' never lasted for more than an hour. This was possible only because I personally visited each section myself once a fortnight. The controller of the section then gathered every member of his staff—down to the office-boys—to discuss with me any question they wished regarding their own programmes or other problems.

In moments of political tension outside — and there were many during the last three years of the Mandate — I held a mass meeting of all the staff, of all sections and all ranks. There I would announce, for example, what new measures I was taking to assure their personal safety and would then hear any suggestions for further improvements.

I also made a practice of keeping *all* the staff informed, by circular on the notice-boards, about promotions, transfers and dismissals as soon as they were decided. Whenever I had to make a disciplinary inquiry, the charges and the results were at once notified to the rest of the staff, especially where the charges were dismissed. This reduced the rumours floating around and materially raised morale in the office.

But I soon discovered that all these formal channels of communication were still inadequate. Six years of strained wartime management had left nearly every member of the staff with some personal grievance or other — leave duly earned but arbitrarily cancelled; anticipated salary increments not paid on due date; all kinds of promises left unfulfilled. The P.B.S. staff had been treated like G.P.O. staff and even fined for lateness. But the general educational level of postmen, telegraph boys, postal clerks and telephonists — the bulk of the G.P.O. staff — was far lower than that of the broadcasting staff. They had been nominally supervised by the deputy P.M.G.; but he had only visited Broadcasting House on rare occasions. Hence I announced that any member of the P.B.S. who had a personal problem could come and see me at any time, without notice. I invariably kept my office door open so that anyone could see at once if I was free. No one had even to ask my secretary. After stopping all incoming phone calls and other possible interruptions, I listened to the problem at length in all its details. I then read through all the previous papers and reopened every case that seemed to require it. The fact that this was being done, often with highly satisfactory results for the staff member — such as backpay or additional paid leave — raised staff morale immensely. As I had by then had twenty-five years experience in applying staff regulations, there was little I did not know of what was possible and what precedents had been established in other departments. I even managed, by using personal advocacy in the right quarter, to get some new precedents established. For example, one experienced married woman producer was very unhappy because she had no children and had had several miscarriages. I got the medical board to recommend that she should be granted nine months maternity leave on full pay before her child was born, in addition to the standard maternity leave given afterwards. Such unheard-of generosity by the Palestine Government made the position of all married women civil servants throughout the country much easier from then on.

Another collective problem I had to cope with was the grievance felt by the P.B.S. studio orchestra — some 15-20 whole-time employees of many years standing. They complained bitterly that they were not pensionable civil servants. I had been warned that the orchestra committee was unmanageable, and was always threatening mass resignation. At my first meeting with the whole orchestra, I announced that any resignation that was tendered in future would be at once accepted. I then persuaded them that artists like themselves should not lower their status by becoming civil servants. I worked out a special contract which would entitle them each to compensation, in the event of termination of appointment, at the rate of a month's salary for every year's service. This was then the regular practice in the Jewish community but had never been recognised by the Government as far as its own employees were concerned. I got this special contract through the Treasury myself with the result that, when the P.B.S. was disbanded at the end of the Mandate, all the senior members of the orchestra received a whole year's salary in advance. They were thus able to tide over the dislocation caused by the War of Independence far better than would have been possible had they received a modest pension at a steadily devaluted rate of exchange.

★   ★   ★

At the same time that I was trying to raise the morale of the P.B.S., I laboured to increase its efficiency. Broadcasting is as much a public service as the electricity or water supply. The slightest interruption is widely felt and hotly resented. Many of our listeners were indignant because some P.B.S. programmes did not start on time, or were replaced by others without adequate warning. There was thus a ready measure of P.B.S. inefficiency in the number of seconds that any programme was late in beginning. The average length of programmes was fifteen minutes, which meant that we were broadcasting some fifty programmes a day on the two transmitters. The studio engineers kept a record of the exact moment when each programme started; and I was supplied the next morning with particulars of any substitute programme the day before or of any programme that had started over five seconds late. When I first began my investigations, there was an average of two such delays each day. In each case, I called the producer or announcer in charge of the delayed or substituted programme and proceeded patiently to determine what, in fact, had caused the delay or last-minute substitution. The causes were often very remote. For example, why had the early morning Hebrew news bulletin at 7 a.m. yesterday started eleven seconds late? The announcer said that the P.B.S. car that picked her up from her home before dawn every morning had not arrived on time. I thanked the announcer and called our transport officer who explained that the P.B.S. car had had a puncture on leaving the garage. All our tyres were worn out and there was no reserve. Our supplies officer reported that our indent had been held up pending Treasury approval of the special financial authority needed under the new budget. So I called the Treasury on the phone and got the authority issued at once and the new tyres delivered. But what was more important, I devised measures to prevent such delays from happening again in the future. In most cases, no one in the P.B.S. was even blamed or warned. In fact, everyone knew he was allowed to make any mistake *once*. But, if after due investigation and rectification, a programme was delayed for a second time for the same reason, then there was trouble. Yet, by putting an extra strong patch on every weak spot in the administrative machine, this hardly ever happened.

These inquiries in depth took up a lot of my time. But, through them, I learned a great deal about every corner of the P.B.S. and of all the other Government departments on which it had to rely for supporting services. In the process, I met almost everyone connected in one way or other with broadcasting. By the end of six months, I had reduced the number of delayed or substituted programmes from two a day to one every fortnight; that is, to about one thirtieth of the original frequency. By this time, staff morale was so high and the administrative machine was working so smoothly, that I decided that it was really unnecessary to try to reduce delays and substitutions any further. We had almost reached the limit of human perfectability.

I had to provide a broadcasting service seven days a week, at intervals throughout each day from early morning till late at night. Yet, every member of the staff — Moslem, Christian and Jewish — had to have daily time off for meals and relaxation; his weekly day of rest; his annual leave; occasional sick leave, as well as eight days of religious festivals during the year. Broadcasting, with its split-second timing, is a rather nerve-racking occupation; so I insisted on all staff taking their full annual leave. I was particularly careful to arrange that every single member of the staff had at least one relieving officer — and that those holding key posts had two, three or even four replacements — all fully trained to step into the vacant post at a moment's notice. The names of all relieving officers were recorded in circulars kept constantly up-to-date. Everyone knew what to do if someone had not turned up by the appointed hour. This worked so well that those busy with programming or office organization often were not even told what had happened until afterwards. The proper training of replacements was simplified by a requirement that no-one could go off on leave until he had personally trained all his replacements and could certify that they were ready to take over.

★ ★ ★

Broadcasting House in Queen Melisande Lane was built around a derelict courtyard which I turned into a garden, tended by a P.B.S. gardener. (The Treasury usually disallowed such luxuries.) I put the supervision of the garden, of the canteen caterers and our own library under the direct control of our staff committee, with power to spend the maintenance budget that I provided. This gave the committee something practical to do, apart from endless arguments over salary scales.

I also made one member of the staff in each block of buildings personally responsible for the proper functioning of everything within it. This involved the immediate reporting of anything needing attention — from broken chairs and window-panes to dirty latrines, lack of soap and wet towels in the wash-rooms. In the company of the head of our administrative section, I minutely inspected once a week the whole of our premises. I am inclined to think that the standards of cleanliness, good repair and comfort that we achieved were higher than in any other public offices in Palestine. I refused to allow any calendars or ash-trays bearing advertising matter to be used: all the equipment needed was bought with Government funds and was of standard, well-selected design. All office corridors had to be kept clear of cupboards. No files were ever allowed to be piled up on tables or on the tops of cupboards. Enough equipment was bought to accommodate everything needed for daily work: the rest was put in archives in the basement or weeded out periodically and destroyed. This is common practice in every modern office; but it was a novelty in Palestine at that time for everything to be kept ship-shape. We achieved a high aesthetic level in the offices, which, I am sure, had some influence on the aesthetic level of our programmes. In any case, the staff felt that they were being treated as ladies and gentlemen and behaved as such.

The national Jewish bodies in Palestine — the Jewish Agency and the National Council of the Jewish Community — had been particularly concerned, ever since the P.B.S. had been founded in 1936, with seeing that 'Jewish rights' were protected. A Jewish advisory broadcasting committee had been appointed by these bodies and was recognised by the Palestine Government. It was in existence when I took over, but, as I was Jewish myself, it was immediately obvious that *I* did not need to be told what were Jewish interests. In fact, I was by now sufficiently trusted — not only by the Jewish national bodies but also by the Jewish press — as to make an advisory committee really unnecessary. We were usually far ahead of public opinion in our programme planning. Nevertheless, I arranged for Mordechai Zlotnik, Karl Salomon, and our Hebrew news-room staff and producers to accompany me to meetings to which I regularly invited the members of the advisory committee. Anything difficult I arranged beforehand privately with the chairman of the committee, Mr Zalman Shragai, a leading member of the Orthodox Jewish community, later to be a Mayor of Western Jerusalem. The only thing that the committee persistently requested that I was unable to provide was an additional Hebrew *short*-wave service. As this was wanted as an additional means of contact between the *Yishuv* (the nascent Jewish state) and the Diaspora, the British administration in Palestine would not authorise it. They feared that it would increase the pressure of Jewish immigration on Palestine, in defiance of the White Paper policy that the Cabinet in London had decided to maintain. It was only after 1948 that the Jewish Agency was able to establish *Kol Zion* ('The Voice of Zion') as Israel's short wave service to the Diaspora.

It was in collaboration with the committee that we introduced broadcasting in Hebrew to the independent Jewish school network. I think we were the first station in the Middle East to broadcast to schools. After the end of the Mandate, such broadcasts were dropped by *Kol Yisrael* ('The Voice of Israel' — our successor) owing to lack of interest by the new Ministry of Education and Culture. It was not until many years later, thanks to support given by Mr Abba Eban when he took over that Ministry, that they were restarted. I had exactly the same difficulty with the Mandatory Department of Education, who were strongly opposed at first to broadcasts in Arabic to Government schools. But in view of the success of the Hebrew broadcasts, school broadcasts in Arabic were eventually approved and radio receivers bought by the Government for a number of its schools.

★ ★ ★

The P.B.S. tried to maintain close relations with its listeners in Palestine. For that purpose, three illustrated radio weeklies were published jointly with the Public Information Office, which supplied the illustrations and half the articles and undertook the printing and distribution. One had been a privately-owned English language weekly in Jerusalem, entitled *Jerusalem Calling* which was taken over by the P.I.O. During the war, an illustrated British propaganda magazine in Arabic was founded by the P.I.O. in Palestine which was eventually called *Al Kafileh* ('The Caravan'). A similar illustrated Hebrew weekly was called *HaGalgal* ('The Wheel'): this was the only one of the three that became self-supporting. Each of these three magazines — in English, Arabic and Hebrew — was a combination of advance programmes (like the B.B.C. weekly *Radio Times*) with reprints of talks and so on (as in the B.B.C. weekly *The Listener*). Each language issue was different; but all three developed a high level of discrimination among many listeners. Regrettably, our successor, *Kol Yisrael*, has never been given a Government grant big enough to enable it to publish its own Hebrew radio magazine: several attempts to do this on a commercial basis have failed. I regard the absence of such a radio magazine today as one of the few defects in the present admirable broadcasting service in Israel.

We tried to keep in touch with our listeners by every other possible means. Shortly after I took over the P.B.S. in 1945, I went to England to study B.B.C. methods. I was not only in London but was sent to one of the B.B.C. regional stations — the Western Region at Bristol — which was of a size comparable with that of the P.B.S. Its remarkable head, Mr Beadle, spent much of his time attending meetings of all kinds of associations in his area — for example, farmers' clubs — in order to find out, as an observer, in what people were really interested in. He then geared his broadcasting programme accordingly. I also studied the B.B.C.'s excellent listeners' research bureau in London. On my return to Jerusalem, I appointed someone in the Hebrew section to do listener research, which was a great help to us in our forward programme planning. All sections of the P.B.S. took steps to answer every listener's letter and to weigh carefully every single suggestion for future programmes.

In order to help serious listeners to understand our programme policy, I gave a weekly fifteen-minute talk myself called *Between Ourselves*. In it, I publicly thanked listeners by name for any suggestions that we had decided to adopt. I also explained in detail why other suggestions could not be used for one reason or another. The controllers of the Hebrew and Arabic sections gave their own weekly talks in those languages under the same generic title — *Between Ourselves*. They incorporated some of what I had said but included much new matter of their own. From time to time, the controller of music conducted a similar dialogue with the many serious listeners to our musical programmes.

As with all radio stations, our listening audience was very mixed. We had listeners who wanted more music and less talks; and listeners who wanted more talks and less music. Among the music-lovers were those who wanted more classical orchestral music, more opera, more vocalists, more light music, more dance music, more popular songs, more oriental music, more Jewish cantoral music. In order to induce a more tolerant attitude by each set of enthusiasts towards all the others, we embarked on a series of public meetings on programme policy. We persuaded different Jewish municipalities in turn to hire a hall. We ourselves advertised on all our Hebrew programmes that, on a given evening, a team from the P.B.S., including myself, would appear on the platform and answer criticisms from the floor, of our programmes. The admission ticket to the meeting was merely a paid-up radio licence. As the P.B.S. team of about a dozen always included several popular announcers with whose voices the audience was very familiar, but whom they had never *seen*, the hall was invariably packed out.

Every member of the P.B.S. team on the platform had a microphone in front of him, connected both to loud-speakers in the hall and to our radio transmitters at Ramallah. In order to eliminate silly questions and prevent members of the audience 'hogging the mike', all questions had to be sent up to the platform on slips of paper, which ushers moved around the hall to collect. One of our producers went through the pile of questions and read out the most interesting. I then indicated which member of the team should reply. As the proceedings were being broadcast simultaneously all over Palestine, a very wide listening audience was obtained. Similar meetings were held from time to time by the music section (for music lovers only) and by the Arabic section.

I was told by the B.B.C. that these public meetings were, at that time, the most imaginative effort at establishing close relations with listeners ever attempted. They only wished that they could do the same; but their listening audiences were far too big.

In addition to my weekly talks on programme policy, I allowed myself, from time to time, a short series of English talks. One series was on current civic affairs. Another was a series of readings from selected English prose. But the most successful was a series of broadcast poetry readings, inspired by listening to a reading given in Jerusalem to a small group by Christopher Scaife, from the British Institute in Cairo. I rehearsed these talks over and over until I was satisfied that I was able to convey every shade of the poet's meaning as simply as possible. To do this, I had myself to understand all the implications of the poem. I went through dozens of anthologies in order to select poems for this programme, and I asked listeners to send in their own suggestions. But it gradually became clear that few poems in English were suitable for broadcasting to non-British audiences. Long poems were no good, as also poems with many place-names unfamiliar to foreign audiences; or poems which touched on Christian dogma that either Christian listeners might find offensive coming from a Jerusalem station or that grated on the ears of Jewish listeners — the majority.

I started my first programme with short lyrical poems; but I eventually tackled abstruse and complex modern poets. In those cases, instead of reading many poems in one programme, I devoted the whole fifteen-minute programme to one short poem, explaining the meaning of every uncommon word and of every line. I re-read every two or three lines over and over again until the whole poem became clear. To help listeners, the text of the poem was printed in advance in the English radio weekly. This I am afraid, was in complete disregard of overseas copyright laws; but no one objected. I still give public poetry readings from time to time at the Y.M.C.A. and the Khan Theatre in Jerusalem.

CHAPTER 12

THE END OF THE MANDATE, 1948

The last three years of the Mandate were, politically, the most difficult of all. The Jewish population was up-in-arms against the White Paper policy of restrictions on Jewish immigration and land purchase. In addition to the *Hagana*, two dissident Jewish terrorist organizations were operating — the Revisionist *Irgun Zvai Leumi (Etzel)* ('National Military Organization') and its even more vindictive off-shoot, the Stern Group *Lochamey Herut Yisrael (Lehi)* ('The Fighters for the Freedom of Israel'). Members of *Lehi* confined their vendetta largely against the British police. But to the *Etzel*, the P.B.S., as the Government radio station broadcasting Government communiques, was anathema and a natural target. The studios in Queen Melisande Lane were on the edge of the Jewish quarter and were heavily wired in and guarded. Although most of our staff, participating artists and listeners were Jewish, our resident guards were, of all things, a detachment from the Arab Legion (originally trained by Glubb.) They had been brought over from Trans-Jordan to form part of the British garrison. One detachment was stationed with their machine-guns on our roof. I inspected them from time to time, but always in the company of one of their own Arab officers. Otherwise, when they saw the trap-door to the roof being opened, they were apt to shoot first and then ask who you were. They were very well-disciplined; and, although we had dozens of Jewish men, women and children visiting the studios at all hours of the day and night to participate in programmes, we never had a single complaint against any member of the Arab Legion, in spite of the excited state of public feeling outside.

However, one day, another Arab Legion unit passing through Ben Shemen — a Jewish village in the foothills — thought it was being attacked and opened fire, with casualties on both sides. Expecting reprisals, I moved the whole of our Jewish staff overnight to the *Beth HaHalutzot* ('Pioneer Girls' Hostel'), well inside the Jewish quarter of Rehavia, where (Jewish) G.P.O. radio engineers installed new studios. And there the Hebrew and music sections stayed until the end of the Mandate.

Before the end of the Mandate, Arab hostility towards the Partition plan, even though it had been rejected by the British Government, endangered the lives of all my British P.B.S. staff. Alex Josey, who had replaced Roy Elston as controller of news, was *plus royaliste que le roi:* his political commentaries infuriated Jewish listeners. So the British P.B.S. staff were all moved to a wired-in British security zone in the German Colony, where so many British families lived.

As a result of this split-up, no member of the P.B.S. (except myself—see page 227) was ever attacked during my three years of office.

A lot depended on the ability to keep one jump ahead. In November, 1947, I was in my cottage near Tiberias when the radio announced that Partition had been approved by the U.N. There was dancing in the streets in every Jewish town and village: but I was sure that very soon there would be Arab reprisals. So I came back home to Jerusalem the long way round, through Tel Aviv, instead of by the far shorter route through the fanatically Moslem town of Nablus. The police announced later that, that morning, a car with several Jewish passengers on the main road through Nablus had been ambushed and all the occupants murdered.

★ ★ ★

Meanwhile, Sir Henry Gurney had taken over as Chief Secretary, his principal function being to liquidate the Mandate. He had had no previous connection with Palestine nor any special affection for it. Summoning a meeting of all heads of department, including myself, he cold-bloodedly announced that there was to be no formal handing-over to any Jewish or Arab nationalist body or even to any local authority. Before Britain pulled out of Palestine, all lunatics were to be released from Government asylums and all convicts from the gaols. Some of the senior (Christian) heads of departments present at that meeting, who had devoted much of their lives to building up Palestine, protested vehemently against this scorched-earth policy. But they were overruled.

Subsequently, I had a somewhat ridiculous personal interview with Gurney. One Saturday morning, when I was in a dirty pair of grey flannel trousers, messing about with my car, I received an urgent telephone call to see Sir Henry. I was very annoyed and rather ostentatiously went as I was, still wearing a frayed pull-over.

'I suppose you realise, Sir,' I began, as soon as I got to

Gurney's office 'that this is my day off!' He motioned me to a chair and mildly said: 'I've been instructed by the Secretary of State for the Colonies to inquire whether you're prepared to accept a C.M.G. The Honours List is being published on Monday.' 'Oh, well, Sir,' I stammered. 'In *those* circumstances, of course, Sir . . .'

The Mandate was shortly coming to an end, and I had to decide what I should do next. I had offered my services to the U.N. as director of their radio station, should Jerusalem become internationalised: but it did not. As an established (i.e., pensionable) British Colonial civil servant, I was eligible for transfer, with or without promotion, to some other overseas dependency. But there were few such dependencies left. Furthermore, I had to remember that, in fact, I was in the Colonial Service primarily in order to be in Palestine, and not in Palestine because I was in the Colonial Service. I had only another five years to go (55 was then the maximum retiring age): it seemed pointless to eke out my remaining days in Hong Kong. The minimum retiring age was fifty; so I decided to take my pension and go. That would reduce by one the number of British officials in Palestine for whom harassed Colonial Office had to find new jobs elsewhere. My application to resign, in consequence, was warmly received. I was even given an extra gratuity to compensate me for 'interruption of career'. When I told the Colonial Office that I was not eligible for this as my career had come to its natural close, they said, in effect: 'Look, we have quite enough problems as it is, so take the gratuity and shut up!': which I did.

While waiting for our turn to be evacuated, Hadassah and I drank up all our remaining cases of good French wine. We sat, night after night, gently sozzling, on the floor of our sitting-room, to avoid the risk of being hit by a stray bullet coming through the window. It was economical, enjoyable and morale-building. The situation in Jerusalem as a whole a month before the end of the Mandate is given at the end of this chapter (pp. 232–251). I wrote it at the time for my own record.

★　★　★

Some five years earlier, during World War II, I had already given some thought to what I should do when I retired. I then planned to stay on in Palestine and run some kind of training-school for Palestinian civil servants. During my visit to Britain in 1943 (see page 193), I had consulted a friend of my father's at Oxford, Sir Richard Livingstone, then Master of Corpus, and one of the leading authorities on adult education. He advised me to concentrate on supplementary in-service training. Otherwise, if I indulged in pre-entry training, I should become little more than an employment agency.

I followed his advice and, immediately after the war, in 1945, started by establishing the Jerusalem Tutorial Classes. These were a series of adult evening lectures, given at the Y.M.C.A. in English. Eight parallel series, each of 22 weekly lectures, were given to groups limited to a maximum of twenty-five students for any one series. No student was allowed to enrol in more than two courses at a time. Of the 150 students who enrolled (mostly civil servants) about a third were Arab and two-thirds were Jewish. Every six months, we started a new series of courses. Our lectures included Palestinian Jews and Arabs, British civil servants and even the United States Consul in Jerusalem. All the administrative work was undertaken by volunteers, led by Mordechai HaCohen (then a civil servant, now a Ph.D. on Wall Street, New York). The whole operation was started on £100 given to me by my friend Sir Simon (later Lord) Marks, then managing director of Marks and Spencer in London. He and his fellow directors, and various other friends in Britain, the U.S.A., Italy and Israel, have given me continuous support on a small scale ever since this administrative training venture was started. It was the first to be established and is older than the State.

Encouraged by the success of the tutorial classes in Jerusalem in English, the following year (1946) I started similar courses in Tel Aviv in Hebrew. There I had the co-operation of the Municipality. The key role was played by Miss Gila Uriel, who had started her career as secretary to the first Mayor of Tel Aviv — Meir Dizengoff. The following year, in Jerusalem, I invited some of the more serious tutorial students to join an eighteen-months' diploma course in public administration, involving six subjects, each with an examination, a pair of subjects every six months. The level of the course was that of the then London University diploma of public administration. Our course was intended for central and local government officials with from five to ten years' service who had not had a complete higher education before entry. They had, however, acquired a practical knowledge of office management, so it was not necessary to teach that: what they lacked was a theoretical background. The six subjects, all obligatory, were the history of political thought; introductory courses on economics and statistics; the structure of government in Palestine (later in Israel); the relations between central and local government; and, finally, the economic and social development of the Middle East.

Before Britain decided to pull out of Palestine, I had hoped to remain in Jerusalem, running an institute of public administration. I had persuaded the Palestine Government to provide me with free accommodation in the (Arab) Mamilla district — two seminar rooms, a library and office on the top floor of an existing rented Government office-building. They also gave me a small grant with which I had made some specially-designed furniture. In view of the interest shown in this diploma course by other countries — in particular the British administration of the Sudan—I had hopes of students from abroad and hence called it the Middle East Institute of Public Administration. I set up a nominal board of governors, headed by my friend Walter Eytan, then on the political staff of the Jewish Agency, now Israel Ambassador to France. In addition to the eight tutorial classes (two a night), we started the diploma course with twenty-five students of whom twenty were Jews and five Arabs. I myself gave the course on the structure of government in Palestine.

But, with the deterioration of public order in the city, we had to move from the Mamilla district to a Jewish area to which the Jewish students could safely come: but the Arab students had to drop out. Then the Jewish students themselves began to be involved more and more in *Hagana* duties in the evening and we had to suspend the courses altogether.

★　★　★

I was due to be repatriated to England in May, 1948, at the end of the Mandate. But, in February, I was wounded in a bomb explosion while visiting the Jewish Agency building. I had gone to discuss with Eytan the provision by the Jewish American Consul-General's car—well-known to the be, in place of that at Ramallah, already in Arab hands. My visit coincided with the arrival in the courtyard of the American Consul-General's car — well-known to the Jewish Agency's security guards. They allowed the Arab driver to enter and park it just below Eytan's office window. The driver — who had been suborned by Arab terrorists — sauntered away. The car, however, somewhat blocked the traffic in the courtyard and one of the security guards moved it to the other side, luckily for me. For, a few minutes later, a time bomb in the boot blew up, with terrific force, shattering the wall above. Eight people in all were killed, including everyone in the courtyard. All the windows facing the courtyard, including those in Eytan's office, were blown in and I was rather severely wounded about the face by splintered glass. I remember being afraid of a second bomb going off, and, half-dazed, making my own way out into the street through the shambles of the more se-riously wounded, the dying and the dead. My wife was in town; but, hearing the explosion and knowing where I had gone, came to look for me. She found me wandering in the street and took me to the house of a surgeon friend near-by to be sewn up. I was subsequently consoled by one of my Arab P.B.S. staff members who assured me that there had been nothing personal in this attack.

Three weeks later, I was involved in a further incident that was definitely personal. I was at Thomas Cook's office, just outside the barbed-wire fence of one of the British security zones, registering my heavy baggage for shipment back to England. I was recognised by an Arab clerk, a nationalist at heart. I was told later that he had telephoned through to the headquarters of the Arab terrorist movement in the Old City that I was on Cook's premises. As I came out on to the street, some Arab caught me by the arm. I dislike being handled and threw his hand off. I then noticed two other Arabs standing by, one with a pistol — a little pearl-handled affair. Between me and the armed British sentry at the gate of the security zone, a heavy lorry had been drawn up by a fourth Arab. It had been ingeniously parked so as to prevent the sentry from seeing what was happening. Lower down the street, a smaller car was waiting, with a fifth Arab, in which, as I learned later, I was to be bundled and taken, as a hostage, into the Old City, then wholly in Arab nationalist hands.

Luckily for me, that day I did not have on me my own pistol. If I had tried to draw it, I would probably have, first, shot myself in the foot and, then, been shot dead. (Unless one is a professional gunman, it is almost impossible to draw a pistol from a holster and fire it before one's assailant can himself shoot.) I decided to run for it and whipped round the back of the lorry, covering in record time the few dozen yards to the barbed-wire fence, over which I somehow managed to leap. As I ran, the man with the pistol fired at me three times point blank. Two bullets were luckily duds; the third went wide. I found out later from one of my Arab P.B.S. staff members that my assailant was a well-known gang-leader. He had subsequently been demoted for failure of a mission: I was not very sorry for him. He had then apparently taken the pearl-handled pistol to the dealer and demanded his money back as it had not shot straight.

By this time, after two escapes within three weeks, I was feeling rather the worse for wear. The Government consequently advanced the date of my repatriation from May to April. Hadassah was very disinclined to leave Palestine at all at this juncture; but I said I would not go until she had gone. We eventually agreed that she could return later, if she wished, when things had settled down a bit. This she did with our younger son Dan who came out from Balliol as a volunteer to participate in the Israel War of Independence.

It was not easy for either of us to escape from the besieged city. Hadassah went down to the Dead Sea with the last potash lorry convoy, escorted by British troops. From there she was flown by a Jewish Agency two-seater Piper Cub communications plane to Tel Aviv, whence she was ferried to Lydda airport, by then almost surrounded by armed Arab irregulars. The Piper Cub was so small that it had to go back and pick up her suitcase.

A week after she was flown out, I was due myself to leave. My non-Jewish colleagues were being taken by road to Lydda airport in motor-buses under British police escort. In spite of the police escort, these buses were being searched for Jews at Arab nationalist road-blocks in the hills outside Jerusalem.

The British police decided that there was quite a risk of my being taken out and shot. So, together with another Anglo-Jewish civil servant, Henry Baker (now back as President of the Jerusalem district court), I was hidden in a British police armoured car and taken along the Ramallah road to the Kalandia air strip some eight miles away (since 1967, the airport of reunified Jerusalem). The police driver had instructions to crash through any Arab nationalist road-blocks and not to stop on any account whatsoever. From

Kalandia we, and a few other evacuees, were flown by a small R.A.F. communications plane to Lydda.

Unfortunately, the big plane that was due to take us and all our other British colleagues to England had not arrived. (I was told later that someone had forgotten to order it!) So we all had to wait in the airport and were given some of the staff quarters there to sleep in. I was woken in the middle of the first night by the clandestine *Hagana* intelligence officer in the airport. He had been tipped off by one of his Arab agents that I had been recognised once more by Arab nationalists on the airport staff who might try to shoot me or kidnap me. I went up to the top of the airport control tower where I found a young Englishman named Frank Butler in charge of air traffic control (he was later to marry the daughter of Chaim Arlosorov). It took two more days for our plane to arrive, during which time Butler guarded me while I slept and I guarded him whenever he slept. Eventually, I was escorted by the *Hagana* intelligence officer to the plane and gave him my pistol as a parting present. That night all Jewish airport staff were evacuated: next day the whole airport fell into Arab nationalist hands. After its recapture by Jewish troops in the Israel War of Independence, it became the first Israel tank training school under Brigadier Haim Laskov (later to be a Chief of Staff). My son Dan (who had been in a British armoured unit) became Laskov's chief instructor; the old generation handed over to the new.

★   ★   ★

My wife and Dan met me in London. I was by now in a sorry state of nerves. I remember that it was the Queen's birthday and we strolled in Hyde Park. As the procession went by, we stood on a bench to see better. At that moment, an artillery battery behind us fired a royal salute. I did not hesitate and seconds later was taking cover under the bench.

★ ★ ★

Although I had retired from the Colonial Service at my own wish, I was then heartbroken at the turn of events. All my life's work in Palestine seemed to have gone down the drain. Today, those thirty years of British rule are seen to be the foundations on which the State of Israel has now been built. In order to get the chagrin out my system, I decided to write an *administrative* history of Palestine under British Mandate. Chatham House agreed to publish it and, in fact, gave me office accommodation and a typist. During the year in which I taught at Dropsie College in Philadelphia, I continued working on the book on week-ends in the Library of Congress in Washington, D.C. I wrote to some of my former colleagues in the Palestine Government and got them to check each chapter as it was written. Eventually, Chatham House decided *not* to publish the book, ostensibly because of a rapid increase in costs. But I fancy that the real reasons were, first, that the book was either too late or too early and, secondly that I was not senior enough to write it. I now realise that it was, in fact, not a very good book; but I was very disappointed at the time.

I did not like living alone in a hotel room in Philadelphia. Nor did I like the absence of proper office facilities at Dropsie College, in spite of the fact that I was a visiting professor. At the end of the first year, I refused President Abraham

Neuman's invitation to stay on for a further year in the so-called Israel Institute that he had established, with two other professors from Jerusalem and myself. It was by now clear to me that Neuman had no real intention of allowing the Israel Institute to develop. So I returned to London in the summer of 1949. Hadassah was back in Israel. I stayed for a while with my parents to await developments. I had little hope of employment by the new Israel Government as I had been, first, a British colonial civil servant and, secondly, I was well-known to have been opposed to partition. But Hadassah persuaded Zeev Sharef, then secretary to the Cabinet, and Gershon Agron, then head of the Israel Government's information services, to invite me out as an advisor on the new Israel broadcasting service. Before the end of the Mandate, I had supplied Sharef with several memoranda on the future government for a Jewish Agency committee of which he had been chairman. These included notes on the Ministry of Finance and, in particular, its personnel division; on staff recruitment and training; on the Ministry of the Interior and the passport office. I had a high opinion of Sharef's abilities and was glad to work again under his aegis (he is now a Cabinet Minister). The late Gershon Agron, founder and editor of the *Palestine Post* (now the *Jerusalem Post*) and, later, Mayor of Jerusalem, was an old friend. So, in the autumn of 1949, I returned to Israel, not knowing if I would be shot by *Irgun* or *Lehi* terrorists as a 'traitor', as had happened to some of my colleagues, for example Witold Hulanicki.

THE LAST DAYS OF MANDATED JERUSALEM

The security situation in Jerusalem began seriously to deteriorate in 1946, when a wing of the King David Hotel was blown up. By the beginning of 1947, all British wives and children were evacuated and all other British subjects, with the exception of journalists, missionaries etc., were required to live and work in Security Zones .

Talbia was almost the only area in Jerusalem where Jews, Arabs and British residents still lived together in peace. It formed a little zone of its own, surrounded by a barbed-wire perimeter fence, with the entrance guarded by two armed British police constables and armed Jewish and Arab municipal police patrols wandering about inside in separate groups of two or four. But the strain of living in a mixed area was considerable. Although we had lived there for fourteen years, I had been on the Arab list of Government officials to be assassinated in the First Arab Rebellion. Since that time, we had been very cautious: we never sat near lighted windows at night, unless the shutters were down: we always looked out of the window by day when the front door bell rang in order to see who was there, before opening the door. The front door was of iron and was locked at night: when the Second Arab Rebellion began, we had keys made for the iron back door which we also began to keep locked at night.

Still, I developed a habit of constant listening, whenever I was at home, for cars passing down our street and even for footsteps outside. I looked out of the window each time to see whether the visitors were strangers or residents — friends or foes. If they were unknown, I watched to see where they went and what they did. This was quite a strain: I could never relax; but one's first preoccupation all the time was the primitive desire to keep alive; always to be on one's guard and never to be taken unawares. Even when walking in the Jewish quarters, I developed the habit of glancing back to see who was walking behind me; of being cautious when young men in motor cars drew up nearby: being kidnapped by the *Irgun Zvai Leumi* or the Stern Gang was always a possibility.

This constant sense of awareness was accentuated by the sporadic shooting that took place all over the city. At night, the rattle of fire echoed loudly round the hills. I acquired the art of estimating whether it was Yemin Moshe or Mekor Haim that was the scene of attack; whether it was Jews or Arabs who were firing; whether they were using rifles, sten-guns or machine-guns. Occasionally there was the loud crunch of mortar bombs, or the even louder crack when the army fired a round from one of the guns at an Arab or Jewish defence post that persisted in indiscriminate shooting. Every day or so, sometimes several times a day, there was a pro-longed roar as some building was blown up by bombs. If at night, the attackers would be greeted by a hail of rifle and machine-gun fire from the defenders, rising to a crescendo: then the bomb would explode, the attackers would with-draw and there would be silence.

Wherever one went, there was the risk of being hit by stray shots: one developed the habit of choosing the more sheltered side of the road, of avoiding certain roads and open spaces altogether, of taking short cuts through well protected alley-ways. The guards at road-blocks would warn you if there was sniping nearby: you then waited behind a wall until it stopped; or you ran for it.

Very few people went out after dark: the cinemas were almost deserted. The risk of their being blown up by bombs brought in motor vehicles was considerable. All approaches were sealed off by barriers, and public meetings and crowded halls were discouraged.

At the beginning of the Second Arab Rebellion, the road-blocks at the entrance to the Jewish quarters were wooden trestles: but after the *Palestine Post*, Ben Yehuda Street and Jewish Agency explosions, sections of iron girders were set vertically in concrete in pits dug in the roads all over the Jewish areas. As Jewish hostility to the British security forces mounted, breast-high barricades were built of dressed stone blocks taken from bombed buildings: (I saw one such barricade of which the lower courses were stone: on top were piled several more courses composed of packets of *matzot**, of identical size, being unloaded from a lorry prior to being taken into a nearby shop). Later still, these barricades were provided with loopholes and covered by *Hagana* men in uniform with tommy-guns in concrete pill-boxes to the rear. To prevent *Irgun Zvai Leumi* and Stern Gang raiding-parties in stolen vehicles from forcing their way out of the Jewish quarters, and to prevent British army and police

---

* Unleavened Passover bread.

234

vehicles from forcing their way in, all Jewish roadblocks were provided with heavy iron bar swing gates, which were only lifted when the vehicles had been stopped and searched. The rear compartments of all cars were also searched.

At all British security zone gates facing the Jewish quarters, a Jewish road barrier was also erected, so that there was a double check. When the Arabs adopted the technique of rolling lorries filled with explosives down-hill into Jewish quarters, more iron bars were set vertically in the roads beyond the Jewish road barriers wherever the road sloped down towards them. As I left Jerusalem, a tall massive concrete wall, with loop-holes, was being built all along one side of King George Avenue as defence against Arab snipers firing from the Mamilla road over the cemetery.

Under pressure of events, the *Hagana* in Jerusalem was considerably reinforced from outside and acquired more and more authority. They introduced their own system of identity cards — for example, for British press correspondents. No Jew of military age was allowed to leave Jerusalem by *Hagana* convoy without a *Hagana* permit. They refused to let Jewish-owned cars go outside the Jewish areas (even into the British security zones) without a permit. Luckily, I had sold my car to the International Red Cross the day this new control was introduced. All British army and police vehicles entering the Jewish quarters were not only searched by the *Hagana* but escorted, if necessary; and sometimes even refused admission.

As a result of Arab attacks on Jewish road convoys and on the railways, there was an acute shortage of petrol in the Jewish areas of Jerusalem; and similarly in the Arab areas, owing to Jewish attacks on Arab traffic. The Jewish authorities introduced a rationing system in March: first priorities were given to *Hagana* transport and the food and arms convoys returning empty to Tel Aviv and the armoured convoys for Tel Aviv. Second priorities were given to other essential users in Jerusalem — doctors, for example. Many private cars were laid up or had to try to get petrol from Arab-run petrol-pumps in Zones A and B, at risk of being kidnapped or the car stolen by armed Arabs. Some Jewish taxi-drivers were buying black-market petrol from soldiers at double the normal price. Even so, there was always an enormous queue at the two remaining petrol pumps in the Jewish quarters, and filling up, even for priority users, involved a wait of several hours.

Earlier, I had laid my own car up in my garage partly for this reason, partly owing to the risk of theft by either Arabs or Jews, and partly because my licence and insurance expired on 9th April, and I did not want to renew them in view of my imminent evacuation. As a matter of fact, the Prudential Insurance Company refused to extend my riot insurance in any case, in view of the constant deterioration of the situation. Every day, half-a-dozen more cars were stolen and their particulars broadcast nightly by the P.B.S. to warn people in case some of the cars would be used for carrying explosives for further surprise bomb attacks on buildings. Other cars were stolen by Arab guerillas or Jewish terrorists for the transport of their fighting squads. Both the P.B.S. cars were stolen in this way by armed Arabs, as well as the private car of one of my news staff. Armed British traffic policeman had to be stationed in the car park outside the Public Information Office: even so, cars were stolen from there. Several consular cars were also stolen, as well as most of the General Post Office, Public Works Department and Public Health Department cars and many police armoured cars.

Hagana armoured cars were also stolen by the *Irgun Zvai Leumi*. In some cases the Government suspended postal services until postal vans were returned.

In any case, having a private car in Jerusalem was quite useless after December, 1947. It was impossible for me to drive anywhere outside the Jewish quarters; my maximum range for the previous months had been a strip about three miles by two. When the High Commissioner asked me to come out to Government House to lunch and to discuss his broadcast appeal for a truce, I had to go through the Arab road-blocks in a Government House car with an armed British police sergeant driver.

As the Arab bomb attacks on Jewish buildings in Jerusalem intensified, more and more road-blocks were set up and more and more roads were closed to traffic: Jewish parking regulations became more and more stringent. Every time I passed into the Jewish quarters from Talbia or from Zone B, I had to get out and open up the rear luggage compartment of the car to be searched for explosives. All parcels were suspect, while a suitcase was almost enough to warrant summary arrest by the *Hagana* and detention. Even to take my heavy suitcase on foot from Rehavia to the Chief Justice's house to be picked up for despatch in the police road convoy to Lydda airport was a delicate operation. I got someone to help me carry it by a circuitous route which avoided all Jewish road-blocks. To take things *out* of the Jewish quarters was almost as suspect as to bring them in; although I must say that, as soon as the *Hagana* guards recognised me or saw my name on my identity papers, they were usually very helpful and polite. I then had to negotiate the military road-blocks at the western entrance to Zone B: the corporal of the guard required the suitcase to be searched before admitting it. The Chief Justice's housekeeper was equally suspicious, although the Chief Justice had told her that I was coming

I also had fantastic difficulties in moving some of my furniture and household effects from Talbia to Rehavia before I left. A small pick-up was used, and two porters: three journeys were made. The distance between the terminal points was less than a thousand yards: the charge was £20 for a morning's work.

But before the furniture could be moved at all, I had to get special *Hagana* permission, as no Jews were allowed to move their furniture from mixed areas into Jewish areas as this meant 'abandoning Jewish positions.' I only managed to secure permission because I was leaving some of my furniture behind in Talbia and had sub-let my flat to another Jewish family. The fact that I had been ordered by the High Commissioner to leave Palestine before the termination of the Mandate was no argument: if anything, it made the situation worse.

Hagana permission having been given to move the furniture (and only through a specified road-block), I had great difficulty in getting the pick-up, the driver and the porters admitted to the Talbia Zone. The British police guards at the entrance to the zone refused to allow them in without permits issued by the army: the army refused to issue permits unless the driver and porters appeared before them in person. In the end, I had to persuade the major in charge of the Pass Office to come in person to the Zone gate at 7.30 a.m. to issue the permits as the pick-up rolled in. The drivers and porters were scared to come to Talbia in any case, so the armed Jewish municipal police patrols in Talbia had to come down with them to my house. There was shooting in Katamon, a few hundred yards away all through the loading operations.

Some of the furniture was being stored in an empty flat opposite the Jewish Agency: and, although I had arranged with the *Hagana* area commander for Talbia to inspect my packing cases before they were closed, the *Hagana* guards near the Jewish Agency (the holy of holies) refused to accept his word and insisted on re-opening all the cases (they had taken weeks to pack). It took two hours of negotiation to persuade them to drop that demand.

Hagana pressure on Jewish residents increased continually. I lived in a mixed quarter and, as a Government official, was expected to have no contact with or even knowledge of *Hagana* operations. Nevertheless, as early as January, 1948, I was being pressed to allow a *Hagana* defence post, complete with hand-grenades, to be established in my flat. I was told that my house was strategically so situated that the protection of the ninety Jewish families in Talbia could not be guaranteed unless a defence post was established in my flat. After much discussion, I agreed to an unarmed look-out post being established there for a fortnight in February when feelings in Talbia were tense following an idiotic attempt by the *Hagana* to force all the Arab landlords to leave. The *Hagana* area commander behaved with much more consideration than was normal; in purely Jewish quarters the *Hagana* just occupied any flats they took a fancy to, whether the occupants agreed or not. But the *Hagana* were very anxious that I should not leave Talbia. I had lived there for fourteen years and, if I left, many other Jewish families would leave too.

The trouble in dealing with the *Hagana* was that every-thing was wrapped in secrecy. As they were still not a legally recognized organization, this was inevitable. But whenever I challenged a local *Hagana* decision (such as the attempt to force the Arab landlords of Talbia to leave) I was told that this was 'on instructions from headquarters.' (In this particular case, I subsequently discovered that this was untrue and was the light-hearted and unauthorised decision of the *Hagana* sector commander). As I was the head of a Government department, I felt it wiser not to ask any direct questions about *Hagana* affairs: I was voluntarily told a little and inferred a good deal more; but my situation was very awkward.

There were *Hagana* levies, supposed to be voluntary, but actually based on house-rate assessment, which also had to be paid. This I did willingly, as the *Hagana* never descended to the *Irgun Zvai Leumi* and Stern Gang methods of naked extortion.

The relations of the *Hagana* with my P.B.S. Jewish staff were also a matter of considerable delicacy. Officially, no Jewish Government officer was expected to be a member of the *Hagana;* but, in fact many of them were. As long as they were only on part-time duty and their *Hagana* work did not interfere too seriously with their official work, I said nothing. A few of the younger members of the staff were 'conscripted' and resigned: one or two, however, went off on whole-time operations without notification and had to be dismissed. One was killed in a punitive field operation against Arabs on the Ramallah-Latrun road near Atarot: it was not easy for me to explain to the Government, when officially reporting his death, how it was that, as a Government officer, he had been involved in this operation.

Jerusalem was packed with *Hagana* reinforcements, mostly from Tel Aviv. I am reliably informed that there were from two to three thousand of them. They wore winter khaki battle-dress and grey or brown knitted woollen head-dresses or khaki tam-o-shanters. Some jackets had the shoulder badges of their former owners (I saw a girl with the pale blue badge of the British Army Palestine Regiment). Most of the Tel Avivians wore a badge of brass crossed-rifles over their breast-pocket. Others wore a blue-and-white enamel Zionist flag on their collar-flaps.

The Tel Avivians were mainly billeted and fed in private Jewish houses in Jerusalem. The war-time Service Men's *Menora* Club was reopened for them. Cinemas offered half-price admission for 'soldiers'. They seemed very well disciplined, with high morale. Their courage under fire was beyond question.

The smartest *Hagana* men in uniform were the newly-established military police, with white lanyards under the shoulder-straps of their pressed khaki jackets and a specially devised regimental cap-badge. But most men on operations dressed as commandos, with jerseys under their tunics, and heavy grey socks outside their trousers. They careered through the streets in armoured troop-carriers, sten-guns pointing out of the loopholes, singing lustily.

The *Irgun Zvai Leumi* mostly wore summer khaki drill and carried tommy-guns. They looked much more sinister. When they went on the rampage, *Hagana* mobile squads would rush out and try to chase them away. But, at other times, there would be tacit agreement between them: for example, the Jewish houses facing the Sheikh Jarrah quarter were an *Irgun Zvai Leumi* sector. In some cases, there was actual co-operation between the *Hagana* and the terrorists. In spite of the official *Hagana* denunciation of the Deir Yassin massacre, it is now established beyond doubt, and admitted by the *Hagana* commander, that he ordered the *Hagana* units nearby to give covering fire to the *Irgun Zvai Leumi* attacking squad who were pinned down by Arab fire from Deir Yassin. When asked why, he said it was not good for Jewish prestige for a Jewish unit, even of terrorists, to be forced by Arabs to retreat. And this was after the *Hagana* had twice told the *Irgun Zvai Leumi* that, in no circumstances, were they to attack Deir Yassin, which was friendly and quiescent.

The *Hagana* military communiques were broadcast daily from their own 'illegal' low-power transmitters in Jerusalem, Tel Aviv or Haifa, They were widely listened to by the Jewish population and accepted as wholly accurate, even the detailed figures of Arab casualties which were usually exaggerated and, in most cases, could not be based on anything more than assumptions. They were, however, much less exaggerated than the Arab claims of Jewish casualties. The Government communiques were based on British military and police reports, sometimes taken from Arab sources; they were disbelieved by most Jews when they ran counter to *Hagana* claims. But even the *Hagana* communiques, which sometimes omitted local defeats and withdrawals, were not so firmly accepted by the Jewish public towards the end of April; rumours of heavier Jewish losses than those publicly admitted received some credence.

The Jewish public in Jerusalem spent much time glued to its radio receivers. The Hebrew daily press from Tel Aviv arrived late, if at all, and a joint Jerusalem edition of the main Tel Aviv dailies was published in Jerusalem under the title of *Yediot Yerushalayim* ('Jerusalem News'). It was snapped up at once, as was also the local Jerusalem edition of the lunch-time newspaper *Yediot Aharonot* ('Latest News'). The latter was usually sold by newsboys on the streets with the invariable cry in Hebrew: 'Dozens of Arabs killed.' However, the anti-Arab feeling in the Jewish community seemed to be much less acute than the anti-British feeling.

With the continual disintegration of Governmental authority, the Jewish authorities took over in the Jewish areas of Jerusalem. At the best of times, loyalty to the Palestine Government, as such, was never very deep among either Jews or Arabs. Among Jews it was now almost non-existent. What the Jewish authorities decided superseded anything that the Palestine Government might decide. Partition, even in Jerusalem, was almost complete *de facto* and often *de jure* (such as splitting up Government departments, the Municipality, the banks and the police force). Although British security forces were still protecting the Jewish quarters of the Old City and patrolling the main Jerusalem–Tel Aviv road, the Jewish community was convinced that the *Hagana* could undertake these duties not only equally well but very much better and with much less interference in the matter of transporting arms. Meanwhile, there were frequent conflicts of jurisdiction between the 'old authorities' and the 'new authorities', such as the searching by the *Hagana* of British convoys through the Jewish quarters; dual roadblocks where the security zone gates abutted on Jewish quarters; and food and petrol rationing.

Food rationing in Jerusalem was under the control of the Jewish Community Council's Emergency Committee. Before November, this Council played a very minor role in Jewish affairs, being overshadowed by the Jewish Agency, the *Vaad Leumi**, the Jewish District Officers and the Jewish

* The National Council of the Jews of Palestine.

243

staff of the Municipality. The Emergency Committee contained a number of leading lawyers, merchants and transport experts who had worked feverishly to lay in supplies for a long siege and to organize rationing schemes. The work had been fairly well done, but they had learned the hard way and their public relations work was deplorable. The sudden introduction of bread rationing without any prior announcement, and the seizure of all bakers' stocks of flour, threw the Jewish population of Jerusalem into a complete panic. The executive side of the work was partly in the hands of the Civil Guard *(Mishmar Ha'am)* which was run by men seconded from the *Hagana*. It was an overt organization, the members of which wore distinctive armbands. They were part-time volunteers working on the same kind of roster system as Civil Defence workers in England during the war. They were mostly in the older age-groups.

The food and passenger armoured convoys between Tel Aviv and Jerusalem were organized jointly by the Emergency Committee and the *Hagana*. Their protection was a major military operation and involved the temporary occupation by the *Hagana* of several Arab villages between Jerusalem and Bab el Wad. For a week or so, the convoys ran very irregularly, owing to Arab attacks, and for some days they were suspended altogether. The effect on Jewish morale was disastrous, as the suspension was accompanied by heavy losses in the field and the sudden introduction of bread rationing and general panic. There was nothing in the food shops for sale, even tinned food; and for those who were too poor to have laid in reserves earlier, the situation was desperate.

As far as the food supply was concerned, the last few weeks

in Jerusalem were grim. There was practically no fresh fruit or vegetables or butter or milk or eggs: no fresh fish or meat whatsoever. (The only fresh meat I had was a cutlet one day at lunch at Government House and that involved my passing through Arab road-blocks.) All cakes and white flour vanished from the shops and the only bread was heavy, grey and indigestible — half a loaf per person per day. Sugar was severely rationed and, in cafes, saccharine only was served. I lived almost entirely on tinned food from war-time stocks and handed over quite a large part of them to my friends and relations before I left. They were very warmly received.

People with dogs were finding it almost impossible to feed them. No fuel oil for central heating was available in the Jewish quarters and we could have an occasional hot bath only by heating a tin of water over a kerosene stove. Kerosene was strictly rationed; but luckily we did most of our cooking with electricity. When I left Jerusalem, there was only three days' reserve of fuel oil for the electric power station; but some further supplies were brought in by the army after I had left. At my brother-in-law's house in Rehavia to which I moved for the last five days, there had been no water supply for a week and no baths at all until two days before I left.

The fuel shortage in the Arab quarters of Jerusalem was equally acute; but the supply of fresh fruit, vegetables, eggs, butter, milk and meat was much easier and the prices correspondingly lower.

With the gradual disintegration of the Palestine Government, one public service after the other was discontinued. Incoming surface mail was officially suspended and other postal services were discontinued daily. The trunk telephone lines from Jerusalem were out of action more often than not. Inland mail between the main towns took a week and more (when the mail bags were not stolen on the way). The quickest and safest route for letters was by *Hagana* armoured bus convoy: the fee for a letter from Jerusalem to Tel Aviv by this method was 3/–.

The progressive collapse of Governmental authority had its effect even on the most unsophisticated. An Arab peasant riding on a donkey on the wrong side of the road to Bethlehem justified himself by saying that there was no more Government (*Mafish Hakume*) and he could now do what he liked. Arabs and Jews in Jerusalem both carried arms openly in their respective quarters with or without permission: private motor vehicles were stopped and searched by anyone who claimed the right to do so: guards shot at sight if they thought fit: reprisal raids were carried out by any group that felt sufficiently vindictive.

The British military and police forces in Jerusalem were so reduced in strength that they could barely maintain existing guard and escort duties and protect themselves against theft and armed attack by both Jews and Arabs. There was no longer any mobile striking force available for restoring order or for punitive measures. Although about 200 armed members of the *Irgun Zvai Leumi* and the Stern Gang were in occupation of Deir Yassin for several days after the massacre of some 250 men, women and children, the army had not enough troops in Jerusalem to surround and capture the terrorists for whom they had waited so long. By the time bomber planes had been brought in from outside Palestine and permission obtained from the Air Ministry for the terrorist-occupied village to be bombed, the terrorists had withdrawn. In the same way, when three armoured vehicles in the *Hagana* convoy to the Hebrew

University and the Hadassah Hospital were destroyed by Arabs and eighty of the occupants were shot or burned alive, the Army units that arrived on the spot could not cope with the number of Arabs involved without recourse to artillery bombardment of the Arab positions for which authority did not come until it was too late. British authority was at the end reduced to 'negotiations' with the two contending parties, as in the rescue of the 120 *Hagana* men returning from Kfar Etzion and trapped in a house near Bethlehem by several thousand Arabs.

Not only was there constant theft of Government cars by armed Arabs and Jews, but Government stores and offices were being pilfered daily. Telephones were ripped out, furniture removed in lorries: no one even troubled to report such acts to the police as the few remaining police were powerless to intervene. As Government buildings were evacuated, they were promptly occupied by either armed Jews or armed Arabs as part of the plans for seizing strategic points in anticipation of the coming battle for Jerusalem after the end of the Mandate.

Under conditions such as these, running a Government department such as the Palestine Broadcasting Service became increasingly difficult. In earlier years, I expected a crisis a month: after November, 1947, there was a crisis a week and sometimes a crisis a day. When all this took place within a beleaguered city and my own personal safety was by no means secure, it was little wonder that I began to lose weight, to suffer from nervous strain and sleeplessness.

By the middle of December, I had to evacuate all Jewish and British staff from Broadcasting House, which was situated on the edge of the Arab quarter of Musrara. The Hebrew and music sections and the Jewish part of the administrative staff were regrouped around temporary studios in Rehavia: the English section worked wholly from branch studios in Security Zone A: the Arabic section and the Arabic part of the administrative staff continued to work at Broadcasting House under Arab Legion protection, with reserve studios and offices at Ramallah. These were for use on days when the firing at Sheikh Jarrah was too intense for Arab buses to bring in those members of the Arab staff who lived in or who had moved to Ramallah. The only place where British, Arabs and Jews still met was in the Public Information Office to which we transferred our three news-rooms.

All control and liaison had to be done by telephone or by personal visits by the British news editors to either the Jewish or the Arab areas, often at considerable danger to their own lives. I visited the Public Information Office daily to sign letters and pick up mail. I could meet there British staff from Security Zone A and Arab staff from Broadcasting House. Similarly, the General Post Office was used as a common meeting place for Jews and Arabs (including a Jewish tailor who used to come there to measure his Arab clients in the lobby).

Payment of the Jewish staff of the P.B.S. was difficult. At the end of December I could still go myself to the police station near Broadcasting House to fetch British police escorts to accompany me to the Public Information Office where I met the Department of Broadcasting accountant with £2,000 in cash for the Jewish staff whom I paid at their temporary offices in Rehavia. But, by the end of January, the British police were not allowed to venture into Jewish areas, so I took Jewish regular police escorts. At the end of February, I varied the procedure and went on an unexpected day, without escort, and paid the Jewish staff in their own homes (all strictly against Government regulations). At the end of March, so many hold-ups of Government and Municipal payrolls had occurred that I paid out the staff at a small table inside the heavily-guarded Anglo-Palestine Bank premises where I cashed the pay cheque.

It was amazing that, all this time, the Palestine Broadcasting Service was still on the air. The main studios at Jerusalem and the transmitters at Ramallah were operated by Junior Arab engineers, all the more senior Jewish engineers, having been withdrawn by the Postmaster-General in December. In spite of the open warfare between Arabs and Jews in the streets and environs of Jerusalem, the Arab engineers continued to transmit all English, Arabic *and* Hebrew programmes without interruption. There were several reasons for this: they had to go on working if they wanted their pensions or gratuities: they were afraid that, if they discontinued the Hebrew broadcasts, Broadcasting House and its studios would be attacked by Jews; and lastly, they were genuinely anxious to show that they were just as capable as the more senior Jewish engineering staff whom they were temporarily replacing.

But, when the telephone and electric power lines to the Ramallah transmitters got shot away in the frequent battles along the Ramallah road, the P.B.S. had to use its emergency transmitters as it was impossible to get Army escorts for the linesmen. The Arabic programmes were transmitted by short-wave radio link to Ramallah and thence by a diesel-operated reserve generator working on half-power. The Hebrew programmes were transmitted by an even lower-powered emergency transmitter in the General Post Office building in Jerusalem itself. The Hebrew programmes were barely audible outside Jerusalem. They could be heard to some extent in Tel Aviv, but there were many complaints from listeners in Haifa and the north. This forced even more Jewish listeners to listen to the *Hagana, Irgun Zvai Leumi* and Stern Gang transmissions.

As it was clear that, in the absence of any central governmental authority, the Arab engineering staff at Ramallah would seize the transmitters at the termination of the Mandate, the Jewish authorities began to set up yet another temporary Hebrew transmitter near Tel Aviv. At the request of the Jewish authorities and with the consent of the Chief Secretary, I set up an executive committee composed of five senior Jewish members of the P.B.S. staff and five more junior members to plan the new transmissions and to tide over the transition period. They also made arrangements for the Hebrew radio paper published by the Public Information Office to be taken over by private enterprise.

I had similar difficulties with the Middle East College of Public Administration. The winter term had begun in October in the new premises of the College in the Mamilla Road; but, even by December, this had become a dangerous area for Jews. The courses were transferred to Broadcasting House until that, too, became unsafe. With great reluctance, it was then decided to split the classes on a racial basis. Tutorial classes for Arab students, with British or Arab tutors, were transferred to the Y.M.C.A., but even these were attended until the end of the term in April by a few of the more adventurous Jewish students. Tutorial classes for Jewish students as a whole, with Jewish tutors, were held in a hotel, then in the premises of the British Institute of Engineering and Technology and finally in the Berlitz School. Out of nine tutorial classes, six were continued to the end of the term, but the number of students who attended fell very sharply, as most of them were engaged on Jewish 'national defence duties' of one kind or another.

Such was the situation in Jerusalem when I left on the 20th April, 1948, for Lydda airport and England, in anticipation of the termination of the Mandate.

CHAPTER 13

ISRAEL, 1949–62

In the autumn of 1949, I went back to what had meanwhile become Israel. Hadassah had already been there for a year, in a small rented flat in Tel Aviv, resuming her chairmanship of W.I.Z.O. (the Women's International Zionist Organization). I had no idea what reception I would receive. But the Government now in power was firmly seated and included many old friends, so I had no difficulties.

Before I had left Palestine in the spring of 1948, I had carefully prepared plans for the management of the future Israel broadcasting service. I had intended that Mordechai Zlotnik (now Avida), in my time head of the Hebrew section in Jerusalem, should take over the new Israel service: but he remained trapped in Jerusalem. He was not a member of *MAPAI*, the ruling Socialist party, and hence was personally unacceptable to them. Another, much less experienced member of the P.B.S. had taken over in the new broadcasting studios in Tel Aviv under the general direction of an old Zionist leader, Shalom Soloveichik (by now Solieli), a well-known Hebrew writer. Unfortunately, he knew nothing about administration and was quite unable to comprehend the particular problems of a public broadcasting service. The level of efficiency had sadly deteriorated in the past months and there was discontent among listeners and staff.

At the invitation of my old friend Gershon Agron, now head of the Government information services, I made a careful investigation and presented him with a long list of recommendations. Solieli, when asked for his observations, rejected every single one. Great pressure was then brought to bear on me by Agron and others (including many of my former P.B.S. staff) to resume control. I was told that my British citizenship was no bar and that I would not be required to change it. (This liberal attitude to foreign subjects in Israel Government employ has since been abandoned, and rightly so.) But I still held the view that the head of *Kol Israel* must have an impeccable command of Hebrew, as well as strong *MAPAI* party backing. I possessed neither and was unlikely ever to acquire them. Lastly, having retired from the Administration after twenty-eight years' service, I was unwilling to pop back again. Later, my friend 'Moish' Perlman, an English Jew who had been the very effective Israel military spokesman during the War of Independence, took over the direction of all the information services. He tried in addition, to run *Kol Israel*, directly, himself. But the *Kol Israel* offices had meanwhile moved back to Jerusalem when the *Knesset* (Israel's Parliament), the Cabinet and the Ministers had returned there. (This move was intended to defeat the United Nations resolution to internationalise the City, opposed also by the Government of Jordan) Perlman's own office remained in Tel Aviv, the press centre of Israel, and he dashed up to Jerusalem once or twice a week to deal with *Kol Israel*. But the service did not improve. Then Harry Zinder, the able American-Jewish wartime Middle East correspondent for *Life* and *Time*, was persuaded to take over the running of *Kol Israel* for a year. This was a great improvement, although he was no

Hebraist. At one point, the Minister for Education and Culture, Zalman Aranne, without even notifying Zinder, asked me to come in as an adviser. After lengthy discussions, this proposal fell through, because I was not prepared to give advice unless Zinder himself asked for it. But I did manage to persuade Zinder to take over permanent control of *Kol Israel*, in spite of his personal desire to return to journalism. Eventually, Hanoch Ovsienko (now Givton), a Hebrew University graduate whom I had taken into the Hebrew section of the P.B.S. as a producer and announcer, was made director of *Kol Israel* and ran it very well indeed until he was posted to the Israel delegation to the U.N.

The position of the head of any Government broadcasting service in a democracy is particularly vulnerable. He must follow in general the Government's political line yet allow all opposition parties a chance to express their views. He must accept suppression of news by the military censorship while trying to give the public a clear and balanced picture of what is really happening.

★   ★   ★

As soon as the Government moved back to Jerusalem, I moved too, as I had now been engaged to start training courses for senior Israeli civil servants. But, while I was still in Tel Aviv, I restarted as well my own diploma course for civil servants in the middle ranks. I followed the exact lines I had adopted in Jerusalem towards the end of the Mandate. The Tel Aviv diploma course, however, was given solely in Hebrew. In this enterprise, I again had the active collaboration of Miss Gila Uriel with whom I had started the Tel Aviv tutorial classes in 1946, which she was still running. Eventually, we had two parallel diploma classes in Tel Aviv, one for military officers, the other for civilians. We even organized, on one occasion, a special nine month diploma course for local government officers. Gila Uriel and I also successfully introduced the first training courses for hospital administrators, both Government and *Kupat Cholim* (the *Histadrut* health insurance fund, the biggest employer of doctors and nurses in Israel.) We also arranged the first training course for bank officials, in the head office of the *Bank Leumi* ('National Bank') the former Anglo-Palestine Bank in Tel Aviv where Yehuda Grasovsky, my father-in-law, had been deputy manager forty years earlier.

It was a critical moment in the development of the new state. Hopes ran high; but administration proved to be far more difficult than the new regime had anticipated. Everyone was keen to learn the secrets that I was supposed to have acquired during the Mandatory period. I had already published in 1946 a small book entitled, rather pretentiously, *The Theory of Administration* (Rubin Mass, Jerusalem). It was, in fact little more than some elementary hints on the methods of administration for middle-rank Palestinian civil servants. It included a few of my own 'patents' that have since become common practice. It was translated into Hebrew by Gila Uriel and published the following year. The Hebrew edition is now out of print; but the English version has proved to be useful to central and local government officials from Asia and Africa being trained in Israel.

But I was not satisfied merely with the publication of a book on administration in both English and Hebrew editions, as well as giving oral courses in both languages to public officials at senior and intermediate levels. So I arranged with Gila to publish a Hebrew quarterly on behalf of what had by now become the Israel Institute of Public Administration. We called the journal *HaMinhal* ('Administration') and managed to get many of Israel's leading experts to write articles on subjects of current administrative interest. We also followed carefully developments overseas and either had translated into Hebrew informative articles published abroad on matters of special interest to Israel, or commissioned Israelis to write such articles. I wrote several myself, following visits to many institutions overseas. In order to make the journal less heavy, I wrote a short satire for each issue. This series of satires — collectively entitled *How Not To In Israel* — was republished in 1957 by *Kiryat Sepher* in Jerusalem, with cartoons by my friend, Mike Ronnen, then cartoonist and feature editor for the *Jerusalem Post*. I have found that, no matter how sensitive Israelis may be to direct criticism, however justified, they will accept it in satirical form, the wilder the better. *HaMinhal* ran for ten years. We departed from the usual practice at that time by having the cover, format, layout and type-face carefully designed or chosen by another friend of mine — Immanuel Grau — a talented graphic artist in Jerusalem. I imported paper of good quality from Finland. (I visited Finland several times in these years in connection with *The Conquest of the Desert* Exhibition. Wood products are by far the most important Finnish export and all Finnish paper manufacturers are organized in a single federation with show-rooms in Helsinki. I was amazed at the trouble they took in handling my miniscule order and the efficiency with which it was executed.) We employed one of the best printers in Tel Aviv, believing that administrators should pay special attention to aesthetics, and thus practised what we preached. For a long time we even stood out against the acceptance of any advertising matter whatever. But constantly rising costs eventually forced us to abandon this principle; yet no advertising was allowed to interrupt the text. We gathered around us, largely in Tel Aviv, a small group of public officials who voluntarily gave much time to proof-reading, distribution and accountancy.

However, after ten years, Gila found that she was unable to continue giving so much time to the journal. By then, she had taken on ever more important duties, and had, as well, her own literary activities. So, after the 40th issue, we merged *HaMinhal* with another Hebrew journal, published six times a year—*Netivey Irgun* ('Paths of Organization')—that had meanwhile been founded by the department of the Prime Minister's Office (later the Treasury) dealing with all civil service matters. Gila Uriel and I went on to the editorial board of the combined journal together with Dr (now Professor) Yehezkel Dror, the leading expert on public administration on the Hebrew University's faculty of political science. (He had previously joined Gila and me on the board of *HaMinhal*.) The combined journal became *Netivey Irgun uMinhal* ('Paths of Organization and Administration') and flourishes to this day. My Institute of Public Administration continues to give it a small annual subsidy, as do a number of other bodies in Israel interested in this subject.

Since 1953, I have been a member of the delegation from Israel to several congresses of the International Institute of Administrative Sciences. This is a translation from the French title—*Institut International des Sciences Administratives*—which I find pretentious: to me, administration is anything but a science. But the French and Belgian delegations approach administration from a purely juristic point of view: to them, administration is merely a branch of law. When the American and British delegations insisted that the congress should deal with practical administration, a committee was set up (of which I was a member) 'for Administrative Practices'. The French and the Belgians set up a parallel body which they insisted on calling the 'Scientific Committee' to maintain their traditional attitude.

The Institute itself has its headquarters in Brussels and now has triennial congresses, with smaller 'round-tables' in intervening years. I have attended meetings at Istanbul (1953), The Hague (1954). Oxford (1955), Madrid (1956), Lisbon (1960) and Paris (1965). At Istanbul, in 1953 the organization of the congress was largely in the hands of the Turkish members of the Institute: they were very slow in getting under way. For example, on the *last* day of the congress, they produced the signs, in English and French, directing delegates to the halls where meetings would be held. So the Israel delegation took its coats off and we ourselves arranged the rooms put at the disposal of the congress In consequence, I was personally elected chairman of an international five-man committee to devise better methods for organizing future congresses. Our report was accepted and was put into effect, resulting in fewer subsequent complaints.

★　★　★

Hadassah and I had moved back to Jerusalem in 1950, to a rented furnished flat in Rehavia. We had failed to dislodge our Armenian landlord from our former flat in Talbia which he had occupied while I was in America in 1948-49. He maintained that his tenant had been the now defunct Mandatory Government and that I was only a sub-tenant and hence unprotected in law. I decided not to persist in a court action for recovery. My lawyer said that, as my land-lord was *not* Jewish, the upright Israel courts were bound to find in his favour and not mine. Eventually we moved to an unfurnished flat in Rehavia and got out all our furniture and books that had been stored for safety in a friend's house when we had left for England in the spring of 1948. We are still in this flat sixteen years later. It is conveniently situated near the main road to the Hebrew University where I have been teaching.

Life in Israel in the early years of the new State was at times very uncomfortable. It was a period of austerity, with both food and petrol rationing enforced. Jerusalem was then a very different place from the undivided city as we had known it under the Mandate. It was a constant irritant to be cut off from our former British and Arab friends on the Jordan side. We were also very unhappy at being excluded from the Old City we had known so well: in 1967, that exclusion ended.

★   ★   ★

As soon as I was re-established in Jerusalem, I restarted the Jerusalem diploma class. I had the help of Dr Joseph Funkenstein of the G.P.O. (now a Reform rabbi back in Germany) and, later, of Joseph Auerbach, a town-planning official of the Jerusalem Municipality. We engaged a number of lecturers, either senior civil servants or on the faculty of the Hebrew University. As there were then no Arab civil servants in Western Jerusalem, Hebrew replaced English as the language of instruction. These courses are still running in Jerusalem, twenty years since they were first started. The tutorial classes and the Tel Aviv diploma classes, however, have meanwhile been wound up, in view of the large number of other evening courses now provided by other organisations, especially in Tel Aviv.

In 1965, I was both surprised and grateful to receive for that year the prize awarded annually in memory of the late David Rosolio, an exact contemporary and friend of mine, who had been civil service commissioner from 1954 till 1961. The prize is given for contributions in Israel to the practice and theory of administration. It is announced at the annual two-day conference of public administration held at the Hebrew University. Till now, prizes have been awarded to seven persons and, on all other occasions, I have been a member of the three-man selection panel under the chairmanship of Reuven Shari, till recently the civil service commissioner.

Shortly after my return to Jerusalem, I was invited by Walter Eytan, by now director-general of the Ministry for Foreign Affairs, to design a course for senior members of that department. I arranged that the heads of several divisions of the Ministry should themselves be some of the lecturers. But some apparently feared that their own shortcomings might come to light in the process. The whole proposal was mysteriously blocked at the last moment and the course never took place. I was indignant; but Eytan could do nothing about it.

★ ★ ★

It was about this time, in 1950, that I was approached by that visionary, Alexander Ezer, to join him in a grandiose project—to organize the first international exhibition in Israel. This exhibition, *The Conquest of the Desert*, was to be held in a convention centre being built in Jerusalem under the auspices of the Jewish Agency, for future Zionist Congresses.

I had known Ezer (then Yevserov) as one of the editors of an English-language economic periodical published in Tel Aviv between the wars. It had published several of my articles on nineteenth-century development in Palestine under the Turks: I felt that I owed him some help in return. I was impressed by the sheer audacity of his latest proposals for which *he* had undertaken himself to raise the money, both for the convention centre and the exhibition. I agreed to become his European manager, with an office in London, which I would use as a base for travel to thirteen other European countries. My job was to persuade governments and exporters to exhibit in Jerusalem. These countries were Eire, France, Belgium, Holland, Switzerland, Denmark, Sweden, Norway, Finland, Italy, Austria (then still under Four-Power control), Greece and Turkey. In addition to getting the participation of various U.N. agencies as well — in particular U.N.E.S.C.O. in Paris, I.L.O. and W.H.O. in Geneva and F.A.O. in Rome — I also had to get the exhibition registered with the international bureau of exhibitions in Paris, no easy matter.

From Ezer's point of view, I had several advantages. I had a British passport and could travel freely around Europe, largely without visa, financing provisionally my own trips. Then I had useful contacts, not only in London and Paris, but also among the Israel diplomats in the countries that

I visited. The exhibition was to be held in 1951; but, in 1950, an economic depression hit Israel, due to the arrival of 240,000 largely penniless immigrants in 1949. This seriously reduced the amount of capital obtainable by Ezer from the sale of shares in the *Binyanei HaOoma* ('Buildings of the Nation') company that he had formed to build the convention centre and organize the exhibition. The construction of the walls of the vast hall stopped for lack of funds and the exhibition could not be held until the hall was at least roofed over. So the exhibition had twice to be postponed. On each occasion, many prospective participants whom I had lined up cancelled their applications: I had to start all over again to enrol new ones. What had seemed at the beginning to involve eighteen months' work, in the end took three years. It involved many visits to each of the centres included in my 'parish'. To some of them I had to go back half-a-dozen times. In the process, I learned a great deal about the terms of trade and its organization. I was particularly impressed with the forceful methods used in Belgium, Switzerland and Finland. (At that time, Western Germany was still beyond the pale, as far as Israel was concerned.) I only wish British export trade was promoted in such a manner. I received much help from the Israel chambers of commerce in London, Paris and elsewhere. In London, Sir Isaac Wolfson helped me to open an office. He put at my disposal his buyers; he helped me acquire some of the furnishings needed for the convention centre and for the exhibition. This was the start of a personal friendship that has lasted till today. It was fascinating for me to hear from Sir Isaac himself the various factors that have contributed to the successful establishment of his world-wide financial empire. These factors include, first, his eye for well situated properties and his willingness to fly, at any hour of the day or night, to any part of the U.K. to clinch a deal. Another factor was his realisation that the grandchildren of many Jewish business-owners had been educated at universities and were disinclined to go into the family business, which could thus be bought at a low price. A third, his retention of the original boards of these companies, subject to his personal supervision. He has an amazing capacity of being able to run his eye down a long list of goods in stock and pick out the one item that is eventually shown to be over-stocked. Lastly, there are the very high salaries paid to his buyers, the key-men in the organization. This makes them immune, not only to all corruption or disloyalty, but also to any desire to leave him, as they could never get a comparable income elsewhere.

In the course of my travels, I got as far on one side as Ankara — a weary train journey across the hot, endless plateau of Anatolia. On the other side, I reached Tampere, the snow-covered centre of heavy industry in Finland. I even went over to Dublin, although Israel had then not received *de jure* recognition by Eire. I was asked by the Israel Embassy in London to take up that matter with the President, the gaunt and humourless Eamon de Valera. He explained to me that, as a Catholic country, Eire was primarily interested, as far as the Middle East was concerned, only in the sufferings of the Arab refugees, some of whom were Catholic. Any exchange of ambassadors with Israel (and any Irish participation in the Jerusalem exhibition) were out of the question.

My travels from one European capital to another occasionally involved my acting as courier between one Israel embassy and another. The fact that a courier with a

British passport was carrying an Israel diplomatic bag was occasionally regarded by customs officials with the deepest suspicion, particularly in Vienna, where the airport was in the Russian zone.

As a matter of fact, I was far more security-minded than they were. It took me a long time to cure the Israel embassy in Rome, for example, of the practice of leaving the key in the door of the safe containing the Foreign Ministry cypher books. The safe stood in the room of the first secretary who was continually being called in to the ambassador's room next door. Very little dexterity would have been needed to make a beeswax impression of the key — a matter of seconds. Once the cypher was compromised in this way, a new one would have to be prepared, at great expense.

The *Conquest of the Desert* exhibition eventually took place in 1953, in the roofed but unfinished convention centre. (It is now complete and serves as well as the city's magnificent concert hall. Although there were many participants both from within Israel and from abroad, the cost of maintaining exhibition staff for three years instead of eighteen months swallowed up all the profits. Before closing down my office in London, I managed at least to pay all bills outstanding out of the rentals I had received from all over Europe.

In February, 1954, I was invited by the Jewish National Fund to go on a fund-raising tour in South Africa. The J.N.F. office there was run by Alan Rose, twenty years my junior. He had come out from England after serving in North Africa, with distinction, as a sergeant in the British armoured corps. We travelled together all round South Africa, Southern Rhodesia and Northern Rhodesia, visiting the stupendous Victoria Falls, and raised quite a lot of money

I was fascinated and horrified by what little I could learn, while on tour, of Southern Africa's racial problems. This filled me with a desire to know more, and the late Israel Hayman (then a leading lawyer in Johannesburg) and his wife Ethel (a distant relative of mine) arranged for me to come out to teach public administration at the University of Witwatersrand in Johannesburg. The professor was then 'Copper' Le May, a Balliol man like myself: I taught in his department for four months. During all this time, I was the Haymans' house guest.

It so happened that my room in the University was next door to the common-room of the anthropological department. I became an honorary member of it, with access to their splendid library. I spent much of my time reading widely about Bushmen, Hottentots and Bantu.

My students were very young: most were English-speaking South Africans. They included some bright Jewish boys who had matriculated from school at sixteen and came straight to the University. A few were Afrikaners, and there were at that time even some coloured students.

I had many talks with leading Afrikaners, whose fanatical, ingrained Dutch Calvinism is basically responsible for South Africa's racial prejudices today. I left South Africa with an undying hostility to *apartheid* in all its forms.[*]

The only thing that was a failure during my visits to South Africa was a week-end in the Kruger National Park, where I had been promised lions galore. For some reason, they failed to turn out; but I did see two beetles.

★　★　★

[*] See my speech in the House of Lords on 22nd July, 1964: Hansard Vols. 695-702.

In 1954, I was invited to become a lecturer at the Eliezer Kaplan School of Economics and Social Sciences. Kaplan had been treasurer of the Jewish Agency and, in 1948, became the first Minister of Finance in the new Government of Israel. When he died in 1952, a large sum of money was raised, largely in the United States, to endow a faculty at the Hebrew University in his memory. It is a component part of the University but has its own budget and board of trustees. In this way, it resembles the London School of Economics in its relations with the University of London. I had already lectured on British institutions at the Hebrew University during World War II, while in the Imperial censorship. I then replaced Professor Jack Isaacs who was sent out from the University of London but took months to reach the Middle East by sea, round the Cape. During all this time I lectured in his stead. He had undertaken to learn some Hebrew during his voyage; but, arriving eventually in Jerusalem, he announced that all his Hebrew books had been in his heavy baggage, stowed underneath some tanks, and he had not been able to get at them. When he did begin to lecture, he concentrated on English language and literature, while I continued to lecture on British institutions.

Then I began to give courses on public administration in the Kaplan School's department of political science. The course was obligatory and the class was very large — up to 150 students: it was difficult for me to control such a mob. So, one year, instead of my lecturing to the class, I asked my students to conduct a survey of the major causes of inefficiency in those Government offices situated in Jerusalem. I divided the class up into some twenty teams of four or five students, each allotted a specific office. Some of the senior civil servants were rather put out when a team of eager young men and women arrived and asked for an interview 'on behalf of Mr Samuel'. But most teams managed to collect interesting material. Each team then had a series of closed sessions in which the material was analysed and conclusions reached. At each of my classroom lectures, the spokesman of a team was invited to present his team's conclusion orally, for discussion by the whole class. We had lively sessions and some of these students who subsequently became civil servants themselves, managed to avoid later several of the pitfalls they had earlier encountered.

The Kaplan School approach to public administration, however, rapidly became too advanced for me. Some of my younger Israeli colleagues on the faculty, who had returned with doctorates from foreign universities, particularly the brilliant Dr (now Professor) Yehezkel Dror, began to take over. So I moved back to British institutions once more as part of the university courses given on comparative government. Eventually, I organized my material into a three-year cycle: first year — Britain; second year — the Commonwealth (which needed frequent rewriting as new pieces dropped off) and, third year—the Welfare State and its alternatives. The last course involved a comparative study of New Zealand, Sweden and Britain as the prototypes; Israel and India as would-be Welfare States; and the alternatives: free enterprise (more or less), the United States; totalitarianism of the left, Russia; totalitarianism of the right, Mussolini's Italy, Hitler's Germany and Peron's Argentina; and the *anti*-Welfare State, South Africa.

But I am not really an academic. I have no doctorate and started as an external lecturer at the University only after I was forty. By 1954, I was fifty-six and too old for regular appointment to the faculty, even if I had been fully qualified academically. So I have been on special contract, annually renewed till 1969 when I reached the age of seventy-one. This has given me the advantage of being able to limit the number of my hours of lecturing per week and to allow me to drop a semester or even a whole year whenever I want to. I must here thank the successive heads of the department of political science — Professor Benjamin Akzin and Dr Martin Seliger — for their courtesy and kindness in fitting my courses into their general programme.

As a senior lecturer I was entirely content. My mass courses were reduced to seminar groups of between thirty and 75 students. I tried to keep the group down through the elimination of those whose knowledge of English is inadequate for speedily reading the necessary books, nearly all of which are in that language. As I lectured only three hours a week, I could devote an average of some six or seven additional hours weekly to individual tutoring. Few of the permanent faculty members are in a position to do this, as they have to give at least six to eight hours of lectures or seminars a week. They must also participate in many university and departmental committees. Most are deeply engaged in their own research and writing, without the publication of which they cannot hope for academic advancement. Luckily, I was not involved in university administration at any level. Nor am I in the running for promotion to a professorship, Hence I was able to arrange for every single one of my students to come alone to my flat in Jerusalem for an hour or so's talk on his past, present and future. Each selected, from the subjects to be dealt with during the course, an essay subject which I then narrowly defined. The books for study were prescribed from the detailed bibliography I had already distributed. If the student

268

wished, a second interview was arranged to discuss the outline of the essay before it was written. When it was completed, the student came again to read it and was subjected to oral examination, to make sure that it was the student's own work.

No additional examination was held at the end of the year: the student's mark was determined solely by his essay. In addition, about twenty students were invited, if they so wished, each to give up to half an hour's presentation in class of part of one of the subjects to be dealt with. This was intended to provide them with practice in public speaking. The students concerned came individually to discuss with me beforehand which aspects they would deal with in their presentation and which I would include in my own subsequent lecture. Each student was expected, after his presentation, to answer questions from the class. In some cases, this was the first occasion on which the student had ever spoken in public. On the other hand, some of the students were already accomplished lecturers, having been officers or N.C.O. instructors during their compulsory military service. As most students come to the University only *after* their military service, when they arrived in my class as second or third-year students, most were between the ages of 21 and 23. They were much more mature than my students in other universities, for example, at Johannesburg, nearly all of whom were still in their teens. Hence it was a joy to teach at Jerusalem. Some students, in fact, were senior civil servants or regular army officers getting their degrees in their late twenties or early thirties. The Israel Defence Forces have a scheme whereby officers doing their compulsory military service, interested in staying on for a further period, are put through the University for three years at Government expense (including the provision of an apartment in Jerusalem) in return for three additional years of military service.

★ ★ ★

I am not very happy about the way in which the Hebrew University has developed. It started in 1925 as a research institution, granting only doctors' degrees and, later, masters'. After a long internal struggle, it decided in 1949-50 to award bachelors' degrees, but without insisting on adequate preparation of students before admission. High school matriculation alone is considered sufficient to secure entry, except to such departments as science and medicine, where there is limited laboratory space. For these disciplines, competitive entrance examinations are held. Elsewhere, the admission of any high school student who chooses to enter, without even a qualifying examination, may be very 'democratic'; but it results, as far as the department of political science is concerned, for example, in a drop-out rate of *forty per cent* at the end of the first year. This is a waste of space, time and money for both student and teacher. This applies, in particular, to students who take economics and are not mathematically equipped to grasp it.

One of the chief weaknesses of most students is in their poor knowledge of English. Supplementary English is compulsory for the majority of students in their first year. This means that, at the *end* of their first year, they are more or less equipped to read some of the text-books in English that they were supposed to read from the *beginning* of that year. Even so, second and third year students read so slowly, with so much reference to the dictionary, that they cannot possibly get through all the required reading set by the various professors and lecturers — incidentally with little or no co-ordination between them. I have long ago given up any attempt to require students to read set books. I am happy if they read some of what I prescribe to each as a basis for his or her essay.

A second problem is the overloading of the students' curriculum. While it is good that undergraduates should not specialise too early, they are required at the Kaplan School to take two full subjects — for example, either economics and political science, or sociology and statistics, or any other combination of five different subjects. This is far too ambitious. In fact, the University tries to keep *down* the number of classroom hours a student may take to twenty-four a week. This must be compared with the normal sixteen in the United States, an average of ten in most universities in the United Kingdom, and much less at Oxford and Cambridge. This twenty-four hours a week in Jerusalem is in addition to the time needed for reading (both required and optional) for thinking, for discussion with fellow-students, and for writing essays. There are, also, far too few scholarships available. Most students have to work their way through the University; so they a full-or part-time job in addition to their studies. Some are married, with children. As a result, there is little time left, as in other universities in the world, for student activities, such as sport. Two hours a week of exercise is required of all students: but they have to be closely supervised to make sure that they take it.

I published a paper on this subject in the 1965 volume of *Public Administration in Israel and Abroad*. It also came out in Hebrew in *Maariv*, the noon-time daily paper published in Tel Aviv. My major suggestion was the provision of high-standard evening university classes at Tel Aviv and Haifa, whence the majority of Hebrew University students come. This would enable many students without means or scholarships to work by day in their own home towns and to study at night. They could then graduate in four, five or six years instead of the normal three. Neither scholarships nor hostels would be required for such students. Teaching them in Tel Aviv or Haifa would take the pressure off Jerusalem and enable the Hebrew University to reduce its student population of about 12,000 to, say the 6,000 which is all that it is equipped at the moment to handle.

★ ★ ★

In the spring of 1960, my father decided, at the age of nearly ninety, that he wanted to visit Australia and New Zealand. He chose what was advertised as a cruise ship. It was, in fact, a fast immigrant ship that went out via the Panama Canal and came back via the Suez Canal, stopping at a few places on the way. As he could not go alone, or even accompanied only by a nurse, he asked me to go with him. I had never been to these two countries myself and was glad of the opportunity to visit them, however briefly. I arranged with the Hebrew University — and my father — that, while the ship sailed along the Australian and New Zealand coasts, I should fly from Auckland to Sydney, Melbourne, Adelaide and Perth, fund-raising for the Hebrew University with the help of its local Jewish committees. In the event, my father's doctors would not give him the certificates of adequate health required by the shipping company from elderly passengers; his sea-trip had to be abandoned. But as I was already booked to speak for the Hebrew University in these countries, I flew via Singapore to Australia and New Zealand and fulfilled my commitments. One of the things in Australia that surprised me was the relative antiquity of its universities: I had not expected to find the universities at both Melbourne and Sydney surrounded by ancient trees. Both institutions are over a century old and, in fact, more venerable than any red-brick university in Britain.

★ ★ ★

In 1957, I was approached, as a publicist, by the *Magen David Adom* ('Red Shield of David'), the Israel equivalent of the Red Cross, to produce a pamphlet for them in separate English, French and Spanish editions. It was to support their claim, at a forthcoming International Red Cross congress in New Delhi, for their recognition as a national Red Cross Society, even though they used another symbol. The pamphlet I produced pleased the M.D.A. executive committee, although their symbol is still not recognised by the International Red Cross. The M.D.A. thereupon invited me to become their permanent adviser, on a ratainer, for publicity and public relations, a post that I retain till today. For many years I produced for them a duplicated monthly bulletin in separate English, French and Spanish editions: more recently, I have been co-editor of a printed and illustrated M.D.A. quarterly. During this period I have paid regular visits to M.D.A. headquarters in Tel Aviv (and now in Jaffa) and to most of their branches overseas.

M.D.A. has great organizational difficulties. It was started in 1936 as the medical wing of the *Hagana*, the clandestine Jewish defence organization. At first, it had only one motor ambulance in the whole country, stationed at Tel Aviv: the first-aid service was then managed by a voluntary committee of a few Tel Aviv doctors. Today, M.D.A. has over 200 ambulances at dozens of first-aid stations all over the country. It also has at its disposal several thousand trained first-aiders as well as a blood transfusion service with its own laboratories at Jaffa and blood banks in the principal cities. Although it now employs a number of paid whole-time motor ambulance drivers in different parts of Israel, the management of M.D.A. is still highly centralised. It remains in the hands of a central committee still including some of the doctors who helped to found the organization thirty years earlier. But they are employed whole-time in other organizations in which, over the years, they have risen to positions of responsibility. It is difficult for them to give adequate time to M.D.A. especially as they are all thirty years older. The solution of course is to devolve the management of many of the local branches on to the local authority, only too anxious to take it over. At headquarters, well-paid administrators should be employed, allowing the present central committee to become a policy-making board of trustees and not an executive body. So far, I have not been able to convert the committee to my point of view.

★ ★ ★

In 1962, I decided that I would take sabbatical leave from the Hebrew University. This enabled me to accept an invitation to teach for a semester at the Graduate School of

Public Affairs at the Albany campus of the State University of New York (it has several other campuses.) This invitation came from Dean O.B. Conaway Jr, whom I had met at an international conference of the International Institute of Administrative Sciences. Before the beginning of that semester, I would visit the Centre for the Study of Democratic Institutions at Santa Barbara in California at the invitation of Robert Hutchins, former President of the University of Chicago. Our younger son, Dan, was then general manager for the Shell Company in Thailand and Laos. So Hadassah and I decided to go round the world by air, starting with a few weeks with Dan at Bangkok, followed by a side-trip to the jungle temples of Angkor Wat in Cambodia. From there, we visited Hong Kong as guests of Lawrence and Horace Kadoorie, who took us to see their remarkable Chinese refugee resettlement project on the mainland.

During our three weeks in Japan, we had the choice of asking for advice and help from one of three sources — the British Embassy, the Israel Embassy, or (through Dan) the Shell Company. We chose the last and were not disappointed. One of Shell's Japanese public relations officers at Kyoto arranged for us to stay for a week in a Japanese inn, where no one knew a word of English. We were given kimonos to wear, *tatami* mats to sleep on and Japanese food to eat while sitting on the floor, huddled round a charcoal brazier and covered by a quilt. We tried to get accustomed to Japanese baths and latrines. On the last day, I slid open by chance a panel in the corridor and found myself in that section of the inn reserved for *real* Japanese. *They* were all sitting on sofas looking at television.

I came back from Japan with a pronounced dislike of

Japanese culture. While appreciating the beauty of its art, its people seemed to be still feudal in outlook and hardly touched by the humanity derived by Western and Middle-Eastern peoples from the Old and New Testaments.

We flew from Tokyo to Los Angeles on 1st January 1963, and stopped to refuel at Hawaii, which had recently become part of the United States. There we were processed as non-immigrants by U.S. immigration officers. As we had passed the international dateline, it was still December 31st. When we reached Los Angeles, it was January 1st again and we were processed once more. When I protested and said that we had been processed only a few hours previously at Hawaii, the immigration officers said: "Ah, but that was *last* year."

When I left Santa Barbara for Albany, Hadassah flew to Mexico City to stay for a second time with her friend, Mrs. Geraldine Morris. But, no sooner had we both arrived at our destinations than we had news that my father, now 92, was dying. So we flew independently to London to be at his bedside. His will to live maintained him, although unconscious, for several more weeks. During this time I had to return to Albany briefly to get my seminars started. I came back for his funeral, having crossed the Atlantic four times in a month.

The tributes paid to my father in the press were remarkable. With him, a whole age came to a close. I now found myself heir to a viscountcy, interested in taking my seat in the House of Lords, and in participating in the debates. So, before I returned to Albany to complete my courses, I called on the clerk in charge of the printed paper offices, and asked him if he would send me the weekly *Hansard*—the stenographic record of parliamentary proceedings — so that I could keep in touch with events until I came back to London. He said: "Of course, my Lord: to what address?" I gave him my address in the United States at Albany. "Oh, my Lord!", he replied. "What's the matter?" I asked. "I am given to understand" he said, "that the United States is no longer part of the British Empah".

"What has that got to do with it?"

"We are not allowed to send printed papers outside the British Empah at public expense."

"I have no intention of asking you to do so. I'll pay the postage myself."

"Ah, my Lord, I'm afraid we're not allowed to accept payment from peers."

"Well, what do you propose to do about it?"

"It's becoming quite a problem, my Lord: we had another case ten years ago."

However, the problem was solved somehow; I not only got *Hansard* while in Albany, without payment of postage, but I also receive it during those months of my stay in Jerusalem.

I spent the next three months at Albany, teaching both British and Israeli institutions. My seminar students were largely New York State civil servants taking advanced degrees. For nearly the whole time, Albany lay deep under snow; but I found life in that small provincial state capital very pleasant.

In May, 1963, I returned to London as Edwin Herbert, second Viscount of Mount Carmel and Toxteth (the quarter of Liverpool where my father had been born). I took my seat as a Labour peer and made a maiden speech in June on raising the age of compulsory education to sixteen. We then returned to Jerusalem after nine months absence.

CHAPTER 14

THE HOUSE OF LORDS, 1963

My father had been leader of the Asquithian Liberals, but I did not follow him into the Liberal Party. No one who has lived most of his life, as I have, in contact with the egalitarianism of the *kibbutz*, the *Histadrut* and the co-operative movement generally, can fail to be influenced by Socialist philosophy. As long as I was a British colonial civil servant, I could not be active in politics, either in Palestine or in Britain. But I had retired in 1948, and, in 1950, began working part of the year in London for the *Conquest of the Desert* exhibition. I then joined the London Labour Party. As I was staying with my father in South Paddington, I became a party member in one of the wards in that consitituency. My father knew of this decision and accepted it at the time: but, ten years later, before he died, it made him unhappy. Till the end, he believed that the fortunes of the Liberal Party were just about to recover: I did not share his optimism.

I gradually made the acquaintance of some of the South Paddington Labour Party organizers. At one stage, they invited me to become their candidate at the next election; but such a proposition had little appeal for me. First, South Paddington was a hopelessly Conservative seat, with many well-to-do people living around the Park. (North

Paddington, with its slums, votes Labour.) Secondly, my father would have to support any Liberal candidate in an election in the constituency in which he himself lived. The only beneficiaries of such a family controversy would be the popular press. Thirdly, I was already over fifty, too old to start a political career. It would take at least two or three elections to get in, by which time I should be over sixty. My father was already over eighty and his life expectancy was limited (actually he lived on for another twelve years). On his death, as his eldest son, I would be automatically excluded from the House of Commons. This was before Wedgwood Benn's success in getting the law altered to allow hereditary peers to 'disclaim' their titles during their own lifetime, if they wished to start or to continue a House of Commons career. Lastly, I did not want to give up living at least part of the year in Israel. I consulted Lord Nathan, a leading Labour peer, and he endorsed my decision not to stand for election.

I found Labour Party activities at ward level of little interest. So I enrolled in the Party's panel of speakers available to address club audiences anywhere in London. Most of these were groups of a dozen or so, mostly women, who met of an evening in chilly church halls. After some time, I realised how defective was the Party's machinery for political education at constituency level. Apart from the training of organizers, there was nothing like the extensive system of party political education that exists today. I worked out the system that I thought should be introduced and discussed it with the organizers of my own and adjacent constituencies, as well as with the secretary of the London Labour Party as a whole. With his endorsement, I submitted a memorandum to Herbert (later Lord) Morisson, the Labour leader, and even went to see him about it. He was enthusiastic and said I must be co-opted to the London Labour Party's education committee. I agreed to serve; but I never heard anything more of it. That somewhat disillusioned me about the effectiveness of the Labour Party's organizational capacities.

When I eventually succeeded my father in 1963, I had to decide what use, if any, I should make of my new position as a second generation peer in the House of Lords. My old friend, Philip Rea, with whom I had been both at Westminster School and Oxford University, was now leader of the Liberal Party in the House of Lords, in succession to my father. Philip suggested that I should sit with the Liberal peers, or at least, on the cross-benches. But I felt that I was already committed. In any case, I had observed, when attending meetings of the House in my father's lifetime (I then used the privilege as a peer's eldest son of sitting on the steps of the throne), that the Liberals rarely had a policy of their own. They were forced to vote with either the Government or the major opposition party. It was clear to me that the gap between the policies of the Conservative and Labour Parties today is already very narrow. It is thus impossible for the Liberals to find a distinct policy of their own between the other two.

The Labour Party in the House of Lords was delighted when I turned up, though somewhat surprised: they had not previously known of my existence. There were then only 64 Labour peers, almost all first creation. As they were faced by over 300 Conservative peers then in power, they were glad to have any reinforcement that they could find. But, for the third time, I had to decide whether or not to try for a political career in Britain. It was important not to fool myself with false prospects. I was already nearly sixty-five, far too old for junior office: such minor Cabinet posts are meant for men in their forties, or, at latest, in their fifties. As a back-bencher, with no salary and only a meagre allowance for every day that I attended, I would have to find a directorship or two in order to maintain myself in London. Once more I consulted Lord Nathan who confirmed my own private view. If I had been a Conservative, and not Jewish, my chances of getting a directorship would have been much greater.

In the event, I decided to spend only three months in the U.K. each year. I chose May, June and July — the last three months of the parliamentary session, when Bills come up from the Commons with a rush. By then, those Labour peers who have attended daily since September are getting very tired. They are glad to have one colleague more to help keep up the Party's voting strength in critical decisions.

When I got back to Jerusalem in August, 1963, I arranged with the Hebrew University to let me give my course of sixty lectures each year during two trimesters (at three a week instead of during three trimesters at two a week). Each trimester lasts for about ten weeks. This would enable me to lecture at the University from October until March. During this period of my absence from the House of Lords I fancy my Party leaders consider that I am probably better employed in teaching Israelis about British institutions than in sitting in one myself. I am thus free from teaching each year from the end of March. As I do not come to the House of Lords till May, this enables me to go on a lecture tour to the United States and Canada.

I have now maintained this annual pattern for five years. Hadassah found a block of flats in London, only eight minutes from Parliament. Dozens of M.P.'s live there, as well as several peers. Some M.P.'s even have division bells in their flat and can reach the House in time to vote and then return to finish their supper. We rent one or other of the vacant flats for three months each summer.

During my London period, I go to the House of Lords every day that it sits, usually for lunch. When unaccompanied by guests, we peers all sit at a long and narrow table. (Someone should write a doctoral dissertation on the influence of the refectory table on English social life — prep school, public school, university, army, Inns of Court and, finally the House of Lords.) The facilities provided for peers, and the whole atmosphere, are those of a very good London club. There is, however, no entrance fee and no annual subscription. (One does not pay to belong but is paid to belong.) As the kitchen department is not charged for rent, heat, water and light, prices of meals are moderate. If the staff were not paid when the House is not sitting, the prices would be even more moderate.

At lunch, one has different peers on either side, and opposite, at each meal: there are no reserved places. As the table is narrow enough for conversation across it, one can pick up quite a lot of what is going on behind the scenes. That often relates to difficulties with the roses in some noble peer's garden.

I sit in the Chamber as a back-bencher. At first we were in opposition; but, since 1964, we sit on the Government side of the House. I am not a skilled parliamentarian, who has come up from the House of Commons. I take no part in the detailed discussions in committee on each clause of new legislation. (The Whips did give me one formal little measure to get through in 1965, just to keep me happy.) Nor do I ask parliamentary questions. But I attend daily and am always there whenever a three-line whip is out, in order to give the Party the requisite voting strength in case of divisions. On Thursdays, I attend the Party meeting in a committee room, upstairs. There, the legislative programme for the ensuing week is outlined by the Chief Whip and the names of those who wish to speak are recorded. On several occasions, when arriving in May, I have been asked by the Leader of the House — till recently the Earl of Longford (formerly Frank Pakenham) — briefly to report to the Party meeting on the situation in Israel and the Middle East.

I would here like to pay a tribute to Frank for the great kindness he has shown to me. He has consistently encouraged all of us back-benchers to participate in the general policy debates, usually held on Wednesdays on a motion usually proposed by the Opposition. As I have lived abroad for most of my life, I do not feel competent to speak on most domestic issues. I confine myself to such matters as education, broadcasting and television, exhibitions, the future of the House of Lords, South Africa and, of course, the Middle East. As a back-bencher, I limit myself to fifteen or twenty minutes. Even that requires much preparation, including discussions with Government departments or other bodies concerned. The rest of my time in the Palace of Westminster I spend largely in the House of Lords library, preparing my lectures for the following winter at the Hebrew University in Jerusalem. As I talk there largely on British institutions, the excellent range of reference books in the Lords' library — and, if necessary, in that of the Commons — enables me to do in a day what it would take me a week to do in Jerusalem. For material on Commonwealth countries, I use the library of the Royal Commonwealth Society, and, for other countries, that of the Royal Institute of International Affairs (Chatham House).

★ ★ ★

I am full of admiration for the small teams of former M.P.'s, now in the House of Lords, who sit on each side through all debates. These are the professionals who keep legislation moving. Even though I am not in the Chamber for nearly as many hours as they are, and then for only part of the year, I find my three parliamentary months very tiring. In May, the House still sits only on Tuesdays, Wednesdays and Thursdays, beginning about 2.30 and rising before dinner. But the pressure of work mounts the nearer we get to the summer recess before which all legislation coming up from the Commons has to be got through. Gradually the House of Lords begins to sit on Mondays as well, then on Fridays too, and eventually till late in the evening, sometimes up to midnight. There are three-line whips day after day, which means that I must also dine in the House. Private plans for dinner parties or the theatre have to be abandoned.

I do not believe that my presence in the House really makes very much difference to anyone. After several years of careful examination of the reporting in the press of parliamentary proceedings, it is now clear to me that the influence on public opinion of any back-bencher — M.P. or peer — depends largely on his influence *outside* Parliament. For example, a TV personality who speaks in either House will get a couple of inches in the *Times* report of the previous day's proceedings, in place of the usual inch given to other participants. Some speeches are not reported at all. Every word, of course, is printed in *Hansard;* but who reads *Hansard*, except officials and the admiring friends to whom one sends a marked copy? One is supposed to address only the House: but back-benchers as marginal as I am cannot hope to be given a place in the list of speakers during 'prime listening time'. I usually come on, either between four or five p.m., when almost everyone is in the tea-room; or after supper, at an hour when most peers have already gone home. As I did not get into the House on my own merits, I do not have any real cause for complaint.

As an administrator myself, I was chiefly interested, on arrival in the House in 1963, in seeing how it is run. I do not mean the legislative procedure, but the management of all the services provided for Parliament. Not only is it a venerable institution (in June, 1965, I participated in its 700th anniversary), but responsibility for its administration is divided between a great many different bodies. For example, the Lord Chamberlain (a Palace official) supervises the admission of visitors to the galleries, as it is still officially the *Palace* of Westminster. Other departments are controlled by the Lord Chancellor, the Clerk of the Parliaments (now Sir David Stephens, C.M.G.), the Minister of Public Buildings and Works, the Postmaster General, Her Majesty's Stationery Office, and the Metropolitan Police. I visited every one of them, saw in the basement the plans of every floor and studied the use made of every room in the huge building. I even crossed the River to be taken round the parliamentary printing works. Two hundred printers are employed there, all night, to get the *Hansard* of the previous day's proceedings (up to 10.30 p.m.) on to the breakfast table of every M.P. and peer who asks for it. My enquiries into the plumbing were regarded as rather unladylike — or, perhaps, unlordlike. But I was, in the end, able to write a detailed article on the administration of the House of Lords. After it had been carefully checked by all the departments concerned, I published it in my own Annual — *Public Administration in Israel and Abroad* — for 1963. The librarian of the House now accepts it as the definitive article on the subject. It is required reading for every new peer who is interested in knowing how the establishment is run. It seems that, for me, once an administrator, always an administrator.

I do not find the House of Lords very interesting. It is very impressive from the outside; but I am glad that I did not give up Jerusalem for it. Today, I can see, even more clearly, that it has only vestigial powers, like those of the Crown. Originally, the King governed. Then, he, the barons and the bishops ruled the country. Gradually, the power of the House of Commons increased but, even by the 18th century, it was still the Lords who dominated. By the 19th century, however, power was equally divided. But, even before World War II, it was established (by the rejection in 1922 of Lord Curzon in favour of Mr Baldwin as leader of the Conservative Party) that the Prime Minister must sit in the Lower House and there face criticism by the elected representatives of the people.

In the last four centuries, the whole concept of a ruling caste of nobility has largely disappeared. In the reign of Queen Elizabeth the First, there were only seventy-five peers. Today, in the reign of Queen Elizabeth the Second, there are over a thousand. Even after making an allowance for the massive increase of population over the intervening period, there has been quite a devaluation of the peerage. It is no longer tied to feudal ownership of vast estates. In the

17th, 18th and 19th centuries many of the King's favourites (or if feminine, their sons) were ennobled. Even in the 20th, some peerages were notoriously conferred in return for payment to public institutions or even party funds (e.g., in the days of Lloyd George.)

Under the Parliament Acts of 1910 and 1945, the House of Lords had been deliberately shorn of most of its remaining power. It cannot touch the Budget, while other legislation can only be deferred nowadays for a year. Even that power of deferment is largely illusory. In 1967, Lord Carrington, when leader of the Conservative Opposition in the House of Lords, said that, with a Labour Government in power, the Opposition in the Upper House had only one shot left in its locker. If it used it, the whole House might be deprived of even that power: hence, it must be reserved for a really vital occasion.

The less the real power of the House of Lords, the fewer the peers interested in attending its daily sessions. The bishops are busy in their dioceses (they take it in turns to come to London for a week at a time to read the daily prayers in the House.) Those peers who are engaged in business or a profession have to 'mind the shop'. Many are permanently resident in northern England, or Wales, or Scotland, or Northern Ireland or even abroad. Some have never even bothered to take their seats. Hence, out of a thousand peers, 150 today is a full House, while even an attendance of fifty is considered creditable. Votes by such a small proportion is clearly unrepresentative of even a highly unrepresentative body. It is thus obvious to even the House itself that it is indulging, most of the time, in shadow-boxing. Any amendments it makes to the House of Commons Bills that the Lower House dislikes are rejected when the Bills are sent back to the House of Commons for its assent: the Upper House can do nothing more about it — today it is largely an august debating society. Some London clubs have a sauna: we have a debating society. Having originally been in favour of the abolition of the House of Lords, I was converted by a speech by Eick Crossman to be a reformist. It is a pity that the reform bill was defeated by a filibuster in the House of Commons.

The House of Commons itself is little better off. A new, young M.P. arrives after fearful political battles, full of hope. As a back-bencher, he is immediately engulfed in a lot of hard work. But, with the continual increase of Government business, little time is left for him. Out of 630 members, only a quarter may at one time or another reach the front bench and have some power as junior Ministers. Only perhaps five per cent will ever become Cabinet Ministers. The rest will never exercise much authority; for the House no longer has the Cabinet at its mercy. Party discipline is now so strict that it is the Cabinet that completely dominates the House. To relieve the pressure on the House, much local legislation should be devolved on to subordinate legislatures in Scotland and Wales as already in Northern Ireland, the Isle of Man and the Channel Islands.

But, today, it is not speeches in Parliament that primarily influence public opinion. Articles, leaders (and even letters in the press) — and broadcasting and television appearances are far more potent. Winston Churchill was a good House of Commons man. He always made his great speeches first on the floor of the House. But then he broadcast to the Nation. In the days of the Greek City State, none had more citizens than could be addressed by a single voice. Today, a whole nation of millions, tens of millions or hundreds of millions can be addressed simultaneously by one man. His face and gestures may also be seen on the domestic TV screen. The response to his words can be measured the next day by public opinion poll. We have now technically reached the point where representative government is no longer essential as a means of eliciting public opinion. Nor is it really necessary as a link between the governors and the governed.

★ ★ ★

In spite of my growing doubts whether my presence in Parliament serves any real purpose, Hadassah and I very much enjoy our three months in London. We can have our fill of everything we miss most in Israel — the theatre, the ballet, the opera, all the music in the world. We can see the latest and best films in every language. Then there are art exhibitions of all kinds, many friends to see. For me, there are meetings of those bodies with which I am connected — the Parliamentary Group on Israel, the Labour Friends of Israel, the Anglo-Israel Association, the Friends of the Hebrew University, the Bridge (that sends young non-Jews on fellowships to Israel), the Chatham House Middle Eastern Group, P.A.T.W.A. the *Jewish Chronicle* and its publishing house Vallentine Mitchell, Balliol College, Oxford, and so on. I am always invited by one or other of these bodies to speak during my three months in England and generally accept. Week-ends we spend in the country, either with my sister or at the houses or cottages of friends. If it rains, it does not seem to matter, as we have a surfeit of summer sun and drought in Israel. The English country-side from May to July is lovely: by now both Hadassah and I have become hopeless chlorophyll addicts.

By the end of July, however, we grow tired of the hectic life of a London season. The House of Lords may play at politics, and I may merely play at playing at politics; nevertheless, I am glad when Parliament rises. It is too hot to return then to Israel, so we go somewhere north of the Alps for a few weeks holiday. We usually go to two countries for about ten days each. In this way we have been three times to Ireland—Connemara, Bantry Bay, and Wicklow. I had myself been many times to Scandinavia while working for Ezer on the *Conquest of the Desert* exhibition. I started going in 1946, when I accompanied my father, who led the British delegation to the first post-war P.E.N. Club congress in Stockholm. Hadassah, however, had never been in any part of it. So we made a two-year plan — the first summer to Denmark and Sweden; the second to Norway (on a cruising ship) and Finland. I have always been fascinated by Finland, that country of forests and lakes and drowned islands. The Finns are brave people, with Communist Russia to the East and the Arctic to the north: and they still manage to survive. We returned another year to stay on a particular Norwegian fjord we had admired earlier, and it is there—at Ulvik on Hardanger—that I wrote this chapter. Twice we have spent eight or nine days at quiet places recommended by friends — in the French Alps, the Loire Valley, the Engadine. I write, Hadassah sleeps and we go for little walks or drives; it is very restful.

To Jerusalem we get back before the beginning of September. I start at once editing the articles for the next issue of *Public Administration in Israel and Abroad*, due out in January. In October, the Hebrew University begins and I have ten solid weeks of lecturing and tutoring. The first ten days of January, during the University's winter recess, we go to Tiberias where I do more writing. From January to March I have another ten weeks of lecturing and of listening to students' essays.

★ ★ ★

In Israel, most people get up very early. All Government offices open at 7.30 a.m. and the banks at 8.30. (In London, I find it intolerable to have to wait till 10 a.m.) My newspaper—the *Jerusalem Post*—arrives at about 5.30 a.m. so that is when I get up and read it. The City is quiet then, and cool in summer. I put in an hour's work before breakfast without interruption by the telephone. Not only do I get my own breakfast, but take Hadassah's to her bed, every morning. In return, she makes mine on Saturday, including scrambled eggs. At seven we listen to the Hebrew radio news. I am out by 7.30, which is when our cook Devora Zadok arrives. She is a Yemenite widow who has been with us for some thirty years and is Hadassah's devoted confidante. I suppose that, in part, having always left for the office at 7.30 a.m., I am loth to admit to myself that I am no longer a civil servant. For nearly twenty years, after I had left the administration, I lugged around the shabby old black leather official pouch bearing the British royal cypher. It had been issued, new, when I became head of the Palestine Broadcasting Service, and has at last been given an honourable funeral.

My car is parked in the street outside our flat. Most mornings, till the end of the year I drive first to Max Nurock's *pension* nearby, before he goes to the Foreign Ministry, to hand over to him new material or proofs for the Annual, and take back those he has done. Then I go to the apartment of Miss Edith Sachs, now pensioned, who does my typing in her spare time. I take her my work every morning and fetch it the following morning. By eight, I park down town near the G.P.O. — one can still find a parking place there — and fetch my mail from the sorting office. The postman does not deliver till lunchtime and the half day I save thereby enables me to reply to urgent letters before noon. I also take mail from the Post Office box of the Institute of Public Administration. Orders for the Annual, and cheques, I hand over to Moshe Bilu, our part-time accountant. He is a middle-rank executive in the Bank Leumi next door. I also visit the printing-press to deliver copy and collect proofs for the Annual. Then I take the car again to visit various Ministries, wherever I have business, or to lecture at the University. Usually I get home by 10 a.m. for coffee, having walked up and down enough flights of stairs to provide me with sufficient exercise for the whole day. At home I work at my desk till an early lunch, after which I drive the cook home. I rarely go out again. After a siesta, I read the previous day's arimail edition of the London *Times*, as well as one or other of the many periodicals I receive — the *Jewish Chronicle* and *Jewish Observer and Middle East Review* from London; *Time* magazine, *Commentary* and the *New Yorker* from the United States, and many others. Then I do more work at home, until the evening radio news at 7 p.m. After an early dinner, I smoke my solitary daily cigar and read till bedtime. I so arrange my writing commitments as never to have to work after dinner in order to fulfil them;

I am thus very much a creature of habit. I like an iced (local) vermouth and soda before lunch and dinner and a couple of glasses of local wine at each of these meals — red in winter and chilled white in summer. In London, I conform more to British tastes — a sweet sherry or gin and tonic before lunch and dinner, and cider with my lunch, and whatever my hosts provide if we dine out. In Jerusalem, we dine out but rarely and ourselves entertain mostly at lunch, when we have a cook. Our own suppers at home, heated up by Hadassah, are light. Like most husbands today, I fancy myself to be a highly proficient washer-upper in the evening and all day Saturday. At least I am speedy, with a low breakage rate and the minimum of splash either on myself or the kitchen floor.

Usually I go to bed at 9.30–10 p.m. or but, once or twice a month, in winter, I accompany Hadassah to a concert of the symphony orchestra that comes up from Tel Aviv: we have been seat-holders for years. Most films I want to see I have already seen in New York or London: Jerusalem's cinemas are rather too uncomfortable for relaxation; and tickets for good seats have to be bought in advance. On Sutardays, all offices and shops are closed: I am not observant and do not go to synagogue. So I sit at home and work, going to my friend Mordechai Kamrat, the Hebraist, for a hilarious hour of philology before lunch. He has the heartiest laugh of any man I know. We are writing together two Hebrew-English books: one a philological lexicon, the other on the origin and meaning of boys' and girls' Hebrew first names in use in Israel today. The rest of Saturday I work, or visit friends, or receive visitors.

Now that the Old City, since June, 1967, has been rejoined to the New, I am able to resume my Saturday walks inside the Walls. But I must confess that, in my wildest dreams, I never imagined the unification of the two halves of the city as a result of war, in spite of my admiration for the prowess of the Israel Defence Forces (to give them their official title).

Every few weeks our elder son David and some of his family come up from Rehovot and stay with us over the Sabbath: and we frequently go to Rehovot to see them. It is pleasant to have at least some of our grandchildren within easy range.

Once a fortnight or so, I drive, with increasing unwillingness, down the tortuous and overcrowded main road to Tel Aviv. On these occasions I invariably give a lift to some Israeli soldier on leave, thumbing a ride. The soldier knows he will never meet me again; and, if there is no one else in the car, he is only too willing to tell me his life story. Much of what I know about social conditions in Israel today, I have learned, either from such casual companions, or from my students at the University.

I usually leave Jerusalem very early and go first to the head offices of *Magen David Adom* (see page 273) in Jaffa to discuss their forthcoming periodicals, both in Hebrew and in English. I then go to Tel Aviv to see Hermann Ellern, the German-Jewish banker. In 1963, after I had succeeded to the viscountcy, he and his elder son, Uziel, called on me in Jerusalem and invited me to become a director of the Ellern Investment Company. At that time, Hermann thought of raising additional capital and hoped that a director with an English title would help. I joined the company; but, shortly afterwards, a general decline began on the Tel Aviv stock market through competition by Government securities, and no issue was launched by Ellern's. Both

Hermann and, later, Uziel, had been trained at our family bank in London—Samuel Montagu and Co. (Samuel Montagu — who later became the first Lord Swaythling — had been born Montagu Samuel and was the brother of my grandfather, Edwin Samuel, after whom I was named.) Although I had myself escaped becoming a director of Samuel Montagu and Co by moving to Palestine, I could read a balance sheet. Through long residence in Palestine and Israel, and a post-graduate study of economics at Columbia University, I understood something of the economic potentialities of Israel. I am also a director, as Hermann's nominee, of the Moller Textile Company: Ellern's Investment Company owns a large share of the equity, Hermann himself being chairman of Moller's. Erich Moller, the founder of the textile company, is an old friend of mine from Czechoslovakia: I once visited the family textile mills there before they were transferred to Palestine. The cotton spinning and weaving mills are now at Nahariya, near the Lebanese frontier. Two or three times a year I travel there with Hermann for board meetings. Other board meetings are held in Tel Aviv in the new Shalom Tower, Israel's tallest sky-scraper, where Ellern's Holdings Ltd. and another director of Moller's, have their offices. To avoid too much motoring in any one day, I stay the night at the Dan Hotel in Tel Aviv, returning to Jerusalem at dawn the next morning.

My other business interests include a directorship of the *Jewish Chronicle* in London. This weekly — the oldest Jewish periodical in the world — was founded in 1841.

In the same year, my mother's uncle, Jacob Franklin founded the apply named 'Voice of Jacob'. For two and a half years it absorbed the Jewish Chronicle. But in 1844, the

Chronicle regained its independence. The 'Voice of Jacob' ceased publication in 1846: since then there had been no family connection with Jewish journalism. When in London, I regularly attend the fortnightly board meetings which also deal with editorial policy. In Israel, the *Chronicle* has its own correspondents: but I look after its business interests.

Before I became a *Jewish Chronicle* director, I myself wrote a great deal for it — for example, a series of unsigned profiles of leading Israeli and British Jews. I still write an occasional feature article and book review. But I try not to put the editor — now William Frankel and a personal friend — in an embarrassing position by offering to write articles which he would prefer to commission from someone other than myself.

It is Vallentine, Mitchell that, in fact, launched me on my career as a short story writer. In November, 1951, I had an article on my experiences in Palestine under the Mandate published in *The Reporter*, a fortnightly in New York. They gave it the title '*The Old Days in Palestine*' and provided some pen-and-ink sketches. One who read it was Sarai Zausmer, the registrar of Dropsie College, in Philadelphia, where I had taught in 1948-49: she suggested that some of the incidents I had mentioned might be used for short stories. I gave another look, agreed, selected half-a-dozen and lightly fictionalised them: two or three were published in minor Jewish periodicals. I continued writing short stories, with backgrounds only of Palestine or Israel, until I had enough — twenty-seven — for a book.

It is not easy to get volumes of collected short stories published: most readers of fiction want to get their teeth into a long novel. Only omnibus collections by the top writers really sell. Nevertheless, Vallentine, Mitchell were prepared to take the risk, sharing it with a New York publishing firm, Abelard Schuman. This is owned by a Canadian, Lew Schwartz, and his brothers, with whom Vallentine, Mitchell was already doing business. I managed to get Steimatzky, a distributor in Tel Aviv of books and periodicals, to place a firm order for 600 copies. An edition of under 1,000 copies was consequently published in 1957. It sold out, and a second printing of the same size appeared and also sold out: it is now out of print but available in some public libraries. That volume was called *A Cottage in Galilee*, because I had such a cottage, and a piece about it was in the volume. It was illustrated with pen-and-ink drawings by Mrs. Gabriella Rosenthal. She had worked with me in the censorship and had become its private cartoonist.

Encouraged by getting into print at all, I continued to write short stories, some set outside Palestine and Israel. By 1960, I had enough for a second volume. Vallentine Mitchell were then no longer publishing general fiction; but Lew Schwartz decided to go it alone. Because the volume contained stories set in a variety of countries, it was called *A Coat of Many Colours*. My relations with Lew Schwartz have become very friendly and he has since published three more volumes of mixed Israeli and non-Israeli stories.

I have now written about 130 stories, of which 104 have appeared in these five volumes. (A list of my various publications is given on page 319.) Other volumes of short stories are in preparation: I have much fun writing them. Some of the incidents which I write about have happened to me personally, but fictional characters have been used instead. Other incidents have been casually mentioned by friends or acquaintances. Sometimes two or more separate incidents have been combined in the same story.

No-one is making much money out of my stories, and I am grateful to Lew Schwartz for publishing so many volumes of them. (A sixth volume is now being published). In 1965 his wife, Frances, also published one of my children's stories—*Captain Noah and His Ark*—illustrated by Lola Fielding.

I do not think I am a very good short story writer. I have been compared by critics with Somerset Maugham and with O. Henry. Unfortunately, they say: 'Edwin Samuel is no Somerset Maugham: Mr Samuel is no O. Henry.' But I am flattered even to get my name on the same page with those of the Masters. I have, however, long since ceased to be worried about what critics say. A story torn to pieces by one will be praised to take skies by the next: reviewers are very subjective.

I cannot say that writing is, for me, a very profitable enterprise. Including all my short stories, various books and numerous feature articles, I doubt if I have ever made more than £ 200 a year. If I had had to live solely on my literary efforts, I would have died of starvation long ago. I plough back most of what I earn into buying other people's books and theatre tickets.

Since 1966, I have been involved in another enterprise, as a departmental editor for the new *Encyclopaedia Judaica*, a major undertaking. Since 1900, eight Jewish encyclopaedias have appeared in five different languages, but no major one in English since 1939. The present project was initiated in 1959 by Dr Nahum Goldmann (then president both of the World Jewish Congress and the World Zionist Organization). The original editor was Dr Elisha Netanyahu of the Technion at Haifa, who moved in 1962 to Dropsie College, Philadelphia, and began collecting articles from contributors in the United States and elsewhere. In 1965, the material was sent to a new office opened in Jerusalem, and Professor Cecil Roth (we had known each other from Oxford in 1919-1920 when he was at Wadham and I at Balliol), who had come from Oxford to live in Israel, became editor-in-chief. After several false starts, it was eventually decided to issue the encyclopaedia in fifteen volumes, to be published all together in 1971. It is to contain 9,000,000 words, of which 189,000 were allotted to the State of Israel. When I asked whether I should not do the Mandatory period, I was told I was personally too involved to be objective. 'And why the state of Israel?' I asked. 'Because you aren't a member of any Israel political party'.

Allocating the 189,000 words allotted to my department was an interesting task. To ensure comprehensiveness and balance, the first necessity was a synoptic index showing every aspect of modern Israel in rational order. After this index had been approved by the editorial board, I then had to allot to each subject and item a specific number of words within the total given to me. For each article, long or short, I had to suggest a contributor who should be well-informed and well-balanced; in other words, an authority. He had also to be able to write (preferably in English); willing to undertake the work for the fee offered and able to provide the article by the date specified. Some 400 articles were involved, varying from 100 words to 5,000. When all this had been approved by the board, I proceeded to collect particulars of all the articles, long and short, on different subjects, to be written by the same person and to discuss with him what was involved. Once he had agreed, a formal contract was offered to him by the encyclopaedia office. As each article came in, I had to check it for accuracy, edit it and sometimes rewrite it. The board agreed that I should myself write a few articles on subjects within my special competence. All this naturally involved many meetings and interviews. The whole of modern *Eretz Israel*, including the Mandatory period and the Jewish Holocaust in Europe, forms a single division under Dr Benjamin Eliav, a most competent co-ordinator and editor. Our team includes Dr Moshe Avidor (a former colleague in the Palestine Administration, now Israel representative at U.N.E.S.C.O.) His period from 1880 to 1948, together with my period from 1948 to 1968, involves about 250 articles: Mr Ephraim Orni, (responsible for short articles on about a thousand place names in Israel); Mr Benjamin Jaffe of the Jewish Agency (responsible for articles on some 300 contemporary personalities in Palestine and Israel) with Mrs Alice Shalvi, of the English Department at the Hebrew University, as stylistic co-ordinator: we are a happy team.

★ ★ ★

Living in Palestine and Israel for most of a lifetime has left a permanent mark on me in various ways.

The Arab habitually gets up at dawn and goes to bed at dusk to save fuel for light. Jewish farmers, like all farmers, get up early to tend their livestock. In Israel today, everyone, myself included, gets up an hour or two earlier than is habitual in England. Even in London, I find it hard to sleep late.

The long summer, with its midday heat, makes a siesta a habit that is hard to throw off in the House of Lords. But, then, many other noble Lords take a nap in the library after lunch.

Having become acclimatised to heat, I find I am now allergic to cold: perhaps that is merely the setting in of old age. In summer, in Israel, one drinks a great deal of water and fruit juice to make up for loss through perspiration. The water in Israel is so impregnated with limestone that many people—myself included—develop kidney trouble. The fact that water is precious in Israel has left me with an enhanced anxiety over dripping taps.

The rooms in our flat are airy, and we get accustomed to leaving doors open to encourage a breeze: that always used to puzzle my father when I came to stay with him. Although deaf in his later years, he liked seclusion when he worked: I can write anywhere. Tiled floors, with rugs, keep the house cooler in summer than wall-to-wall carpeting: they are easier to keep clean in a dusty land. Rooms are sparsely furnished and we feel cluttered up in the cosier rooms of northern peoples.

Even after nearly a century of immigration and development, Israel is still a pioneering country. As a former district officer, I travel self-contained, even in Europe. I still carry a small medicine chest, oblivious of the fact that a pharmacy exists at every street corner. I still go through life prepared for anything. Having been twice on assassination lists, on entering a restaurant or cafe I automatically choose a chair with its back to the wall so that I may see who comes into the room. I keep the petrol tank of my car full as I never know when I might need a quick getaway. This leads me always to park my car in the direction I will have later to leave, not in the direction I arrive. This, in part, derives from the days when I was a district officer. When I visited a village, it made a poor impression on the assembled inhabitants if I had to do a lot of backing and turning on leaving. Having said my good-byes, I would then sail away, followed by my escort.

In a pioneering country, where everyone works very hard, one feels somewhat ashamed if one is idle. I *can* wholly relax in an English country-house over the week-end; but not for very long. I usually take some writing to do when I need the stimulation of more effort.

Again, in a warm country where everyone works hard, one dresses informally. Slacks and an open-necked shirt are acceptable, except perhaps in the evening if one dines out, especially in a tourist hotel. My wardrobe in consequence is scanty.

In the 1920's practically no clothes were made in Palestine and one bought everything in London when on leave: I still do. Although I may be Labour in politics, I am the most conservative of men as far as my clothes are concerned. I always have been: this is not just advancing age. In London, I still ask in shops for styles and materials that have not been available for decades.

In Israel, strongly influenced by egalitarian *kibbutz* philosophy, feudal titles are out of place. At my own request, I am addressed there as Mr and not as Viscount. In the United States, I am often a professor. Becoming a viscount again on arrival in England from Israel and America has a certain unreality about it.

★ ★ ★

Living in Jerusalem — or even in Tiberias — has for me a particular satisfaction. All the time, the magnificent historical panorama is just below the level of consciousness.

Now, with the recovery of the Old City, that panorama is visible as well. One author, Robert Payne, an expatriate Englishman in New York, has brilliantly captured this mystique in his book, *The Splendour of Israel*★ written after spending only six weeks there. I suppose that mystique, basically is why I stay. Otherwise, life in Jerusalem is not very gay: one lives on the edge of civilisation. For example, it takes months for new books to arrive. The London Sunday newspapers are too heavy to come by air: who wants a Sunday paper a month later? I have had to abandon my favourite *Illustrated London News* for the same reason. One gives up quite a lot — the ballet, new plays, friends, good food, the comfortable habit of speaking in one's own mother tongue. For that, I rely on the constant stream of people who visit us in Jerusalem — acquaintances from Britain and the United States, people whom we have met and liked on our travels, as well as *their* friends, arriving with introductions.

★ ★ ★

A lifetime in Jerusalem has left me with an ingrained sense of urgency. Israel is faced with massive problems and everyone has to work overtime to keep up. It is this sense of urgency that I miss in Britain. During World War II, a sense of urgency existed there also. Perhaps Israel still has it because it is permanently at war, or forced to prepare constantly to meet war. I cannot get used to a five-day week, either in Britain or the United States: nor to offices where no one with authority arrives before 10 a.m.

★ Robert Hale, London, 1963.

New York works harder than London; but the rat-race there is largely the struggle to make enough money to pay for all the expensive amenities of the American way of life.

There is, however, the other side of the medal. Constant overwork in Israel results in a low level of efficiency. Many facets of organization in Israel are infuriating—failure to answer letters, red tape, indifference, even downright rudeness. Some of this derives from the former happy-go-lucky inefficiency of life in Eastern Europe from where many of the founders and leaders of Israel originally came.

One of the most irritating features of life in Israel is chronic unpunctuality. Few meetings ever start on time. Theatre performances can start anything up to half an hour late. Only concerts begin on the dot, because they are often broadcast, and split-second timing becomes essential. As a would-be efficiency expert, I am invariably punctual myself. The result is that I have to wait until everyone else rolls up for a meeting. For me it is not procrastination that is the thief of time, but punctuality. My wife has such touching faith in my keeping to a time-table that if ever I return home five minutes later than I said I would, I find her prepared to ring up the police to know if I have met with an accident.

As long as Israel is faced with the massive problems of defence, immigration and development, it is difficult to persuade Israelis not to overload the machine, not to be so ambitious, to fix priorities, to keep something in reserve, to rest your horses whenever you can. In Israel, human beings are expendable: hence the high ratio of those who fall by the wayside.

The Jewish mind is quick and keen. It delights in hair-splitting. Hence the multiplicity of political parties in Israel and the political in fighting. This politicisation also blocks orderly development. But it is ingrained and one has to put up with the consequences. One of these is the endless committee meetings necessary to get anything done. It is impossible to persuade one political party to allow anyone from another party to have the authority and trust necessary for unhampered and speedy action. In Britain, with its lower tempo, things sometimes get done just as quickly as in Israel, with its frenzied forcing through thickets of its own making. Luckily, I do not now have to choose between London or Jerusalem: or even New York. I can have a little of all three each year and consider myself extremely lucky to have arrived at that solution.

CHAPTER 15

MY CHILDHOOD

Other people's childhoods are usually a big bore, so I have put this chapter at the end. If you have got as far, you may perhaps now be interested to know something of the period in which I grew up and out of which my life developed.

When one grows old, one's childhood consists largely of the especially pleasant moments one chooses to remember, as well as the particularly unpleasant events one still cannot forget. The average happenings are by now a blur.

Sixty years ago, when I was ten or so, everything was possible. Life was new: I had an insatiable curiosity. I was well looked after and had few responsibilities. Having been born at the end of the Victorian period, my well-to-do parents had a large London house with half a dozen servants. At first we lived in Gloucester Terrace, off the Bayswater Road, near Paddington Station. Later, we had, successively, three different houses in Porchester Terrace, ten minutes away. Both these 'terraces' were within walking distance of the New West End Synagogue to which my two younger brothers, my sister and I were taken every Saturday morning by our mother. Driving there would profane the Sabbath, which is why most of my uncles and aunts and their thirty-five children — my first cousins — lived in the same neighbourhood. Bayswater lay north of two of the royal parks —

Kensington Gardens and Hyde Park. It was not as fashionable as Park Lane to the east or Kensington and Knightsbridge to the south

As a baby, I was taken by my nanny in my pram to the Serpentine, the long artificial lake that divides Kensington Gardens from Hyde Park. Later, I sailed my toy yacht on the Round Pond in front of Kensington Palace, or flew my kite in the broad avenue between the chestnut trees.

My first kindergarten was just round the corner in a pokey little house. My mother was a great supporter of the P.N.E.U. (Parents' National Educational Union) which was then trying to modernise the teaching of young children; so I had lots of handicrafts as a child. I well remember my mother's pride in my first water-colour daubs of an acorn sprouting in a jar full of water. But I remember, even more acutely, the day of my arrival in this kindergarten and being told to wait in a room downstairs. I had an irresistible desire to urinate, but I was too shy to look for the right place in the passage outside and used the fire-place instead, putting out the tiny fire. The shame of discovery still haunts me.

Later, I went to Mr Gibb's fashionable prep school, south of the Park, in Sloane Street. I travelled there daily by Inner Circle underground, wearing a cherry-coloured cap and carrying my satchel. The school has long since vanished but, while it lasted, we were in fierce rivalry with the boys of another private school — Mr Wilkinson's — against whom I played unwilling football and cricket. I remember nothing of the lessons except carpentry, which I thoroughly enjoyed, although the tool-box I made for myself was unbelievably crude and clumsy.

I only wish now that I had learnt more skills when young

such as sewing, cooking, typing, plumbing and electrical installation. These are, today, essential in a servantless world, where even craftsmen are hard to find. But, in those days, I would have been chased out of the kitchen of my parents' house had I asked the cook for lessons: such things were not for young gentlemen. Even grown-up gentlemen never typed their own letters then: to be polite you *had* to write your letters in your own hand. And today, when letters are habitually typed by secretaries, the 'Dear so-and-so' and 'yours sincerely' are still inserted by the hand of anyone who is a stickler for exquisite behaviour. My sons, however, did learn to type at school and I envy them. Had I learnt, or had the wit to teach myself later, my literary efforts would have become much simpler and less costly.

I do not remember that, as children, we ever had a dog — London is no place for one. There may have been a cat in the kitchen. I can recollect a tortoise that died and was buried by us solemnly in the garden. Years later we learned that it had merely been hibernating. Our pride was a canary in a cage in the nursery which we four children bought with our Purim money (2/6 each). We called him Mordechai and he chirruped away for years.

Those were the days not only before television but even before sound radio. We had to keep ourselves amused on wet days with all kinds of indoor games. My parents had a fitted mahogany case — some wedding present perhaps. It was called The Compendium and contained chess, draughtsmen and a board for them, packs of cards, a backgammon board and dice, halma men and a board. These were kept in my father's library and we were allowed to use them as a great treat.

One of the pillars of my childhood existence was Grandma

— my father's mother, Clara — who had been widowed six years after my father was born. When I was a child, she lived in a suite of her own, furnished in satinwood, at the Royal Palace Hotel, near the Albert Hall. That hotel was long ago pulled down and has recently been replaced by the Royal Garden Hotel. I bore her husband's first name — Edwin — and was her godson as well as her grandson. It was she who taught me how to tell the time, one summer when she was staying with us in the country.

In London, every few Saturdays, after synagogue, I walked across Kensington Gardens to lunch with Grandma. To my childish mind, she lived in unbelievable luxury. In her satinwood cupboard there were always chocolates, each with a crystallised parina violet on it, such as we never had at home. At lunch in the restaurant I was introduced to further examples of 'high life': toast instead of the bread I was normally given, and lemon squash in place of water. As we left the immense hotel dining-room, the head waiter and the leader of the three-piece string band bowed impressively low. It was only years later that I learnt that she tipped them handsomely every Christmas.

One of the features in her drawing-room was a gilt chair, upholstered in flowered satin: it had a musical box in the seat. When an unwary visitor sat on it, it suddenly began to play *Der Tannenbaum*. After my grandmother died, it went to my parents and gave much pleasure to *their* grandchildren. On my parents' death, it was inherited by my niece, now married in a *kibbutz*, where it hardly fits in. So my younger son Dan has taken it to Brussels where it still amuses the great-great-grandchildren of the original owner, Clara.

In those days, families were parent-centred. When my father carved the chicken, he and my mother naturally took the white meat while we children were left with the dark. But, by the time I had sons of my own, families had become children-centred. So they had the white meat and I continued with the dark. I am now so conditioned to it that I would not change for the world.

In those days, my father was active in politics and employed a male secretary to handle his correspondence. Each secretary became, successively, tutor to my next brother — Philip — and myself. (My youngest brother Godfrey and my sister Nancy were too young.) I remember best Barclay Baron, a muscular Christian who, I suspect, had quite a lot to do with my moral development.

As I approached my *barmitzva* at the age of thirteen, I was taught the elements of Hebrew and the Jewish religion by the synagogue cantor. These lessons were given for months in the dark school-room on the ground floor of my parents' house. The walls were lined to the ceiling with glass-covered mahogany book-cases entirely full of bound volumes of *Punch* and the *Illustrated London News* from their inception. They both served me well as a social history of Britain. I disliked my old-fashioned Hebrew grammar lessons intensely, the more so as the cantor frequently spat into the fireplace. (Have I developed a fireplace syndrome?)

About this time, in 1911, I was admitted to Westminster School as a day-boy. I went there every morning by Underground, continuing two more stations to St James's Park. I was dressed as a little gentleman: in my first years, this meant an Eton jacket; later, as I grew taller, it involved 'tails'. In both cases, a top hat, striped trousers, an umbrella and a brief-case were *de rigeur*. It took World War II and evacuation of the school from London to put a stop to such nonsense.

I hated my early years at Westminster. I was a day-boy in a boarding school; a 'commoner' among 'scholars'; no good at any games; a Jew exempted at my mother's insistence from early morning chapel in Westminster Abbey, Monday morning's divinity lessons and all day on every major high holy-day in the Jewish calendar. I was also expected by my mother to follow her own peculiar version of the Jewish dietary laws by picking the pieces of ham out of the beef rissoles served at school lunches. I was much bullied in my early years, my particular fiend being a boy called Mostyn. I was revolted by the disorder, 'fug' and dirt in the changing-room in the basement of my 'house', where we kept our football shorts, boots and unwashed shirts and stockings. In my last year at Westminster, as a monitor, I shared a study upstairs with other monitors and the bullying stopped.

What really got me down was my parents' decision that I should be on the 'classical side.' This meant my spending hours a day on Greek and Roman history, Greek and Latin grammar, and the endless translation of English verse into Greek or Latin verse as homework, which all seemed to me an utter waste of time. After two years of this torture, I begged my father so hard to remove me from Westminster altogether that he allowed me to transfer to the 'modern side'. This involved an equally unbalanced concentration on mathematics, mechanics, physics and chemistry. As, however, I wanted by then to be an electrical engineer, I was now in my element. My incredibly neat note-books, with their meticulous diagrams and sketches, consistently got me marks of 98 to 100 per cent, week after week and I was always near the top of the class. I lectured to the school scientific society on the torpedo and on the manufacture of coal gas (after I had been taken by my father on a visit to a

311

gas works). For that lecture I made a complete model of a gas works, out of glass tubing, that actually worked. In my spare time, I visited every kind of trade exhibition and came home with piles of advertising handouts that I carefully studied. I thus developed some understanding of mechanical and chemical processes. After a visit to a Yates family lard factory at Liverpool (my grandmother Clara had been a Yates from Liverpool and I had second cousins there), I was able, from memory, to make a complete diagram showing every process involved. These included several secret processes about which I had been told nothing but which I had deduced. When I proudly sent this diagram to the owner, he impounded it and sent me a guinea for my pains. It was the first real money I had ever earned. My pocket-money, even when I was in my teens, was still only half a crown a week.

In those days, Meccano was the great rage among mechanically-minded boys and I invested every penny of my birthday money in acquiring bigger and bigger supplementary sets. In the end, I was able to construct the most complicated and sophisticated machines in the instruction books. I then began designing my own mechanisms, especially model overhead railways. I built one all around the dank boxroom in the basement of our house that I had been allotted as a workshop.

It was there that I assembled my first wireless set — the old cat's-whisker-and-crystal model. I used to sit up till midnight just to hear the time signal from the Eiffel Tower. This was long before wireless telephony: the speed of the commercial wireless telegraphy messages in morse code was far too quick for me to understand. How proud I was when, on the outbreak of World War I (I was then fifteen), Post Office engineers came and dismantled my wireless set as a menace to national security!

Sometimes I believe that I might have made quite a good engineer, had I not decided to go back to Palestine in 1920. I had already developed a patent collapsible motor-car wheel-rim, to make easier the changing of tyres, then a frequent necessity. I also drew up specifications and diagrams for a very delicate electric balance. My father, bless him, arranged for the president of the Institute of Electrical Engineers — no less — to examine it. He said it was ingenious but in advance of its time. Like all boys, I took my budding scientific leanings very seriously.

My education, however, was very lopsided. By some mischance, I studied the reign of Queen Elizabeth I for two years running. But I knew neither medieval nor modern English history, nor any American history, and very little foreign history of any kind. I did learn some French; but even with supplementary home coaching in German by Fräulein von Weech, I failed in German in my London matric.

When I was seventeen or so, I won the Westminster school 'Masonic Prize', for an original piece of research into the decomposition of hydrogen peroxide, of all things. There was only one other competitor that year, a boy named Perkins, who was one of my rivals for top of the class. It is the only school prize I ever won — a set of books of my own choosing, mostly Kipling, specially bound in half morocco: I still treasure them. Yet I knew no biology at all, and nothing about art, or music, or literature, or the theatre. I had never seen a ballet until I was over thirty. It is not surprising that later I was ill-equipped for life, having been pitchforked into the army and only then going, for an all too brief period, to Balliol. As a young married man, I scared

313

Hadassah by my introspection and my insistent inquiries about the meaning of life, why trees were beautiful and how to understand a painting — none of which she could answer. In practically all fields of learning I am largely self-taught and but indifferently at that. I consider myself to be very badly educated.

In 1915, when I was sixteen, I had a mysterious illness, now believed to have been meningitis, from which I nearly died. But that did not deter me later from being passed medically fit for admission to the Westminster School O.T.C. As I liked marching at the head of the column, I joined the band as a kettle-drummer. But I also got my marksman's badge for rifle-shooting.

In July, 1914, I was away in a camp organized by the War Office for the combined public schools' O.T.C. When war threatened, the training officers and N.C.O.'s — all regulars — were called back to their units and the camp hurriedly broke up. We marched in uniform, with sloped arms, from Waterloo Station over Westminster Bridge to the school armoury amid wild cheers from bellicose crowds. Few of those who marched with me survived the holocaust of Flanders: I was one of the lucky ones.

The happiest days of my childhood were the school holidays. At Christmas there were the fascinating lectures given to school-boys by eminent scientists at the Royal Society. Then there were the theatres and the pantomimes to which all four of us children were taken by our parents. Each year, when the curtain went down at the end of the first act and the lights went up, and we sat enthralled, my father would solemnly say: 'Shall we go home now?' And each year we would imploringly say 'No' and then dissolve into laughter at being 'had' once again. At Easter, we went to the south coast — Littlehampton, St Leonards and so on — but I have no recollection of such watering places. The great event of the year was our summer holiday and, for us, that always meant Cleveland, my father's constituency in north-eastern Yorkshire. We all set off from home in a horse-drawn station-wagon, with an incredible number of heavy trunks and portmanteaus. In those pre-Welfare State days, on our return, a tattered casual labourer ran all the way behind our wagon from the station to our house to earn a shilling unloading all our baggage and lugging it on his back upstairs.

We went by train, often to some country-house that my father had leased for the summer. One was the ancestral home, at Hutton Rubby, of Elizabeth Fry, the early Quaker prison reformer. It was full of her relics as well as of chintz-covered arm-chairs, bad water-colours and Victorian books in sober bindings. There was a tower at one corner of the house, with a sun-drenched observatory at the top and a small telescope. There, among the dead flies, I had my kingdom. Much of my time, one whole summer, I spent copying out for future reference the fascinating tables of constants in Ganot's Physics, even then half a century out of date. The rest of the summer, we children — and our friends from neighbouring country-houses — bicycled, played tennis and croquet, ate strawberries and cream or made toffee. Any time, anywhere that I now smell sweet peas, or roses, or honey-suckle, or new-mown grass, or dry hay, a Yorkshire summer immediately comes into my mind.

Once each summer there would be a gymkhana, for all the children of the neighbourhood, with prizes for everyone. But the great climacteric was The Demonstration—a garden-party given by my father, as sitting Member, to all his supporters. I can still sniff the crushed grass in the refreshment marquees. Any brass band playing in a municipal garden today gives me the same thrill as that derived from the band hired by my father's political agent to play during The Demonstration. There may have been speeches, too, but those I do not remember. I do remember, however, seeing my parents wearing big orange rosettes, flushed with excitement, walking through the crowds and greeting old acquaintances.

My father had invested in a heavy old second-hand Delaunay-Belleville motor-car, with a collapsible leather hood. It had reputedly belonged to some Maharajah and had lots of polished brass about it. This was still the day when there were no doors to the driver's seat: I, as the eldest son, was allowed to sit at the feet of whoever sat next to the driver, with my own feet on the running-board, holding on to the acetylene lamp-bracket. It was on this car that, later, my father's chauffeur taught me to drive. Even at seventeen I had to use all my strength to disengage the clutch of this juggernaut.

Occasionally we would drive up to the Yorkshire moors for a picnic lunch among the bracken and the heather. We would come to a halt on the bank of some ice-cold mountain brook, with sheep grazing behind dry-stone walls and birds soaring in the wind.

Once or twice a week we would motor to Saltburn beach. It ran for miles and was so wide and level and firm that it was used for the early motor races. It was also used for sand-yacht racing: a sand-yacht was a triangular wooden frame, with bicycle wheels at each corner, a mast and a sail.

That beach, to us children, was paradise — swings, donkeys to ride, music on the pier, ices to eat, the building of intricate sand castles complete with keep and moat and ramparts on which were stationed our toy soldiers. And, best of all, the lumbering, great bathing-cabins, dragged out by cart-horses into deeper water as the tide went out. And down the wooden steps, all slimy with sea-weed, we lowered our warm and skinny bodies into the cold embraces of the marvellous sea that washed all our youthful tribulations away.

I must have been in Cleveland every summer from 1902 till 1917, when I was already commissioned in the artillery, awaiting my embarkation papers. It was the previous summer, when I was already seventeen, that I tried to get a job making munitions at Middlesbrough, the big industrial, city to the north. Usually, we helped to get the hay in; but, now, munitions had an even higher priority. I had been promised my first motor-cycle to take me to and from Middlesbrough each day. But, somehow the plan fell through; and, till today, I mourn for the motor-cycle I never had half a century ago.

I did work during one war-time school holiday in the basement of the London Polytechnic in Upper Regent Street, turning eighteen-pounder shells on a great lathe. I was not at all skilled and soon put it out of action: so perhaps it was better for the war effort that I did not do munitions work at Middlesbrough. The following year, 1917, I sailed off to Egypt as a reinforcement to Allenby's army, the beginning of my life-time in Jerusalem.

INDEX

319

326

331

332

335